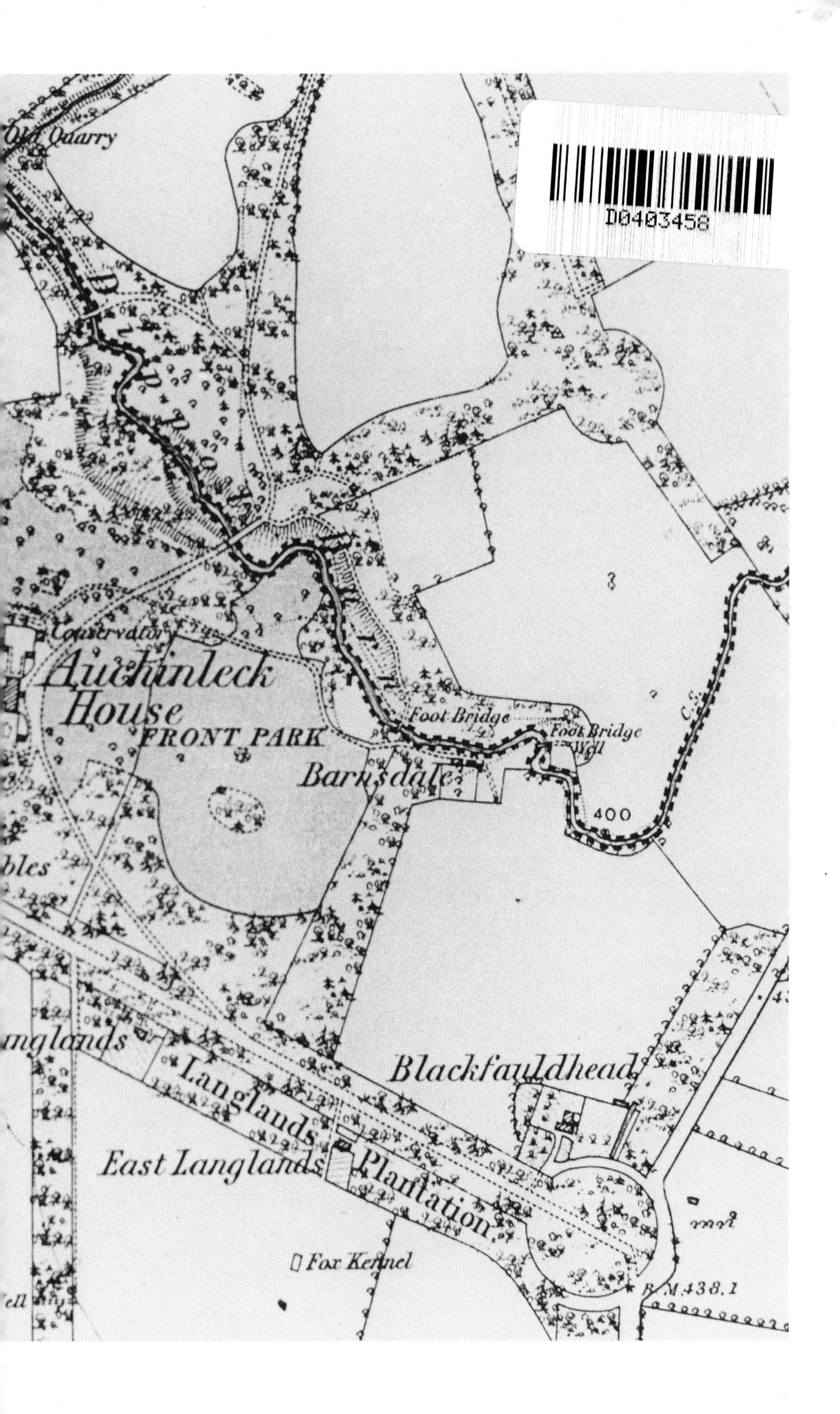
Old Quarry
Auchinleck
House
FRONT PARK
Foot Bridge
Foot Bridge
Well
Barnsdale
400
Langlands
Plantation
East Langlands
Blackfauldhead
Fox Kennel
B.M. 438.1

BOSWELL

1775 And let me add, that citizen of the world (433)
as I hold myself to be, I have that degree of
predilection for my natale solum, nay, I have that
just sense of the merit of an ancient nation which in
old times was renowned for its valour and
maintained its independence against a power:
:ful neighbour, and in modern times has
=celled in all the arts of civilization, that
I should have felt a generous indignation
at any injustice done to it. Johnson treated
Scotland no worse than he did even his best
friends, whose characters he used to give
as they appeared to him both in light and
shade, Some people
who had not exercised their minds suffi:
:ciently condemned him for censuring
his friends. But Sir Joshua Reynolds
whose philosophical penetration and
justness of thinking are not less known to
those who live with him than his genius
in his art is admired by the world ex:
:plained his conduct thus. He dis:
:crimination which he could not shew without
pointing out both the bad as well as the good in every
character, and as his friends were those

BOSWELL

Citizen of the World, Man of Letters

IRMA S. LUSTIG
Editor

THE UNIVERSITY PRESS OF KENTUCKY

Frontispiece: From the manuscript of the *Life of Johnson,* page 433, Boswell's proclamation of himself as "a Citizen of the World." The Beinecke Rare Book and Manuscript Library, Yale University.

Endpapers: A portion of the estate of Auchinleck, the Ayrshire home of "the Citizen of the World." Though the map is reproduced from the *Ordinance Survey* of 1857, the estate as shown is little changed from Boswell's years as laird.

Scholarly publisher for the Commonwealth,
serving Bellarmine College, Berea College, Centre College of Kentucky, Eastern Kentucky University, The Filson Club, Georgetown College, Kentucky Historical Society, Kentucky State University, Morehead State University, Transylvania University, University of Kentucky, University of Louisville, and Western Kentucky University.

Editorial and Sales Offices: Lexington, Kentucky 40508-4008

Library of Congress Cataloging-in-Publication Data

Boswell : citizen of the world, man of letters / Irma S. Lustig, editor.
p. cm.
Includes bibliographical references and index.
ISBN 0-8131-1910-3 (acid-free)
1. Boswell, James, 1740–1795. Life of Samuel Johnson.
2. Johnson, Samuel, 1709–1784—Friends and associates. 3. Authors, English—Biography—History and criticism. 4. Authors, Scottish—18th century—Biography. 5. Scotland—Intellectual life—18th century. 6. Biographers—Great Britain—Biography. 7. Biography as a literary form. 8. Enlightenment—Scotland.
I. Boswell, James, 1740–1795. II. Lustig, Irma S.
PR3325.B65 1995
828'.609—dc20 94-39584

This book is printed on acid-free recycled paper meeting the requirements of the American National Standard for Permanence of Paper for Printed Library Materials.

In memory of
Frederick and Marion Pottle

Contents

Contributors

THOMAS CRAWFORD is Honorary Reader in English at the University of Aberdeen and the author of *Burns: A Study of the Poems and Songs* (1960); *Scott* (1965); *Society and the Lyric* (1979); and *Boswell, Burns, and the French Revolution* (1990). He is editor, with David Hewitt and Alexander Law, of *Longer Scottish Poems, Volume 2, 1650–1830* (1987) and of Lewis Grassic Gibbon's trilogy of novels, *A Scots Quair* (1988–90). Crawford, a member of the Editorial Committee of the Yale Boswell Editions, is editing Boswell's correspondence with his lifelong friend, William Johnson Temple, for its research series.

MARLIES K. DANZIGER is professor of English at Hunter College and the Graduate School of the City University of New York. She is editor, with Frank Brady, of *Boswell: The Great Biographer* (1989), the last volume of the Yale trade edition of Boswell's journals, and has written articles and books on Boswell, Johnson, Goldsmith, and Sheridan. She is currently at work on the Yale research edition of Boswell's journals in Germany and Switzerland.

MICHAEL FRY is an independent scholar and the author of *Patronage and Principle: A Political History of Modern Scotland* (1987); *Adam Smith's Legacy* (1992); *The Dundas Despotism* (1992); and *Scotland in the Age of the Disruption* (1993). He is a political columnist for the *Sunday Times* (London) and a regular contributor to Scottish newspapers and journals.

ISOBEL GRUNDY is Henry Marshall Tory Professor in the Department of English at the University of Alberta, Edmonton, Canada. Her recent works include *Samuel Johnson and the Scale of Greatness* (1986); *The Feminist Companion to Literature in English: Women Writers from the Middle Ages to the Present* (1990), with Virginia Blain and Patricia Clements; and *Women, Writing, History 1640–1740* (1992), edited with Susan Wiseman. Professor Grundy is presently writing a biography of Lady Mary Wortley Montagu.

IRMA S. LUSTIG, research associate in English at the University of Pennsylvania, is a member of the Editorial Committee of the Yale Boswell Editions and editor, in association with the late Frederick A. Pottle, of two volumes in the trade series of the journal: *Boswell: The Applause of the*

Jury, 1782–1785 (1981) and *Boswell: The English Experiment, 1785–1789* (1986). Her essays have been published in scholarly journals and collections in the United States and Great Britain. She has twice directed National Endowment for the Humanities Summer Seminars for School Teachers (1988 and 1992) on the subject of Boswell's journal and the *Life of Johnson.*

CAREY MCINTOSH, professor of English at Hofstra University, is the author of *The Choice of Life: Samuel Johnson and the World of Fiction* (1973) and *Common and Courtly Language: The Stylistics of Social Class in Eighteenth-Century British Literature* (1986). A book is now in progress on "Literacy, Politeness, and Style: The Evolution of English Prose, 1700–1800," a subject on which he has written and lectured extensively.

PETER F. PERRETEN, professor of English at Ursinus College, specializes in biography, autobiography, and eighteenth-century gardens. His essay, "Paradox in Paradise: Nature and Art in the Eighteenth-Century Landscape Garden," was published in *Man, God, and Nature in the Enlightenment,* edited by Donald C. Mell Jr., Theodore E.D. Braun, and Lucia M. Palmer (1988).

JOHN B. RADNER, associate professor of English at George Mason University, is the author of articles on Johnson, Boswell, and Swift published in *Studies in Eighteenth-Century Culture, Studies in English Literature, Eighteenth-Century Life,* and *The Age of Johnson.* A book-length study of the relationship of Johnson and Boswell is in progress.

RICHARD B. SHER, professor of history at the New Jersey Institute of Technology and Rutgers University–Newark, is the author of *Church and University in the Scottish Enlightenment: The Moderate Literati of Edinburgh* (1985) and co-editor of two collections of essays, *Scotland and America in the Age of the Enlightenment* (1990) and *Sociability and Society in Eighteenth-Century Scotland* (1993). Sher is also co-editor of Boswell's correspondence with the Scots literati, a forthcoming volume in the research series of the Yale Boswell Editions. He is the founder and executive secretary of the Eighteenth-Century Scottish Studies Society.

JOHN STRAWHORN, historian, has written extensively on his native Ayrshire since Glasgow University commissioned him to prepare the Ayrshire volume of the *Third Statistical Account* (1951). Among his many local histories are *Cumnock* (1966), *Irvine* (1985), and *Ayr* (1989). Dr. Strawhorn is editor of *Ayrshire at the Time of Burns* (1959); the *Collections* of Ayrshire Archeological and Natural History Society; and, with the late Nellie Pottle Hankins, editor of a fouthcoming volume in the research series of the Yale Boswell Editions, "The Correspondence of James Boswell with James Bruce and Andrew Gibb, Overseers of the Auchinleck Estate."

Hitoshi Suwabe, professor of English at Chuo University, Tokyo, and the author of *Eighteenth-Century Britain* (1988), has translated the *Life of Savage* into Japanese (1975) and written numerous articles on Johnson and Boswell in English and Japanese. Like Johnson, Suwabe is also a lexicographer. He edited the *Kenkyusha-Longman English-Japanese Phrasal Verb Dictionary* (1993) and the translation of the *Kenkyusha-Longman English-Japanese Idiom Dictionary* (1989).

William P. Yarrow, instructor of English at Joliet Junior College, also teaches classes on Boswell and the *Life of Johnson* in the Lyceum program of the Newberry Library, Chicago, where he is Scholar-in-Residence. The recipient of several awards from the National Endowment for the Humanities, in 1991–92 he was the NEH/Reader's Digest Teacher-Scholar for Illinois. Yarrow is the author of varied papers and articles on Boswell, Johnson, and their styles and of a forthcoming volume on Boswell in the English Author Series of Twayne Publishers.

Acknowledgments

The authors of this collection of essays are grateful to Yale University and the Edinburgh University Press for permission to quote so extensively from the manuscripts and publications of the Yale Editions of the Private Papers of James Boswell. We are conscious of an unusual debt.

We are also pleased to acknowledge the unfailing kindness of the office staff of the Yale Boswell Editions, Tulin Faulkner, managing editor, and Irene Adams, in particular, in furnishing materials as we needed them.

For the reproduction of manuscript, portraits, engravings, and photographs, we thank first the University Press of Kentucky, which made the unusual decision of publishing them in a collection of scholarly essays because illustrations, too, are instructive, as well as visually appealing. Our gratitude to the following persons and institutions is equally wholehearted for professional courtesies in providing the illustrations and permission to reproduce them: Viscountess Eccles; Peter F. Perreten; John Strawhorn; Derk Visser; Vincent Giroud, curator of modern books and manuscripts, The Beinecke Rare Book and Manuscript Library, Yale University; Joan H. Sussler, curator of prints, The Lewis Walpole Library, Yale University; Richard Wendorf, librarian, The Houghton Library, Harvard University; the National Galleries of Scotland; and the National Portrait Gallery, London. The Department of English of the University of Pennsylvania, John Richetti, chair, made a gracious and meaningful contribution to the illustrations.

The editor wishes to thank in addition Peter S. Baker, Mary Gillis, Joann Oseroff, Duncan Robinson, and Richard B. Sher for timely assistance of various kinds. Constance Billé and Ben Cohen made inestimable contributions to the index.

Cue Titles and Abbreviations

Unless otherwise noted, references in the text and notes of this volume to James Boswell's manuscripts are cited by the letter and number assigned to them in the *Catalogue of the Papers of James Boswell at Yale University*, ed. Marion S. Pottle, Claude Colleer Abbott, and Frederick A. Pottle, 3 vols. (Edinburgh: Edinburgh University Press and New Haven and London: Yale University Press, 1993).

Applause	*Boswell: The Applause of the Jury, 1782–1785*, ed. Irma S. Lustig and Frederick A. Pottle (New York: McGraw-Hill and London: Heinemann, 1981).
Boswell in Extremes	*Boswell in Extremes, 1776–1778*, ed. Charles McC. Weis and Frederick A. Pottle (New York: McGraw-Hill, 1970).
Boswell in Holland	*Boswell in Holland, 1763–1764*, ed. Frederick A. Pottle (New York: McGraw-Hill and London: Heinemann, 1952).
Corr: Club	*The Correspondence of James Boswell with Certain Members of The Club*, ed. Charles N. Fifer (New York: McGraw-Hill and London: Heinemann, 1976).
Corr: Garrick, Burke, Malone	*The Correspondence of James Boswell with David Garrick, Edmund Burke, and Edmund Malone*, ed. (Burke) Thomas W. Copeland, Peter S. Baker, Rachel McClellan, Robert Mankin, and Mark Wollaeger; (Garrick) George M. Kahrl and Rachel McClellan; and (Malone) James M. Osborn and Peter S. Baker (New York: McGraw-Hill and London: Heinemann, 1986).
Corr: Grange	*The Correspondence of James Boswell and John Johnston of Grange*, ed. R.S. Walker (New York: McGraw-Hill and London: Heinemann, 1966).
Corr: Life	*The Correspondence and Other Papers of James Boswell Relating to the Making of the "Life of Johnson,"* ed.

	Marshall Waingrow (New York: McGraw-Hill and London: Heinemann, 1969).
Defence	*Boswell for the Defence, 1769–1774,* ed. William K. Wimsatt Jr. and Frederick A. Pottle (New York: McGraw-Hill, 1959; London: Heinemann, 1960).
Earlier Years	Frederick A. Pottle, *James Boswell: The Earlier Years, 1740–1769* (New York: McGraw-Hill, 1966).
English Experiment	*Boswell: The English Experiment, 1785–1789,* ed. Irma S. Lustig and Frederick A. Pottle (New York: McGraw-Hill and London: Heinemann, 1986).
Grand Tour I (GT I)	*Boswell on the Grand Tour: Germany and Switzerland, 1764,* ed. Frederick A. Pottle (New York: McGraw-Hill and London: Heinemann, 1953).
Grand Tour II (GT II)	*Boswell on the Grand Tour: Italy, Corsica, and France, 1765–1766,* ed. Frank Brady and Frederick A. Pottle (New York: McGraw-Hill and London: Heinemann, 1955).
Great Biographer	*Boswell: The Great Biographer, 1789–1795,* ed. Marlies K. Danziger and Frank Brady (New York: McGraw-Hill and London: Heinemann, 1989).
Hebrides	*Boswell's Journal of a Tour to the Hebrides with Samuel Johnson, LL.D,* ed. Frederick A. Pottle and Charles H. Bennett (New York: McGraw-Hill, 1961).
In Search of a Wife	*Boswell in Search of a Wife, 1766–1769,* ed. Frank Brady and Frederick A. Pottle (New York: McGraw-Hill, 1956; London: Heinemann, 1957).
Journey	Samuel Johnson, *Journey to the Western Islands,* ed. Mary Lascelles (New Haven: Yale University Press, 1971).
Laird	*Boswell: Laird of Auchinleck, 1778–1782,* ed. Joseph W. Reed and Frederick A. Pottle (New York: McGraw-Hill, 1977).
Later Years	Frank Brady, *James Boswell: The Later Years, 1769–1795* (New York: McGraw-Hill, 1984).
Letters JB	*Letters of James Boswell,* ed. C.B. Tinker, 2 vols. (Oxford: Clarendon Press, 1924).
Letters SJ	*The Letters of Samuel Johnson,* ed. Bruce Redford, 5 vols. (Princeton: Princeton University Press, 1992, 1994).
Life	James Boswell, *The Life of Samuel Johnson, LL.D. Together with Boswell's Journal of a Tour to the Hebrides,* ed. G.B. Hill, rev. L.F. Powell, 6 vols. (Oxford: Clarendon Press, 1934–64).

London Journal (LJ)	*Boswell's London Journal, 1762–1763*, ed. Frederick A. Pottle (New York: McGraw-Hill, 1950; London: Heinemann, 1951).
Malahide	*The Private Papers of James Boswell from Malahide Castle in the Collection of Lt.-Colonel Ralph Heyward Isham*, ed. Geoffrey Scott and F.A. Pottle, 18 vols. (privately printed, 1928–34).
New Light on Boswell	*New Light on Boswell.* Critical and Historical Essays on the Occasion of the Bicentenary of the *Life of Johnson*, ed. Greg Clingham (Cambridge: Cambridge University Press, 1991).
New Questions, New Answers	*Boswell's "Life of Johnson": New Questions, New Answers*, ed. John A. Vance (Athens: University of Georgia Press, 1985).
Ominous Years	*Boswell: The Ominous Years, 1774–1776*, ed. Charles Ryskamp and Frederick A. Pottle (New York: McGraw-Hill and London: Heinemann, 1963).

I am, I flatter myself, completely a citizen of the world. In my travels through Holland, Germany, Switzerland, Italy, Corsica, France, I never felt myself from home; and I sincerely love "every kindred and tongue and people and nation."

The Journal of a Tour to the Hebrides, 1785

And, let me add, that, citizen of the world as I hold myself to be, I have that degree of predilection for my *natale solum*, nay, I have that just sense of the merit of an ancient nation, . . . that I should have felt a generous indignation at any injustice done to it.

The Life of Johnson, 1791

Introduction

IRMA S. LUSTIG

James Boswell was not a vaunting youth but a recognized author forty-five years of age when he assumed in *Journal of a Tour to the Hebrides* the lofty title "citizen of the world." He had aspired from his early years to the urbanity, cosmopolitanism, and wide sympathy implicit in the title of Goldsmith's well-known essays. Boswell, too, would be a "very universal man, quite a man of the world," the praise he accorded Sir Joshua Reynolds (identified in the manuscript of the *Life of Johnson*) because he associated with persons of "very discordant principles and characters." By the date of that remark to Samuel Johnson, 26 March 1779, Boswell had himself associated easily with many "discordant characters," Jean-Jacques Rousseau, John Wilkes, and Margaret Caroline Rudd among them. Indeed, the crowded record of Boswell's journal and his major works, the *Life of Johnson* especially, affirm his extraordinary adaptability and his claim to world citizenship, though "universal" in his terms was chiefly white, male, and western European. He considered himself wiser than Johnson in defending slavery.

Both Boswell's education and his personality fostered his eagerness to erase provincial borders geographically and intellectually. The continental travels which he cites in the *Tour* as evidence of his universal ease followed his introductions to learning almost as a matter of course. For he was literally a child of the Scottish Enlightenment, born of humanism, as the first section of essays in this volume attest. His father had assembled a fine classical library at Auchinleck and rewarded him for memorizing Horace; his first tutor, the Rev. John Dun, also taught him to enjoy the Roman poets. They thereby fueled Boswell's enraptured study of Italian antiquity, which Peter F. Perreten examines within.

By age twenty-one or twenty-two Boswell had been elected to the Select Society of Edinburgh. The most illustrious figures of several generations and a comprehensive range of professions were already his teachers, companions, and intimate friends. From Adam Smith at the University of Glasgow Boswell acquired the principles of rhetoric and style essential to the artistry analyzed by Carey McIntosh and William P. Yarrow in their essays. David Hume's serene skepticism challenged Boswell's uncertain religious orthodoxy and haunted him long after Hume's death. In large part it underlay, intellectually, his questioning of Johnson, Rousseau, and other continental philosophers and theologians whom Marlies K. Danzinger has restored to significant life in her essay. Richard B. Sher and Perreten document Boswell's intimacy with Alexander Home, Lord Kames, a judge, aesthetician, and author who was very influential with Thomas Jefferson and other statesmen of the American colonies. By uniting authority with affection, the combination essential to Boswell's numerous mentors—Johnson, General Pasquale de Paoli, and Sir Joshua Reynolds come to mind—Kames helped resolve Boswell's perilous conflicts with his father and guided his future. Traveling with Kames and reading his published works informed Boswell's enlightened response to nature and formal landscape. When in middle age he became Laird of Auchinleck, a responsibility which John Strawhorn shows him to have taken very seriously, he applied to his Ayrshire neighbor, the eminent agricultural improver Alexander Fairlie, and profited from his advice. In every role of his life Boswell was alert to the new developments of his age, though he also clung to regressive attitudes.

The "enlightened" practitioners who failed him utterly were professional politicians: Henry Dundas, for reasons that Michael Fry explains, and James Lowther, the notorious first Earl of Lonsdale, who multiplied enormous inherited wealth by adopting the new industrial and agricultural methods. Government was of longstanding interest to Boswell, as Thomas Crawford exhibits in his study of the correspondence with William Johnson Temple. Public life held center stage in the eighteenth century; it conferred power, and related to people, not abstractions. Boswell longed for a seat in the House of Commons, but he was unfit for *realpolitik* (though he grasped opportunity when he could), not only because he was erratic and indiscreet but also because of an essential rebelliousness. Had he been poised in character, had he been endowed with a mind for philosophical abstraction and scientific inquiry, he might have found the world in the adventuresome intellects of the Enlightenment among whom he lived at home.

But the field under Boswell's microscope was human. Individuals and society in their uniqueness and variety stimulated him more than formal study. He was a snob and yet indifferent to the respectable. Before he left for his Grand Tour he had been involved in the bohemian world of the theater and published his indecorous letters. He had read more than any one supposed, as he himself said, but his preferred method of learning was social, in conversation with superior minds on important issues. Throughout his life Boswell also traveled in quest of sensation—intensity of experience—and to escape the orbit of his father.

Scholars and critics have anatomized Boswell's restlessness and his inconsistencies. Causes are mysterious and complex, especially in so complex a personality. Boswell's written records, because they are massive and particular, make generalization hazardous as well as tempting. Still (genetics aside), one sees in his contradictions an obsessive conflict between free will and necessity, or fate. Boswell expressed it in religious terms, as was appropriate to his times and to one whose mother and tutors had fixed his mind from early childhood with Calvinist terrors. Suffused with guilt, for he knew himself to have sinned grossly against several of the Commandments, yet craving forgiveness and eternal life (the journal is material witness), he was baffled ultimately by the inscrutable will of God. In "'Over Him We Hang Vibrating'" Isobel Grundy shows Boswell's acceptance of uncertainty as a biographer. He was, after all, an advocate practiced in the weighing of evidence. He knew its limits. But spiritual uncertainty plagued him. He could not yield to Enlightenment skepticism because a void was intolerable. Nor could he be deprived of hope that God would elevate him.

Boswell's religious dilemma parallels a lifelong struggle with his earthly father. The torments reinforce each other. Lord Auchinleck's expectations of obedience as well as responsibility imprisoned Boswell in a paradox. Accustomed to authority from childhood, thwarted when he pursued his own goals, quixotic as they may have been, he never developed adequate self-confidence (strange to say of one so cocky) or self-discipline. Limits had to be imposed from without, by Johnson, Lord Kames, Rousseau, General Paoli, Edmond Malone, and by Margaret Boswell (why else did Boswell record his sexual transgressions, sometimes in obvious code, and leave his journal where she might find it?). The one ambition at which he persisted regardless of opinion was literary fame. He had no doubt of his gift.

The power of authority over Boswell was compounded because he admired his father, a person of obvious stature, and wished to please him. The awe he felt in Lord Auchinleck's presence quieted him (it "put a lid on my mind and kept it from boiling vehemently"), yet it kept him perpetually a boy. As late as 13 March 1778, Boswell was glad to have his daughter Veronica with him when he called upon his father: like a "little footstool to raise one," she elevated him to the rank of a father. Fearful of expressing his anger directly, Boswell defied and vexed his father in middle age as in youth, even on matters so self-destructive as the family entail. Lord Auchinleck, reserved, yet occasionally affectionate, grew cold and bitter. As early as 30 May 1763, when Boswell had already shamed him publicly many times, he could say no more in a reasonable and conciliatory letter than that his criticisms were "not from authority but from friendship. I am bound by the ties of nature to love you." On 29 August 1782, Boswell, forced to stand off from his father's deathbed, "Wept; for alas! there was not affection between us."

In his most formative relationship, to age forty-two, and psychologically to his death, Boswell had neither been embraced nor controlled his fate in matters deeply important to him. He had been denied a commission in the guards, become an advocate against his will, suffered his father's anger when he journeyed to London without his approval, yielded on the family entail (with Johnson's encouragement), and, having opposed Lord Auchinleck politically (and otherwise behaved imprudently), never obtained a seat in Commons. What Boswell achieved was infinitely superior to his frustrated ambitions, but, commonplace or foolish, they were *his* desires.

The contradictory impulses bred in him—toward authority and against it—are evident in many circumstances of Boswell's life and work and in his attitudes on Enlightenment issues. The archetypal relationship is replayed most conspicuously with Samuel Johnson. Olympian in his wisdom and detachment (as, not being kin, he could be), Johnson was also loving, even under demand. His advice and approval were essential, especially when Boswell's decision was predetermined, as in his permanent removal to London with his family. But it was inevitable that as Boswell's accomplishments mounted he should resent intimations of condescension or control. John B. Radner's painstaking study of the visit with Johnson at Ashbourne in September 1777 is a model of the struggle. Johnson could heal Boswell only if he recognized his independence.

The contest with Johnson at Ashbourne over the American cause, like Boswell's defence of Wilkes, is characteristic of his sympathy with the luckless or those he thought victims of injustice. Compassionate and impulsive, he was roused to active relief both in private and public life. His journal and expense accounts record many spontaneous acts of benevolence: small sums to the poor; substantial loans to relations when he himself was in debt; bustling to rehabilitate the depressed by training or employment; waiving an old tenant's arrears, resettling another in a more comfortable dwelling. Equally, if not more endearing to many readers, is his ardor in publicizing the Corsicans' struggle for independence and raising funds for them in Scotland. Emotions are also stirred by Boswell's defense of the disinherited at home, most famously John Reid "the sheepstealer," and Mary Bryant and two fellow convicts escaped from Botany Bay, for whom Boswell won pardons in his very last years. The intensity with which he hurled himself against those with the power to judge and to enforce their decisions is startling. In his own time it branded him an eccentric—even mad—and jeopardized his career at the law.

Modern readers, possessed of Boswell's journals, his anonymous publications now identified, cannot help but recognize in his passion a deep, almost frantic, personal involvement in the causes he took on. The symbolism is not always so clear as in Boswell's defense of Reid. Lord Auchinleck was among the robed justices before whom Boswell argued against Reid's condemnation by "habit and repute." Although the charge of sheepstealing had not been proved conclusively, Reid was found guilty because of a similar unproved charge in the past. What is one to make of Boswell's improbable plot to resuscitate Reid but a refusal to yield a life because of an allegedly bad character? As an advocate he was outraged; as a susceptible individual he fought for Reid as for a surrogate.

Boswell's energetic and voluntary efforts earlier on behalf of the Douglas Cause are also suggestive. He wrote songs, pamphlets, and an allegory, *Dorando*, and, when Archibald Douglas was denied as heir, was rewarded for these early efforts by serving among

Douglas's counsel in the triumphant appeal before the House of Lords. Elated by the reversal, Boswell headed the mob which broke windows in the houses of Edinburgh that were not illuminated in celebration. Lord Auchinleck was among the victims, though Boswell knew that he had voted for Douglas in the Court of Session and had not lit candles in respect to the Lord President. Douglas's success was a metaphor, as Frederick A. Pottle has written, for Boswell's legitimacy as heir to Auchinleck.

In rallying to various national struggles for independence in the 1760s and 1770s and thus aligning himself with libertarian ideals of the Enlightenment, Boswell also expressed a compelling personal need. He retreated in later years because paternal authority had always been central to his ideology. An unwavering monarchist, he was almost slavish in his adulation of the king (Lord Auchinleck retained his "old republican humor" to the end). Nor was Boswell fundamentally critical of the legislative system, though he thought Parliament corrupt in its expulsion of Wilkes after the Middlesex elections. Boswell himself wished to upset established arrangements in Ayrshire and supplant old rivals, but as readers of the *Life of Johnson* know well, he denounced advocates of reform, especially in the late 1780s and 1790s. He was sympathetic to the American colonists on legislative grounds: it was only just that they consent to their taxation, through a representative body under the Crown. If the news of Cornwallis's surrender at Yorktown "inspirited" Boswell at a gloomy period, perhaps the patriotic Scot took pleasure in the wound to the English lion. The old resentment doubtless contributed to his empathy with the Corsicans, though ambivalent as always, he identified himself to them as "English." But even in those early days, when he was fired by Rousseau's plans for a constitutional Corsica, Boswell's ideal was Paoli, "Father of his country," well-intentioned, far-seeing, and authoritarian.

Amidst his contradictions, Boswell was not merely conservative but archaic. Like other members of the landed gentry, he welcomed the wealth generated by commerce. But his allegiance was always feudal and became more intransigent with age, loneliness, and disappointment. The romantic attachment to Auchinleck in his younger years strikes the sympathetic chord of nature and of home. His posturing as Baron Boswell in Germany is amusing. One recognizes early on that hierarchical privilege bolsters his self-esteem. Margaret Boswell thought the whole family's self-importance ludicrous. But Boswell's *enactment* of rights he always assumed—the sexual exploitation of lower-class women, for example—arouses distaste and anger. He was bred a feudal laird and accepted his inheritance unquestioningly. Kind as he was to his dependents, dispensing paternal largesse gratified him, and he looked with satisfaction on the tenants ranged behind him in the family loft of parish churches where he was heritor.

In his essay in this volume on Boswell as laird, Strawhorn quotes my statement in the introduction to *Boswell: The Applause of the Jury* that Boswell's concern for the people of Auchinleck was the "noblest feature" of his tenure. Though I still hold the opinion, I would now qualify it. In preparing the volumes of journal that I edited with Professor Pottle I read extensively in Boswell's estate records and correspondence, but Strawhorn's more exhaustive researches disclose that strangled by debt and inadequate funds, Boswell was also hardheaded and unrelenting. With some exceptions, and in varying degrees, we strive for virtue but succumb to self-interest. The estate of Auchinleck had to pay in order to keep Boswell in London.

Just so, property and privilege swept Boswell up in the hysterical reaction to the French Revolution and its possible consequences at home. We who have lived through the last half century in America suspect the alarms by which dissent is managed and suppressed. Unlike those of his contemporaries who were persecuted and imprisoned, Boswell was easily convinced of official charges. The overthrow of established authority and the resultant instability in France terrified him philosophically and practically. In sending antirevolutionary pamphlets to Auchinleck to be distributed to his tenants, he signals his genuine fear that good father though he had been, he could be dispossessed.

Nothing, no caveats, will dispossess Boswell of his literary stature. His self-display, both willing and compulsive, in the *Life of Johnson*, has been used against him as a man of letters since Macaulay praised the book and mocked the author. Now, also paradoxically, Boswell suffers from good fortune: the popularity of his *London Journal* since its publication in 1950 has fixed his image for many readers as perpetually immature. The studies of the *Life of Johnson* in Part II of this volume emphasize not Boswell's idiosyncracies but his artistic skills. Those essays have been deliberately paired with the studies in Part I of his development as a "citizen of the world," for his sophistication as a writer is inseparable from his cosmopolitanism.

The *Life of Johnson* is a great repository of the Enlightenment in its various strains over almost the entire course of the eighteenth century. Johnson was born in 1709; his mind was shaped before the death of Pope and tested and enlarged by developments in the next four decades. Boswell's presence in the biography and his expansiveness add to Johnson's range of friends and acquaintances another mix of years, types, and opinions. The book seems peopled by all of Great Britain.

Thirty-one years younger than Johnson, Boswell responded effortlessly to the new, particularly in literature. The attention fastened on his persona in the biography, and, understandably, on the dramatic results of his questions, personal and yet philosophic, obscures what he is owed for the "View of Literature and literary Men in Great-Britain, for near half a Century." That quotation is, after all, the climactic claim of Boswell's title page.

In art, as in matters I have discussed above, Boswell united past and present, the established and the evolutionary, the didactic and the affective. Johnson was his literary hero; Boswell held with him to the moral function of literature and to the Enlightenment formula which combined instruction with pleasure. Johnson found these elements in Richardson. Given Boswell's robust appetites, his open affections, and his relish of human diversity, it is not surprising that he preferred Fielding and believed that his works promoted benevolence and generosity. He painted "very natural pictures of human life"; Johnson scorned them as "very low life." But Boswell was so aroused by *The Beggar's Opera* that he feared the effects of its gaiety, its heroic highwayman, and easy means of acquiring property on theater-goers less resistant than himself. He would not ban the work, however.

Boswell's alarmed enjoyment of Gay's satire typifies his visceral response to literature, as to the other arts. He who would be whinstone on the face of a mountain was excited by the rude and the sublime. The "wild peculiarity" of the first fragments of Ossian stirred him to subscribe to Macpherson's search for an epic in the Erse language. Only after considerable disillusionment did he yield to Johnson's skepticism. Johnson derided the abrupt opening of "The Bard"; Boswell admired Gray's poems, though he does not say why. One need not apologize for his taste, but did the flower born to blush unseen bring a pleasing tear to his eye?

For Boswell relished pathos, that "delicate power of touching the human feelings." It was to him the principle end of drama. He lamented that *Irene* contained not a single passage that drew a tear. He was also dissatisfied that Johnson praised Young's "Night Thoughts" highly but failed to acknowledge the pathetic power of the poetry to shake the nerves and pierce the heart. Johnson mocked the tender strains of William Hamilton of Bangour. And so on. Boswell started many conversations in the *Life of Johnson* which reveal his partiality to the sentimental and the pathetic. Johnson dismissed them briskly. Thus, in Boswell's great biography, as in Boswell, "citizen of the world" himself, Sensibility meets the Enlightenment, and the reader is engaged in the enduring drama of age, and youth, and change.

PART I
Boswell and the Enlightenment

Boswell's Travels through the German, Swiss, and French Enlightenment

MARLIES K. DANZIGER

Boswell and the continental Enlightenment? To link the two may, at first glance, seem far-fetched. Yet the journal Boswell wrote while traveling through Germany, Switzerland, and a little corner of France from June to December 1764 gives vivid accounts of several German and Swiss representatives of the Enlightenment, respected in their own day even if unfamiliar to British and American readers today. More importantly, Boswell provides a detailed record of his own intellectual development, revealing the impact of the Enlightenment on an eager, ambitious young man. And most significantly, his interviews with Rousseau and Voltaire, those key figures of the Enlightenment whom he portrays so vividly in some of the best-known passages of his early journals, represent a culminating point in his experiences.

Boswell was fortunate. Among the many acquaintances he made in Germany and Switzerland were several clerics, scientists, university professors, editors, writers, and even a ruling margrave, all of whom showed a remarkable willingness to discuss philosophical issues or literary questions with him. These men, who represented a variety of interests and points of view, may all be regarded as Enlightenment figures in that they believed in reason, religious tolerance, and self-development. But most of them were less radical or skeptical than the French philosophes. Several were, in fact, part of the conservative Enlightenment characteristic of northern Europe.[1] Boswell, with his relatively conventional religious beliefs and deep-seated monarchism, tested his own views against theirs, using his conversations with them to clarify his own thinking.

Indeed, Boswell was at a stage in his life when he was receptive to new experiences. His intellectual curiosity had been aroused by no less a person than Samuel Johnson, himself certainly a representative of the conservative Enlightenment in England, during their meetings in London in 1763. Now, at the age of twenty-four, his year-long homesickness in Holland behind him, Boswell was embarking on travels through which he hoped to develop his knowledge, tastes, and character. The German courts were a sensible choice for such self-cultivation; they were francophile and even francophone—culturally rich and linguistically manageable without the expense and social snobbery of the court in Paris or Versailles. Most of the Swiss cities were also French-speaking, but their main attraction for Boswell was that they lay on his path to Rousseau in Môtiers and Voltaire at Ferney.

As he moved from one interesting acquaintance to another, Boswell became part of the cosmopolitan network that is a hallmark of the Enlightenment. And he contributed to this network, as we shall see, by bringing greetings, transmitting messages, starting correspondences, and finally writing about his experiences in his journal, which he hoped to convert into a travel book. That he was so readily received by a number of prominent people attests to his persuasiveness, perhaps even to a certain youthful charm. Besides, he was a Scot—something of a novelty—and, better still, he could claim to be a baron, at least by the standards of the German courts, and could therefore lay claim to some attention in those rank-conscious societies.

At the beginning of his tour, Boswell made a brief foray into the intellectual world of Berlin. He attended a meeting of the Académie royale des sciences et belles lettres, an august body founded in 1700 with Leibniz as its president and now under the personal control of Frederick II (who insisted on its French name).[2] Boswell heard two papers, one in Latin on astronomy and another in French on ambergris, but was "not greatly edified" (13 Sept. 1764, *GT I* 92–93). At least the Academy's Perpetual Secretary should have been interesting, for Jean-Henri-Samuel Formey (1711–97) was a prolific editor, lecturer, and translator, as well as the intellectual leader of the large Huguenot community in Berlin. But when Boswell dined in his company, Formey spoke so much about his books and lectures that Boswell was struck only by his vanity, not by his accomplishments (1 Aug. 1764, *GT I* 46–47).

His meeting with one of the Academy's scientists was more satisfying. The chemist Andreas Sigismund Marggraf (1709–82), best known for discovering the sugar in the sugar beet, was apparently working on crystallization, for he was able to make a "composition" that looked like precious stones and presented Boswell with a sapphire-like substance. Boswell promised to send him minerals from Scotland in return. It was a fine gesture of international good will, though whether Boswell ever sent anything is not recorded. At the same time, he was gathering interesting anecdotes. In an unusual glimpse that belies Marggraf's reputation as a quiet, restrained man,[3] Boswell saw him greeting a burst of thunder and lightning with the cry, "I love to see my God in flames" (14 Sept. 1764, *GT I* 94). But Boswell was merely sightseeing, and in general was more interested in personalities than in scientific achievements.

Religion was a different matter; on that subject he was really in search of personal enlightenment. Boswell had already experienced one religion, strict Presbyterianism, in his childhood; had explored several others, including Methodism, Catholicism, and deism; and had recently decided to become an Anglican. For a long time he had been troubled by the relation between religion and life; that is, between his yearning for piety and his yielding to temptations, especially to sexual transgressions. And he had given some thought to such religious concepts as revelation, foreknowledge, free will, and the immortality of the soul. His frame of mind is vividly illustrated in several precepts in the "Inviolable Plan," which he composed in Holland on 15 October 1763 and was determined to read "frequently" to regulate his behavior. The admonition "Elevate your soul by prayer and by contemplation without mystical enthusiasm" suggests his genuine spiritual aspirations but also his distrust, by this time, of the highly emotional approach of the Methodists. And the exhortation "Be steady to the Church of England, whose noble worship has always raised your mind to exalted devotion and meditation on the joys of heaven," attests not only to his newfound Anglicanism but also, by its focus on "the joys of heaven," to his attempts to counteract the Presbyterian teachings of hell, punishment, and eternal damnation (*Boswell in Holland* 388).[4] Yet his Anglicanism was not quite secure. On 24 June 1764, for instance, he was finding "Catholic pomp" an aid to devotion and was only tentative about his beliefs: "I see a probability for the truth of Christianity" (*GT I* 10–11). And so, wavering between doubts and the earnest wish to believe, he made a point of seeking out the representatives of several religious denominations.

The remarkable Lutheran clergyman Johann Friedrich Wilhelm Jerusalem (1709–89), whom Boswell visited repeatedly in Brunswick, seemed just the man to reassure him. Known locally as the abbé or Abt (abbot) Jerusalem because he headed a seminary, he combined great personal piety with the ability to reason persuasively about religion; indeed, his particular forte was the soothing of religious doubts. Formerly tutor to the Hereditary Prince of Brunswick and his brothers as well as chaplain to the Duke and Duchess of Brunswick, he had managed to calm the restlessness of the Prince and the momentary doubts of the Duchess by giving them, as he explained to Boswell, "a neat summary of the proofs of Christianity" (15 Aug. 1764, *GT I* 63–64). He even promised Boswell a copy, though he never sent it.[5]

Jerusalem was very much a man of the Northern Enlightenment. He was known for his religious tolerance; he was well versed in the classics, the Bible, and contemporary thought; and he accepted the basic tenets of Christianity, "the genuine Christian religion itself," while refusing to become involved with the sectarian squabbles of the time. Moreover, as an educator as well as a clergyman—he was founder and director of a renowned school, the collegium Carolinum, as well as the head of a seminary—he certainly regarded religion as essential for a moral, happy life. Above all, true to the Protestant tradition, the abbé valued personal religious experience. On their first meeting he told Boswell with disarming frankness how his own faith had been confirmed. Twice, when he was on the verge of death, he had tried to find peace by reading Plato's *Phaedo,* but in vain. It was reading the New Testament that had given him strength. "Thus . . . I had a trial of my religion" (28 June 1764, *GT I* 14). That the New Testament was so important in confirming Jerusalem's faith was no accident; much of his teaching was based on a close reading of the Bible. Boswell was touched by the anecdote, which he recorded in some detail in his journal. But he could not apply it to himself.

Nor were the abbé's religious theories easy for Boswell to grasp, particularly those on revelation, which they also discussed during their first meeting. Jerusalem was drawing on several sources, notably the Leibniz-Wolffian philosophy with its emphasis on the harmonious interaction of reason and revelation, and English latitudinarianism with its emphasis on rational and practical Christianity, an approach to religion he had come to know during a stay in England.[6] His popularizing treatise, *Betrachtungen über die vornehmsten Wahrheiten der Religion* (Reflections on the Foremost Truths of Religion), published a few years after Boswell's visit, gives a good idea of his thinking. In the first volume (1768), Jerusalem interpreted revelation as God's gift to mankind in general; he even paraphrased the passage in the first Epistle of Pope's *Essay on Man* that scorns man's pride in thinking he is singled out by God. Yet the abbé also recognized each individual's wish to be known to God, and he acknowledged a special revelation for individual human beings, at least to the extent of letting them feel that their happiness or suffering serves a purpose in the universe.[7] In the second volume of the *Betrachtungen* (1772, 1774) Jerusalem took the Old and New Testaments as quasi-historical documents and described three stages of revelation: from God the Creator in Genesis, from Moses, and from Christ. Such ideas were surely of interest to Boswell, who had been encouraged to think about revelation by Johnson and had continued to do so during his stay in Holland.[8] But Boswell made no attempt to record the abbé's arguments and simply declared: "My faith was confused. Objections rose thick against revelation. Yet I hoped at last to attain stability" (28 June 1764, *GT I* 14–15).

Jerusalem's explanation that divine foreknowledge was compatible with free will was not reassuring to Boswell, either. After discussing this point in another of their conversations, Boswell noted patronizingly that "the good abbé" could not bear to question divine power. Unwilling to accept Jerusalem's characteristic balancing of opposites, Boswell strongly favored one side: "I boldly opposed prescience, and clearly defended my liberty" (11 Aug. 1764, *GT I* 56). It is noteworthy that in this emphasis on free will, Boswell was rejecting not only the abbé's moderate position but also the much sterner Calvinist teachings on predestination and original sin. However, in a letter to Jerusalem written from Strasbourg some weeks later, on 16 November, Boswell was no longer so sure. Jocularly calling their argument about free will and necessity a mere "sport of the mind" because it was bound to be inconclusive, he admitted to second thoughts: "I used to be a strenuous asserter of the Liberty of man. No Roman ever had a warmer ambition to vindicate external freedom than I had to vindicate internal" (L654). Suddenly, reflecting on how certain memories can come to the fore without one's volition, he was aware of experiences that seemed to contradict free will. And so Boswell was continuing the exchange of ideas begun with Jerusalem in Brunswick, showing that their conversations still germinated in his mind.

Although he could not accept the abbé's religious views, Boswell was touched by the fact that Jerusalem's apparently cloudless piety was actually hard won. This seemingly calm, rational man had suffered from periodic depressions—the "hypochondria" that afflicted so many of his contemporaries, including Boswell—but had borne them with patience, thanks, he said, to God's help. With hindsight, we know that Jerusalem's son was not so fortunate; the model for Goethe's Werther, he committed suicide a few years later. Boswell, relieved to hear that Jerusalem had successfully vanquished "the demon," described his own extreme depression in Utrecht and felt like a hero for not having succumbed. In addition, Boswell was impressed by the abbé's library, one of several created by European scholars in the Enlightenment,[9] and was determined to have a "large and good one" at Auchinleck one day (11 Aug. 1764, *GT I* 56–57).

While in Berlin, Boswell encountered a more skeptical approach to religion in a secular representative of the Enlightenment, the mathematician Jean Salvemini de Castillon (1708–91). A cosmopolitan figure, Italian by birth, Castillon had earned a law degree from Pisa but had then taught mathematics and astronomy in Lausanne and more recently in Utrecht. He had just been appointed to the Prussian Academy and it was he, in fact, who took Boswell to the Academy meeting. Castillon was an active scholar. He had edited Newton's minor mathematical treatises and the Leibniz-Euler correspondence; he had also written an answer to Rousseau's *Discours sur l'origine de l'inégalité* (in 1756, two years after its publication) and had translated Pope's *Essay on Man* into Italian (1760) and Locke's *Elements of Natural Philosophy* into French (1761). Frederick II was sufficiently impressed by him that he named Castillon royal astronomer a year after Boswell's visit and eventually made him head of the Academy's mathematics section.[10]

Boswell had studied with Castillon in Utrecht without enthusiasm, but now that both were newcomers in Berlin, they sought each other's company. On one occasion, Castillon acknowledged with remarkable frankness that he considered God a being to be revered but that he disapproved of emotional worship, which he called "the fancy of fanatics." He also declared that only the Gospels were "truly Christian scriptures," that the Epistles might be useful "sometimes," but that "the Christian religion had not added much to morality." Sounding rather like the French philosophes with their distrust of fanaticism and doubts about the ameliorating power of the Church, Castillon left Boswell wondering: "What would he be at?" (14 Sept. 1764, *GT I* 94–95). Questioning the link between Christianity and morality, in particular, was bound to be disturbing to Boswell, who needed Christian beliefs and indeed the sense of belonging to a church (he was an avid church-goer) even though he changed from one religious denomination to another.

Interestingly enough, Castillon's ideas as recorded by Boswell sound more skeptical than those expressed in his *Réponse* to Rousseau's *Discours sur l'origine de l'inégalité*, published in Amsterdam while he was teaching in Utrecht. In this work, in which he debunked Rousseau's idealization of the state of nature, Castillon was hardly ever critical of religion or the clergy, and he expressed such unsubversive ideas as that God the Creator has endowed man with a soul, with reason, and—following Francis Hutcheson—with a moral sense (99–107, 117). Perhaps Castillon was being deliberately cautious in the *Réponse*. That would explain Boswell's commiserating with him for having had to hide his philosophical thoughts while in Utrecht (29 August 1764, *GT I* 77). Apparently the Dutch were even less ready than Boswell for some of Castillon's ideas.

Boswell expressed his commiseration after he recorded their talk about that other favorite subject of his, free will. At first Castillon maintained that he could "conceive the most perfect prescience without restraining liberty"—the position which Jerusalem had taken but which Boswell now rejected as "absurd." Thereupon Castillon, giving the subject a more philosophical cast, explained that since God has offered man part of His own nature, He has granted man some of this will. And he offered as example the choice between two eggs. Boswell does not clarify this puzzling allusion, which perhaps refers to man's ability to reach a decision even when confronted by identical objects.[11] But he called Castillon's reasoning, which included a justification for free will, "just and clear" (29 Aug. 1764, *GT I* 77). Still, as when confronted with Jerusalem's ideas on revelation, Boswell made no effort to express more of these complicated ideas in his journal.

Continuing his search for a variety of religious views, Boswell sought out a clever Jesuit a few weeks later in Mannheim, which was a Catholic stronghold. According to Boswell, our sole source of information about him, the Père Monier was French, had been in Canada, and had left France when his order was dissolved; that is, some time after the summer of 1761. With Monier, Boswell jokingly raised the question of whether he, as a non-Catholic, was doomed to be eternally damned. This was no idle question, because already as a small child and hence long before his brief flirtation with Catholicism, Boswell had been terrified by the Calvinist teachings about eternal punishment (see *Earlier Years* 2). Monier gave the traditional answer of the Church, that Boswell did not have the excuse of ignorance a peasant might have, thereby implying that Boswell would indeed be damned. But at this stage in his life Boswell was no longer impressed by such an argument nor by Monier's other reasoning (not recorded in the journal). Although he acknowledged his liking for the "grand worship" of the Catholics, he refused to believe in a God so cruel as to withhold salvation from non-Catholics. Their meeting ended with Boswell wittily expressing the hope that he would meet Monier again in heaven, a possibility that the priest had just denied (7 Nov. 1764, *GT I* 168–69). In rejecting the Jesuit's position, Boswell was again demonstrating that he had freed himself from the oppressive ideas of his Presbyterian childhood.

In a more secular vein, Boswell enjoyed a taste of the life of learning and literature when he came to the university town of Leipzig. He had studied at the University of Edinburgh—happily—and at the University of Glasgow—unhappily—and was eager for a look at academic life in Germany. Again he was fortunate, for he immediately became acquainted with several professors, notably Johann Christoph Gottsched (1700–66), who for more than thirty years had labored to improve the public's taste in the arts and above all to make German, rather than French and Latin, the language of literary and scholarly writing. Gottsched had also done much to rescue the German theater from its low repute by encouraging local acting companies to stage serious dramas. He had himself written a few neoclassical plays, including a *Cato* based partly on Addison's drama; had produced several *Spectator*-like journals, some odes, and numerous essays; and had published a number of textbooks, a grammar, a rhetoric, an encyclopedia of literary terms, and an important literary treatise, the *Critische Dichtkunst* (1730), which had gone through four editions by 1751.[12] Openly didactic and successful in improving the taste of a new middle-class public, he had achieved much by the time Boswell came to see him in 1764.

History has not dealt kindly with Gottsched, largely because Lessing's blistering attack on his neoclassical views, begun in Letter 17 of *Briefe, die neueste Literatur betreffend* (1759) and continued in the *Hamburgische Dramaturgie* (1769), as well as Goethe's boredom as his student have made him appear a rigidly conservative fuddy-duddy. His reputation was already waning; he was, in fact, a representative of an earlier generation of German Enlightenment scholars. But Boswell, who described him as "one of the most distinguished *literati* in this country," found that Gottsched was still esteemed in Leipzig[13] and rightly credited him with "the true cultivation of the German language, of which he has given an excellent grammar" (4 Oct. 1764, *GT I* 125).

Boswell was welcomed warmly by Gottsched. They talked about linguistic matters, and Boswell, cleverly finding a topic that would interest Gottsched, described the Scots dictionary he was planning to compile.[14] Now he was not just an observer but an active participant in intellectual endeavors. Gottsched encouraged him in his project and offered advice (6 Oct. 1764, *GT I* 130). Their talk also turned, as might be expected, to Johnson's *Dictionary*, for which Gottsched had high praise. Oddly enough, Boswell made no comment in his journal about the strong resemblance between Gottsched and Johnson, though he could hardly have failed to notice the similarity in age, portly appearance, literary and linguistic interests, and conservative outlook. And, as with Johnson, Boswell quickly established rapport with this formidable scholar.

Boswell was pleased to gain permission to look for bibliographical sources in books on etymology in Gottsched's private library, an extensive collection that was greatly prized in his time.[15] Indeed, libraries became the focus of Boswell's attention in Leipzig. When, at Gottsched's suggestion, he called on Karl Andreas Bel (1717–82), professor of poetry, he immediately noticed another good private library. And since Bel was also university librarian, Boswell was shown the great Leipzig University Library with its treasured German manuscripts and the Bible that had belonged to Luther. Thrilled by these sights, Boswell was confirmed in his interest in collecting books for himself. No longer contented with the "large and good" library he had planned in Brunswick, he was now determined to have a "noble" one at Auchinleck (5 Oct. 1764, *GT I* 126).

Moreover, Boswell was able to learn about a publication that was the pride of Leipzig and a fruit of the Enlightenment interest in learning. The *Acta eruditorum Lipsiae*, begun in 1682, was the oldest periodical in Germany devoted to reviews of recently published scholarly and literary works.[16] Bel, who edited the *Acta*, not only described its history but also read aloud the preface to the year's volume (written entirely in Latin), which he was about to deliver to the printer. Boswell took to the scholarly scene with obvious pleasure: "I was in a true classical humour, quite *doctus.*" As if to demonstrate this immersion in the classics, he sprinkled his talk with a few Latin phrases, as when he jocularly called a simple supper he served to Bel a "*cena Pythagorica*"; that is, a meal without meat as recommended by Pythagorus (5–6 Oct. 1764, *GT I* 126–27, 130). He regretted not having studied in Leipzig himself and promised to send his son there if and when he had one. After Boswell's death his son Sandy fulfilled this promise, at least to the extent of spending some time in Leipzig while on his own continental travels.

Perhaps made unduly proud by his heady intellectual experiences with Gottsched and Bel, Boswell became censorious when he met those he regarded as the lesser lights of Leipzig. He criticized Johann Bartholomaeus Rogler (1728–91), editor of a German-English dictionary, assuming that Rogler had based his text on Johnson's *Dictionary* and unnecessarily introduced additional words, whereas in fact Rogler had worked with a German dictionary and had only augmented it with words drawn from Johnson's work. Boswell was furthermore unimpressed by Christian Fürchtegott Gellert (1715–69), professor of Philosophy at the university and a poet much admired in Leipzig. Boswell described him as "a poor, sickly creature" and was not sympathetic even though Gellert was suffering from extreme melancholia, the very complaint Boswell himself experienced in milder form. He also considered

Gellert's poems mere "versifying," though his own German, he admitted, was not good enough to appreciate them (5 Oct. 1764, *GT I* 127).

Right or wrong in his judgments, he was whetting his critical faculties. When he met Bartholomew Tanner, the first professor of English at the University of Strasbourg, Boswell could apparently hold his own in literary conversation. "I was quite a genteel *literatus,*" he noted in his journal (14 Nov. 1764, *GT I* 178). He set down no details about their talk, but he must have been impressed by Tanner's inaugural speech, published as "A Discourse, showing the Influence, which the Living Languages, Particularly the English, have on the Cultivation of the Arts and Sciences" (1764), since he took a copy along for the library at Auchinleck.[17]

Thanks to another recommendation from Gottsched, Boswell met an additional interesting Enlightenment figure a few weeks later in Basel. Emmanuel Wolleb (1706–88) not only served as president of the Chamber of Justice (*Schultheiss*) but also wrote philosophical and satirical pieces.[18] Some of his writings were collected in a periodical entitled the *Helvetische Patriot,* which appeared from 1755 to 1757 and was dedicated to Gottsched.

Boswell recognized in Wolleb "a German-Swiss *literatus,* full of animal spirits" (25 Nov. 1764, *GT I* 203). He was a mine of fascinating information. In regaling Boswell with explanations for the curious fact that the clocks of Basel had been running an hour ahead of others in the region for many centuries, Wolleb showed a distinctly anti-Papist bent; he impishly suggested, for instance, that the bishops at the Council of Basel (1431–49) had changed the time in order to meet their mistresses at an earlier hour.[19] Furthermore, when Wolleb took Boswell to see a tiny chapel on the main bridge across the Rhine, he pointed to an obscene sculpture just below the niche formerly occupied by a statue of the Virgin. Such anti-Catholic bias reflected not only the spirit of the Reformation that was strong in Basel, previously an important Catholic bishopric, but also the debunking of the Church that was typical of the more radical Enlightenment. Less worldly than Wolleb, Boswell seems to have been shocked by the sculpture of a woman with thighs apart that replaced the Madonna (25–26 Nov. 1764, *GT I* 204, 207).

Wolleb had more intellectual interests as well. For instance, he was familiar with Rousseau's educational theories, which he claimed to have followed in bringing up his own daughter. Hearing about such an experiment was a good preparation for meeting Rousseau himself and also no doubt increased the store of interesting ideas Boswell was gathering on his travels.

Another of Boswell's goals, to meet the enlightened monarchs in his path, proved more difficult to achieve. He had been eager to meet Frederick II of Prussia, whom he initially admired as the great defender of the Protestant cause in the Seven Years War and whom he was thrilled to see exercising his troops (13 July 1764, *GT I* 24). Boswell was particularly struck by the fact that this great military hero also had keen intellectual interests, had played host to Voltaire for several years before they quarrelled, and had published poems, essays, and histories under the pseudonym of *le philosophe de Sans Soucci* (an allusion to his rococo summer palace). The sight of both Frederick's and Voltaire's works in the town palace of Potsdam pleased Boswell greatly (3 July 1764, *GT I* 18). But no matter how hard he tried to obtain an interview through his influential acquaintances, including Frederick's close friends the Earl Marischal of Scotland, the British ambassador, and his secretary (all Scots), as well as the King's reader, Boswell's efforts were foiled. He could not know that he was being deliberately kept away from Frederick; apparently Boswell's acquaintances feared that he might behave foolishly in his enthusiasm and so irritate the short-tempered ruler.[20]

In any case, in spite of his enthusiasm Boswell could not ignore the brutalities associated with Frederick's militarism. At first, seeing a group of soldiers in the guardroom, Boswell was flippant, likening them to "herrings in a plentiful season" or mere canon fodder (13 July 1764, *GT I* 25). A few weeks later, however, he was dismayed to see the beating of a deserter, who was forced to run the gauntlet (4 Sept. 1764, *GT I* 82). By the end of his stay in Berlin, his enthusiasm had waned. Eventually, when he saw the destruction of Dresden caused by Frederick's bombardment of 1760, he waxed indignant: "I hated the barbarous hero" (9 Oct. 1764, *GT I* 133). Even if his judgment was colored by personal pique, by the disappointment of being denied an interview, he became well aware of the pernicious side of an absolute militaristic rule.

Staunch monarchist that he was, Boswell did not give up his hopes of meeting a genuinely enlightened ruler. Yet at least at first, luck was against him. The young anglophile Prince Leopold

Friedrich Franz of Anhalt-Dessau, the first culture-loving member of a ruling family previously devoted to hunting and military life, was away on his travels. Nor did Boswell realize that the Duke and Duchess of Saxe Gotha were actually the sort of rulers he was seeking, especially the Duchess, Luise Dorothee (1710–67), a highly educated woman interested in science and philosophy. She had gathered a group of like-minded intellectuals at her court, had persuaded Voltaire to stay in Gotha for several months after he left Prussia in 1753, and was carrying on a lifelong correspondence with him. A few months after Boswell's visit she also invited Rousseau to Gotha to seek refuge from his enemies.[21] But she was no longer in good health, and for Boswell she and her husband were merely "plain old people" (16 Oct. 1764, *GT I* 141).

Then, at the end of his travels through the German domains, Boswell's highest expectations were met by Karl Friedrich (1728–1811), Margrave of Baden-Durlach, in Karlsruhe. The epitome of an enlightened ruler, the margrave was interested in philosophy, literature, and the other arts. Though somewhat weak-willed himself, he was married to the strong-minded, highly intellectual, artistic Karoline Luise (1723–83), and together they presided over a culture-loving little court. The margrave was pleased to speak English, having visited England twice, and was even familiar with current Scottish literature. Boswell had the opportunity to shine, describing his first meeting with Johnson as well as the Select Society of Edinburgh, to which both David Hume and he himself belonged (9, 13 Nov. 1764, *GT I* 175, 178).

Better still, Boswell could discuss his favorite subject, religion, with the margrave. On fate and free will, Boswell felt he acquitted himself well—"I was clear and lively and strong"—though, as usual, he did not record what his thoughts on the subject now were. Still, as the ensuing conversations made clear, he was not prepared to accept the rational skepticism that seemed to be in the air in Karlsruhe; it was probably no accident that Voltaire had been a welcome guest here, too, a few years earlier. When the discussion turned to the nature of the soul, the margrave exhibited quite advanced ideas and, in fact, echoed those Voltaire had expressed in his recently published *Dictionnaire philosophique*.[22] One knows very little about when and how the soul is created in an individual, the margrave pointed out, and he joked about the possibility that God, using a trial and error method in creating human beings, might take the soul out again "if the experiment fails" (15 Nov. 1764, *GT I* 180). Furthermore, perhaps influenced by Hume, the margrave wondered how one could know that the Bible was really God's word. Boswell recognized him as "a moderate sceptic" (14 Nov. 1764, *GT I* 179) but did not seriously entertain such irreverent notions.

Boswell did not hesitate to make his own position clear. He believed in "the religion of Jesus as displayed in the four Gospels" and vehemently opposed Hume "and other infidels who destroyed our principles and put nothing firm in their place." Continuing these thoughts with a young courtier who declared himself a materialist and rejected the possibility of an afterlife, Boswell opposed him "with firm vivacity" and suggested that such beliefs would lead the courtier to thieving if he could get away with it (14 Nov. 1764, *GT I* 178–80). Confronted with the skepticism of the Karlsruhe court, Boswell reaffirmed the basic beliefs of Christianity and firmly upheld these as essential guides to moral conduct.

Although they were not in agreement on religious questions, Boswell continued to be charmed by the amiable Karl Friedrich, who ruled over a well-run court and country, was devoted to the life of the mind, and was willing to share his thoughts with his visitor. Even without the margrave's Order of Fidelity, which Boswell aspired to but did not receive, he knew that he had made an excellent impression.

Indeed, he had done more by this time. He had held his own in serious conversations with important people and had won their approval. The abbé Jerusalem, Gottsched, Bel, Rogler, and even the Margrave of Baden-Durlach agreed to correspond with him. He was ready for the much-hoped-for meetings with Rousseau and Voltaire.

There is no need to rehearse all the details of these meetings, which are well known from Boswell's own journal and from Frederick A. Pottle's eloquent description (*Earlier Years* 162–97). It will be more fruitful to consider in what sense these indeed represented culminating experiences for the young Boswell, inclined to the conservative Enlightenment of northern Europe and now confronting the key representatives of the more radical continental Enlightenment.

What made the meetings with Rousseau and Voltaire such a high point was, first and foremost, the fact that Boswell regarded them as such. "Voltaire, Rousseau, immortal names!" The phrase his friend William Johnson Temple had used in the spring of 1759 in alluding to their plans to travel together on the Continent still echoed in Boswell's mind on 29 December 1764, when he repeated it in his journal just after completing his visits to the two great men (*GT I* 302). Naturally, his enthusiasm colored the meetings and led him not just to have interesting conversations, as had been the case with the Enlightenment figures he had met up to this time, but to become deeply, personally, involved.

With Rousseau, Boswell's experiences were not strictly intellectual. He felt drawn to Rousseau as the author of the *Nouvelle Héloïse* (1760) and of the profoundly personal religious passages in *Emile* (1762), the "Profession de foi du vicaire savoyard." In his famous letter of 3 December 1764 asking for a meeting, Boswell presented himself as a Scottish Saint-Preux endowed with a sensitive, melancholy temperament and in need of a mentor. And during the course of several days he lived like a Rousseauesque hero, first transported by the sublime mountainous landscape surrounding Môtiers, later experiencing a Rousseauesque idyll while sharing a simple meal with Rousseau and Thérèse Levasseur, and finally gaining the assurance that he had achieved that special bond of friendship with Rousseau that the *Nouvelle Héloïse* had popularized. But side by side with these emotional experiences, Boswell also encountered Rousseau the philosophe, the man with strong, independent opinions, who provided food for thought on several intellectual topics that had already caught Boswell's attention on his travels.

On religion, the subject that had so often preoccupied him, Boswell gained a striking view of Rousseau's highly personal, highly moral, and highly unconventional beliefs. From the start of their acquaintance, for instance, he found Rousseau remarkably outspoken in his disparaging remarks about clerics who offer incomprehensible explanations for already incomprehensible notions and about the "mummeries" of monastic life (3, 5 Dec. 1764, *GT I* 223, 231). Much more explicitly than Castillon or Wolleb, Rousseau was demonstrating the critical attitude toward the established Church that was characteristic of the radical Enlightenment.

Moreover, in a scene that is well known but worth noting here because it reveals a newly found aggressiveness in Boswell as interviewer, he dared to ask the question that many in Europe must have wanted to put to Rousseau since the banning of the *Social Contract* and *Emile* in 1762: "Mais dites moi sincerement: etes vou Chretien?" The result was a far more interesting pronouncement than any he had gained from his earlier conversations on religion: Rousseau's credo, his belief in the clear and simple religion of the Gospels without any later accretions, not even those based on St. Paul. That Boswell recognized the significance of the moment is shown by the dramatic presentation in the journal, complete with eye contact and gestures, foreshadowing his best efforts in the *Life of Johnson*. "I looked at him with a searching eye. His countenance was no less animated. Each stood steady and watched the other's looks. He struck his breast and replied "Oui—Je me pique de l'étre."[23] The whole episode showed Boswell a piety based only on personal feeling. Unencumbered by a reliance on ritual or clerical intervention, this was certainly a more extreme Enlightenment religion than the sort Boswell had encountered in the Lutheran Jerusalem or the Catholic Père Monier.

More significantly still, the meetings with Rousseau led Boswell to review his own religious experiences. Having only skirted his private doubts in his conversations with Jerusalem, Castillon, Monier, and the Margrave of Baden-Durlach, he expressed himself quite openly in the "Ebauche de ma vie" he composed for Rousseau. In this extensive autobiographical sketch written on 5 December 1764, Boswell, clearly inspired by Rousseau's well-known interest in childhood education, unburdened himself about his earliest religious training. He blamed his mother for inflicting on him her stern Calvinist teaching, which had literally put the fear of God into him with its emphasis on eternal punishment for sinners and which must have included an emphasis on predestination. And he recalled the interminable Sundays spent listening to the sermons of the Presbyterian ministers and being forced to concentrate exclusively on pious thoughts (L1107; see also *Earlier Years* 2–3). In revealing the roots of his interest in eternal punishment, predestination and free will, so often the topics in his previous conversations about religion, he was bringing into the open some powerful ghosts from his past.

The response from Rousseau that Boswell had hoped for, though brief, was again pointedly anti-clerical. "Vous avez eté enfariné," Rousseau declared, using an untranslatable term that suggests Boswell had been duped and even brainwashed. "Ne voyez jamais un pretre" (14 Dec. 1764, J6, folio 797; *GT I* 252). But, although Boswell recorded this advice in the journal, he gave no indication that he was prepared to give up his church. Nor could he relinquish his religious preconceptions in another respect. Full of guilt feelings, he had included in the "Ebauche" a vivid description of his adulterous affair with a Scottish lady, and had heard Rousseau's advice to follow his conscience and break the relationship. This seemingly simplistic advice actually encapsulated Rousseau's belief, expressed in the "Profession de foi," that one's personal conviction, conscience, should be one's moral guide. Boswell had then pressed Rousseau about how one should atone for one's misdeeds and had heard Rousseau declare that suffering was not necessary as atonement, but rather that the only way to make up for evil was to do good. Although Boswell found this "a beautiful thought," he could not forego the notion of "satisfaction by punishment," which he termed "a leading principle of Christianity" (14 Dec. 1764, *GT I* 254). Rousseau's ideas on religion and morality were too unorthodox for Boswell.

Literary discussions with Rousseau proved less troubling to Boswell. Indeed, he occasionally felt free to make provocative comments and so gathered more interesting material than he had been able to record after meeting Gottsched and Bel in Leipzig. His mentioning that Voltaire had no liking for Rousseau was surely no accident and elicited Rousseau's bristling comments about Voltaire in turn. Even more daring was Boswell's reference to Johnson's remark about innovative thinkers who try to milk the bull after they have exhausted the milk of truth in the cow (15 Dec. 1764, *GT I* 258, 262–63), a quip Johnson had made about Hume "and other skeptical innovators" shortly after criticizing Rousseau's ideas.[24] Quite apart from running the risk of irritating Rousseau, who sensed that the *bon mot* referred to him (see *Earlier Years* 170), Boswell was creating a piquant situation for himself as he played off the ideas of his much-admired English mentor against those of the new mentor he was now trying to enlist.

On a very different subject, political theory, Boswell found his intellectual horizons considerably broadened by Rousseau. Up to this point he had not shown much interest in this favorite Enlightenment topic. For instance, when he described his meeting with Emer de Vattel (1714–67) in Dresden, he identified Vattel as the author of the *Droit des gens* (1758) but did not refer to his contribution to international law, which included important ideas about the relationship among the rights of the individual, the ruler, and the Church.[25] And although Boswell set down Vattel's remark about writing his book under difficult circumstances during the siege of Dresden (9 Oct. 1764, *GT I* 133), Boswell seemed unaware of the extensive section on the legal ramifications of war in Vattel's treatise. It is therefore amusing to find that in his first interview with Rousseau, Boswell was treated to a full-scale lecture on a seventeenth-century precursor of the Enlightenment, the abbé de Saint Pierre (1658–1743), whose voluminous work on world peace, entitled *Paix Perpétuelle* (1717), Rousseau had published in condensed form in 1761.[26] Boswell, having himself recently seen the destruction wrought by the wartime bombardment of Dresden, should have been interested in the subject, but true to form, recorded only some details about the abbé's eccentric behavior. Personalities, not theory, continued to be the focus of Boswell's interest. Still, he was pleased to be presented with a copy of Rousseau's abstract, another pearl for the library at Auchinleck.

On a more personal note, Boswell found his political beliefs challenged by Rousseau. During his travels Boswell had increasingly insisted on his social position; he had made sure that the Margrave of Baden-Durlach knew of the Boswells' relationship to the royal houses of Stuart and Hanover (16 Nov. 1764; and *GT I* 182 n.), and he had signed himself *baro de Auchinleck* in the visitors' book in the university library of Basel.[27] To Rousseau he boasted that he was "un vieux Seigneur" who demanded respect from his tenants. Not impressed, Rousseau pointedly asked whether Boswell ever spoke to a tenant as an equal, and when Boswell acknowledged that he did, Rousseau approvingly declared that it was then that Boswell was returning to his basic humanity: "Vous vous etes oublié et devenu homme" (15 Dec. 1764, J6, folio 812; see *GT I* 260). Although he could hardly have overlooked Rousseau's needling egalitarian remark, Boswell staunchly retained his feudal attitude, quickly adding that he had usually regretted having lowered himself by such talk with a tenant.

Unexpectedly, however, it was just these feudal instincts as well as his preference for personalities over political theory that led Boswell to another culminating experience with Rousseau: the introduction to General Pasquale de Paoli. The very idea of Paoli, determined to create an independent state in his native Corsica with a constitution formulated by no less a person than Rousseau, was bound to appeal to Boswell. And brash as was his offer to go to Corsica in Rousseau's stead, he must be credited with seizing the opportunity to involve himself in international politics. His visit to Corsica was to have consequences for the rest of his life: another astonishing series of interviews for the journal, the publication of a book about Corsica that made him famous, and a lifelong friendship with the Corsican patriot.

Exciting as the visit to Rousseau in Môtiers had proved to be, it was equalled by Boswell's visit to Voltaire at Ferney. Yet Boswell's expectations were different. As he noted in his journal of 28 December 1764, he knew that he would not agree with "the celebrated Voltaire, the infidel," and he told Voltaire to his face at their last interview a day later that he had expected to meet "a very great, but a very bad, man" (*GT I* 288, 303). Still, such disagreement did not diminish but perhaps rather added spice to the meetings.

The discussions about religion in which he managed to engage Voltaire must have exceeded Boswell's expectations. To judge by his letter of 28 December to his friend William Johnson Temple (our main source of information since Boswell's separate account of the episode has been lost) he again became the aggressive interviewer and asked about Voltaire's "real sentiments." In reply he heard a still more radical statement on religion than he had heard so far. For Voltaire acknowledged only his belief in an all-wise supreme being, an "Author of Goodness" whom he hoped to resemble, and flatly rejected the notion of an immortal soul. To the question of whether he was really sincere—a question that Boswell had already tried on Rousseau—Voltaire gave the theatrical, self-dramatizing answer: "I suffer much. But I suffer with patience and resignation; not as a Christian—but as a man" (L1227; quoted in *GT I* 294). The whole scene showed Voltaire deliberately rejecting any comfort the Christian religion might offer.

As revealed in the surviving "Notes on Voltaire's English Conversation" of 29 December 1764, Voltaire's doubts concerning the immortality of the soul were of particular interest to Boswell, who had already objected to such questioning in his talks with the margrave of Baden-Durlach. Face to face with Voltaire, Boswell did not hesitate to voice his disapproval of the article on the soul ("âme") in the *Dictionnaire philosophique*, which presents the argument that since one does not know what the soul is, one cannot say what happens to it after death.[28] When Boswell declared that the notion of immortality is "a pleasing imagination" and "noble," Voltaire retorted that wishing did not make it so (*GT I* 303). Here was not just the "moderate skeptic" Boswell had encountered in the margrave but an out-and-out questioner of accepted beliefs who remained unyielding in his rationalism. Apparently Boswell could hardly believe what he was hearing, for he interviewed both Père Adam, the Jesuit who lived at Ferney to play chess with Voltaire, and Voltaire's personal physician, Dr. Tronchin, to ascertain whether Voltaire was really prepared to face death without believing in an afterlife. Boswell would later show the same curiosity about David Hume's professed atheism.

When he asked about Voltaire's ideas on public worship, Boswell garnered another unconventional comment—Voltaire's declaration that he favored a barely theistic service: "Let us meet four times a year in a grand temple with music, and thank God for all his gifts. There is one sun. There is one God. Let us have one religion. Then all mankind will be brethren." Again wholly rational, dispensing with the ceremonial, rejecting all sectarianism, wishing for universal brotherhood—this is surely the most drastic Voltairean statement on religion that Boswell could have hoped to capture. And remarkably, even though he did not agree with such a radical rejection of institutionalized religion, he was stirred: "It was truly singular and solemn," he wrote in his journal. "I was quite in enthusiasm, quite agreeably mad to a certain degree" (29 Dec. 1764, *GT I* 303–4). In this instance, at least for a moment, he was moved, carried away, by an Enlightenment idea that was quite different from his own thinking.

Although less startling than the discussions with Voltaire about religion, those about literature, which survive in the "Notes on Voltaire's English Conversation" of 27 December, can be regarded as at least a minor culmination of Boswell's experiences as well. For Voltaire's remarks were certainly more amusing than those of Gottsched, Bel, and even Rousseau, while Boswell, in turn, found some opportunities to display his own ideas. Only a few high points need be recalled here. When Voltaire expressed his well-documented prejudice against Shakespeare, extravagantly calling him a madman or buffoon able to write two good lines but not six, Boswell had a chance to defend the "grand imagination" of the British. When Voltaire made a derogatory remark about Johnson, Boswell could counter with Johnson's joke about Frederick II being no more than Voltaire's "footboy"—a comment that made Voltaire, who felt ill-treated by his former Prussian master, more appreciative of Johnson. And Boswell was treated to such witty aperçus as that Homer was the only poet who ever wrote twelve thousand verses about two or three battles. Boswell was particularly struck by Voltaire's metaphors for the poetry of Pope and Dryden—that "Pope drives a chaise with a couple of neat trim nags but Dryden a coach and six, with postillion and all" (*GT I* 298–301)—an image he repeated to Johnson on his return to England and used to good effect years later in the *Life of Johnson* (Feb. 1766, 2: 5).

Apart from collecting Voltaire's literary *bons mots*, Boswell was actively involved in some minor sleuthing. He hoped to ascertain whether Voltaire had written the sarcastic review of Lord Kames's *Elements of Criticism* which had recently appeared in the *Gazette littéraire.* Although Voltaire refused to answer directly, he gave just enough hints to suggest his possible authorship (24 Dec. 1764, *GT I* 289). Boswell found this tacitly confirmed five days later by the presence of Kames's book in the library and did not take the denial by Voltaire's secretary seriously (*GT I* 302). It was just the sort of weighing of evidence at which Boswell would later excel in the *Life.*

Voltaire's extensive library, a particularly fine example of Enlightenment book collecting, which was purchased by no less a person than the Empress Catherine of Russia after Voltaire's death, naturally intrigued Boswell. Looking through Voltaire's books, he was amused by his host's barbed sense of humor, demonstrated in the titles he had placed on the spine of certain volumes: *Sottises ecclésiastiques* for a set of religious tracts actually entitled *Mémoires ecclésiastiques,* and *Tragédies barbares* for a collection of plays he was damning for being written in English (29 Dec. 1764, *GT I* 302). On a more personal note, Boswell was delighted to read Voltaire's *Mahomet* while at Ferney. Subtitled *ou le fanatisme,* this tragedy, first performed in Paris in 1742 and published in several editions by the time Boswell read it, dramatized the destructive effects of fanaticism on a young man and his family, and so illustrated Voltaire's own hatred of fanaticism.[29] To read this play, which reflected a special interest of Voltaire's, in Voltaire's own house was particularly meaningful to Boswell. He could not resist adding to Voltaire's collection by leaving a copy of two of his own poems, now no longer extant, with a fulsome dedication (28 Dec.

1764, *GT I* 289). Consciously or not, he was inscribing himself into Voltaire's literary collection.

All in all, Boswell's visits to Rousseau and Voltaire provided a remarkable climax for his travels through Germany, Switzerland, and the little corner of France in which Ferney is located. Clearly these visits increased his personal involvement with the life of the mind. He would never be a great intellectual, but he was open to ideas, indeed, he eagerly sought them out, and he tested his own ideas against some that were quite foreign to him. Moreover, no doubt inspired by the very excitement of meeting Rousseau and Voltaire, he became more expansive in his presentation in his journal, able to set down complex ideas more fully than before. At the same time, still true to his interest in personalities, he created unforgettable portrayals of these two famous philosophes.

The tastes that Boswell formed from his encounters with the continental Enlightenment remained with him for the rest of his life. He continued his mild interest in the sciences, at least to the extent of dropping in at breakfast or tea on Sir Joseph Banks, president of the Royal Society in London and owner of a remarkable scientific library. Expanding his own library at Auchinleck, Boswell found a place there for the treasures he had picked up on his trip. He fulfilled his ambition of himself becoming one of the *literati,* basking in the company of Johnson, Goldsmith, Cumberland, and Malone; eventually he created the *magnum opus* that expressed so much of Johnson's and his own conservative Enlightenment. And although he never resolved his religious doubts, the very fact that while he remained a practicing Anglican, he took a keen interest in the affairs of the Presbyterian kirk at Auchinleck on the one hand and enjoyed the Catholic masses at various foreign embassies in London on the other, suggests an open-mindedness, a tolerance, whose seeds were surely sown during his travels. What remained with him, too, was the cosmopolitanism to which he had, in fact, contributed by his travels and which gave him, in later life, the satisfaction of regarding himself not just as a Scotsman but as a "citizen of the world."

Notes

1. The phrase "conservative Enlightenment" is proposed by J.G.A. Pocock in "Conservative Enlightenment and Democratic Revolutions:

The American and French Cases in British Perspective," *Government and Opposition* 24 (1989): 82–83, 91–93. Pocock warns, however, against "reifying" this concept or, indeed, the very term "Enlightenment."

2. See Angelika Menne-Haritz, "Akademien und Universitäten," in *Panorama der Fridericianischen Zeit,* ed. Jürgen Ziechmann (Bremen: Edition Ziechmann, 1985), 68–71.

3. *Dictionary of Scientific Biography* (New York: Charles Scribner's Sons, 1974), 3: 119.

4. For the changes in Boswell's religious beliefs, see *Earlier Years* 32–33, 45–46, 52.

5. Boswell was still asking to see these proofs in a letter to Jerusalem written in Basel on 26 Nov. 1764.

6. Ernst Cassirer, *The Philosophy of the Enlightenment,* trans. Fritz Koelln and James P. Pettegrove (Princeton: Princeton University Press, 1951), 176–77; August Roloff, *Abt Jerusalem* (Berlin, 1910), 54–69; Wolfgang E. Müller, "Von der Eigenständigkeit der Neologie Jerusalems," *Neue Zeitschrift für Systematische Theologie und Religionsphilosophie* 26 (1984): 289.

7. *Betrachtungen* (Brunswick: Fürstl Waisenhaus Buchhandlung, 1773–74), I.iv. 73–74, 81, 101–03, II.i. 25–37; Müller 295–99; and *Johann Friedrich Wilhelm Jerusalem* (Berlin and New York: Walter de Gruyter, 1984), 66–76, 98–99.

8. See *London Journal* 267; and *Boswell in Holland* 50 and n. 7, 183.

9. See Bernhard Fabian, "Bibliothek und Aufklärung," in *Bibliotheken und Aufklärung,* eds. Werner Arnold and Peter Vodosek (Wiesbaden: O. Harrassowitz, 1986), 12.

10. *Neue Deutsche Biographie* (Berlin: Duncker and Humblot, 1955), 3: 174.

11. This interpretation is suggested by Pottle, *GT I* 77 n. 6.

12. Werner Rieck, *Johann Christoph Gottsched* (Berlin: Akademie Verlag, 1972), 39–52, 79, 97–104, 325–32.

13. Daniel V.B. Hegeman, "Boswell's Interviews with Gottsched and Gellert," *Journal of English and Germanic Philology* 46 (1947): 260–63, suggests that Boswell greatly overestimated Gottsched and underestimated Gellert but ignores Gottsched's standing among his colleagues.

14. Boswell repeatedly mentioned this project, notably in his French Theme of c. 24 Feb. 1764, but never completed it (see *Boswell in Holland* 162–67). The manuscript was in the library of James Boswell the younger until that was sold in 1825 (see *Earlier Years* 493, n. to 128).

15. Hegeman, 260–63; Rieck, 124.

16. Georg Witkowski, *Geschichte des Literarischen Lebens in Leipzig* (Leipzig: B.G. Teubner, 1909), 185–88.

17. The professorship in the English language had been established in 1763 (A. Schreiber, *Zur Geschichte der Universität Strassburg,* 1872,

140), and Tanner had begun his course of lectures in January of 1764. Boswell's copy of the inaugural discourse is now among his papers at Yale University (P161).

18. *Die Matrikel der Universität Basel*, eds. Hans Georg Wackernagel, Max Triet, Pius Marrer (Basel: Universitäts bibliothek, 1975), 4:467.

19. The time was eventually changed in 1798. See M. Fallet-Scheurer, "Die Zeitmessung im alten Basel," *Basler Zeitschrift für Geschichte und Altertumskunde* 15 (1916): 297–305, 342–51.

20. Marlies K. Danziger, "Boswell and Frederick of Prussia," *Studies on Voltaire and the Eighteenth Century* 305 (1992): 1654–57.

21. Jenny von der Osten, *Luise Dorothee, Herzogin von Sachsen-Gotha* (Leipzig: Breitkopt, 1893), 140–42. H.A. Stavan, "Voltaire et la duchesse de Gotha," *Studies on Voltaire and the Eighteenth Century* 185 (1980): 27–56.

22. For Voltaire's visit to Karlsruhe, see Jan Lauts, *Karoline von Baden* (Karlsruhe: C.F. Müller, 1980), 129–38; for the ideas on the soul in the *Dictionnaire philosophique*, see below.

23. 5 Dec. 1764, J6, folios 755–56; see *GT I* 230. This passage in the Journal with its curious mixture of French and English is quoted verbatim from the manuscripts at Yale University. Although Boswell was becoming increasingly fluent in French, he was still uncertain about accents.

24. 20, 22, 27 July 1763, *London Journal* 313–15, 317.

25. Ulrich A. Cavelti, *Einflüsse der Aufklärung auf die Grundlagen des Schweizerischen Staatskirchenrechts* (Freiburg, Switzerland: Universitäts Verlag, 1976), 87–116.

26. *Extrait du projet de paix perpétuelle du Monsieur l'abbé de Saint-Pierre*, in *Oeuvres complètes de Jean-Jacques Rousseau* (Paris: Gallimard, 1964), 3: cxxxii–cxxxv.

27. Bibliothek der Universität Basel, AN II 30, B1 228r.

28. Voltaire, *Philosophical Dictionary*, trans. and ed. by Peter Gay (New York: Basic Books, 1962), 1: 29–31, 63–72.

29. Theodore Besterman, *Voltaire* (New York: Harcourt, Brace, and World, 1969), 250.

Boswell's Response to the European Landscape

PETER F. PERRETEN

> We dined in a room on the third floor, commanding a view of the Green Park, St. James's Park, the Queen's House, Westminster Abbey, the Surrey Hills, etc. I said I never before had dined in a room with such a prospect, and I exclaimed, "How delightful it is to see the country and be sure you are not in it. Piccadilly is between us and it!"
>
> *Boswell: The Great Biographer,* 1989

Boswell's disparaging remarks about country life, especially frequent in his later years, color our perception of his feelings for the country and landscape. No doubt he was a city man, mostly interested in people; but, at least in his younger years, when he looked forward to becoming Laird of Auchinleck, and during his continental tour, one sees a Boswell whose reaction to landscape is as sophisticated as that of most young gentlemen on the tour. Boswell's written notes on the landscape during his travels on the continent may be placed into three categories: a direct response, based on a deep affection for what Boswell called the "romantic beauties" of his native Scotland; a consciously developed response to "improved" landscape learned from his friend and surrogate father, Henry Home, Lord Kames; and a complex, indirect response shaped by classical authors and guidebooks.

The origins of the first two of these reactions to the continental landscape may be found in the years of Boswell's late adolescence and early manhood in Scotland. Frequent references in his early letters and journals to several specific locations, including Auchinleck, the Boswell family estate, and Arthur's Seat, the elevation just to the southeast of Edinburgh, show a direct, emotional response which he indicated by using the adjective "romantic." In the earliest surviving letter to John Johnston of Grange, for example, dated 26 September 1759, Boswell says of his ancestral estate, "Auchinleck is a most sweet, romantic Place. There is a vast deal of Wood and Water, fine retired shady walks, and every thing that can render the Countrey agreable to contemplative Minds" (*Corr: Grange* 3). He used the word "romantic" in a similar way in 1761 in "Journal of North Circuit," an eight-page manuscript journal he wrote while accompanying Lord Auchinleck on the northern judicial circuit. The entry for Tuesday, 12 May, contains a detailed account of the Duke of Atholl's estate, including this description of a "Hermitage": "The most compleat thing of the kind that can be imagined—A little House thatched with heath & the Walls cover'd wt. Ivy—situated in the most wild romantic Spot imaginable" (J1).[1]

On 27 October 1762, just a few days before leaving Edinburgh for London and the grand tour, Boswell wrote to Johnston in a nostalgic tone that was to appear frequently during the next three years in letters he wrote to his old college friend. He is trying to entice Johnston to join him in Edinburgh for a sentimental farewell: "You also think of the Royal Palace of Holyroodhouse, the venerable church, the lofty Mountain Arthurseat, the romantic Salisbury craigs and the extensive King's Park, where You and I have had so many walks of pleasing Meditation" (*Corr: Grange* 17). Although Johnston didn't join him on the day of departure, 15 November 1762, Boswell performed his own ceremony, recording in the *London Journal* for that date, "I . . . stood in the court before the Palace, and bowed thrice to Arthur Seat, that lofty romantic mountain on which I have so often strayed in my days of youth" (41, 42). In London, two months later (10 January 1763), he described Auchinleck to Lady Northumberland as possessing "more romantic beauties" than any other place he knew (*LJ* 134). Still later he described as "romantic" natural landscapes in Germany and Switzerland which he associated with the "fanciful" and "wild" landscape of his native Scotland. "Romantic" appears occasionally in Boswell's Italian letters and memoranda also, but in Italy he uses the word in a different sense, a shift indicative of his "classical" response to Italy.

Before Italy, Boswell seems to apply "romantic" to natural landscape according to Johnson's third definition in his *Dictionary of the English Language* (1755), "Fanciful; full of wild scenery." Johnson illustrates this usage by citing Thomson's "Spring" (ll. 1027–28): "The dun umbrage; o'er the falling stream / Romantick hangs." Thomson had also used "romantic" to describe landscape in "Summer":

> Thrice happy he! who, on the sunless Side
> Of a romantic Mountain, forest-crown'd,
> Beneath the whole collected Shade reclines (458–60).[2]

Even more to the point for Boswell's use of the word, in "Autumn" Thomson had associated "romantic" specifically with the Scottish landscape.

> And here a while the Muse,
> High-hovering o'er the broad cerulean Scene,
> Sees CALEDONIA, in romantic View:
> Her airy Mountains, from the waving Main,
> Invested with a keen diffusive Sky,
> Breathing the Soul acute. (878–83)

Boswell had read Thomson's work sometime before 1757, when he himself wrote a poem "October" and described it on the wrapper of the manuscript as "In the manner of Mr. Thomson" (M265). In line 37 of "October" Boswell refers to "sweet Thomson, Nature's bard," though he did not use the word "romantic" in the poem.[3]

Boswell reveals a developing response to "improved" landscape in the journal he kept during a "harvest jaunt" with Lord Kames through Scotland and northern England between 14 September and 14 November 1762. Kames acted as a domestic "bear leader," a guide and tutor whose eye was clearly focused on the landscape. This "little tour" served as the aesthetic training ground for Boswell's grand tour of the Continent, which followed a year later.

Lord Kames, one of the leading figures in the Scottish Enlightenment, sat on the bench with Lord Auchinleck and, as Ian Ross suggests, served as a surrogate father for Boswell.[4] Kames's wide-ranging interests included agricultural improvement and gardening. His *Elements of Criticism* (published early in 1762, just a few months before the "harvest jaunt"), includes a chapter on gardening and architecture. Both the *Elements* and *The Gentleman Farmer* (1776), subtitled *An Attempt to Improve Agriculture by Subjecting it to the Test of Rational Principles,* were enormously influential in changing the economy and shaping the landscape of Scotland.[5] James Truscott, in the introduction to *Private Gardens of Scotland*, credits Kames with pioneering the "use of exotic plants in a romantic, semi-wild setting," and suggests a fundamental philosophical difference between English and Scottish garden styles.

> The truth is that with a few exceptions . . . the concept of the landscape garden as practised in England by Capability Brown and William Kent—that of undulating hillsides, seminatural tree clumps and serpentine lakes—never transferred very successfully to Scotland. What did develop, however, was a very Scottish form of landscape gardening which took its inspiration from the existing surroundings, adapting the concept in a wholly individual way to Scottish topography and conditions. This form of landscape gardening was first advocated by Lord Kames, a contemporary of Brown, in the mid-eighteenth century, and has survived to this day.[6]

At the beginning of chapter 24 of *Elements*, "Gardening and Architecture," Kames observes that most books dealing with those subjects "abound in practical instruction necessary for a mechanic."[7] Kames states that he intends to follow a different process, first considering the matter in the abstract, exploring the "rational principles to improve our taste," and then continuing in a more concrete manner by "illustrating these principles . . . to give a specimen of their application to gardening" (*Elements* 3: 294). He proposed in chapter 24 that "Gardening, beside the emotions of beauty by means of regularity, order, proportion, colour, and utility, can raise emotions of grandeur, of sweetness, of gaiety, melancholy, wildness, and even of surprise or wonder. . . . A garden may be so contrived, as in various scenes to raise successively all its different emotions. But to operate this delicious effect, the garden must be extensive, so as to admit a slow succession" (*Elements* 3: 296–97).

Boswell, who had read Kames's *Elements of Criticism* before the jaunt began in mid-September 1762, seemed especially responsive to the innovative idea of raising a succession of emotions through the variety and arrangement of plantings. His romantic reaction to the variety in landscape appears clearly in his impression of Springkell, the estate of Sir William Maxwell: "Sir William and I walked about the place which, as Lord Chalkstone says, has great Capabilitys. There is a fine walk for near two miles upon the side of a river, and a pretty variety of grounds about his house, which is a very good one. Sir William has a turn for improving and will probably make Springkell much better."[8] The deft allusion to Lord Chalkstone, a satirical character based on Lancelot "Capability" Brown in David Garrick's afterpiece *Lethe*, indicates that Boswell was familiar with the lively dialogue on landscape gardening carried on in eighteenth-century Britain.[9]

Boswell's journal of his harvest jaunt contains other brief descriptions of estates he visited with Kames. For example, Boswell described "Kenmore [as] . . . a very noble Place. The House is situated on a beautiful hill . . . ; behind it are wild Mountains and Woods; before it a pretty Plain with the river of Ken running into a Lake seven miles in Length, of which you have a large stretch under your eye finely diversified with natural Islands" (60–61). He described Kirroughtree, the estate of Lord Kames's daughter and son-in-law, as "a very good mixture, having behind it Wild hills and before it a pretty plain with the bay of Wigtoun" (74).

Boswell worked hard during this tour at the task of educating himself in the language and aesthetics of landscape and agriculture, but about halfway through the journey, on Sunday, 10 October, still at Springkell, he recorded a deep frustration:

> Sir William and Lord Kames went and surveyed the Place. And I sat in the house and read a little and wrote a little. It gives me some concern that I have no sort of turn for farming, for it is a pity that a Being who will probably possess a part of the earth should not know how to cultivate it. Indeed I have lived so much in a town, and have so high a relish of Society and other amusements, that my Attention has had little chance of being employed upon Ploughs and Harrows. But what I regret more is my want of taste for planting or gardening, which are realy noble and elegant Employments. I flatter myself that I may be able to acquire that taste by attention and Study. ("Harvest Jaunt" 91)

The dissatisfaction with himself expressed here recurs many times in Boswell's lifetime. But even if he gained little practical knowledge of planting and gardening on this jaunt with Lord Kames, his journal shows that he acquired an eye for the improved landscape and a vocabulary for recording his observations.

Boswell left Scotland in the middle of November 1762, and spent the next eight months in London seeking a commission in the Footguards. While he dreamed of the cosmopolitan career of an officer in London, letters from Scotland reminded him of his responsibilities toward his family and "romantic" Auchinleck. The country estate would have claimed special attention in the family at this time because the new house had just been completed and was first occupied in August 1762 (*Earlier Years* 454). On 10 January 1763, James Bruce, gardener and overseer at Auchinleck, wrote to Boswell,

> But as now if the propos'd peace [settlement of the Seven Years War] hold I'm hopeful the Guards affair will be over. The Tour of Holland, France & Italy & etc. will answer much better, in my humble Opinion—
>
> But mean time, . . . As now something must be done in finishing about the New House It might be of use [if] at Spare hours you'd purchase some plans of Noblemens Seats, of which plenty will be got in the City, from which several things might be taken that would help us much. (C600)

A letter to Lord Eglinton dated 7 February 1763 shows that Boswell considered combining a career in the Guards with the responsibilities of an "improving" Laird: "O that my grandchildren might read this character of me: 'James Boswell, a most amiable man. He improved and beautified his paternal estate of Auchinleck; made a distinguished figure in Parliament; had the honour to command a regiment of footguards, and was one of the brightest wits in the court of George the Third'" (*LJ* 181). The postscript to a letter from Bruce dated 8 July 1763 indicates, however, that Boswell's attention was not focused on the estate. "Your Honr According to promise has never sent any Plans, & etc" (C602).

William McQuhae, Boswell's friend and former tutor, wrote to him on 26 April 1763 of Lord Auchinleck's displeasure at his scheme to join the army and his lack of interest in the estate. "He is very earnest to have his Schemes for improving and ornamenting his Estate carried fully into Execution. to find his heir altogether inattentive to matters of that kind gives him great uneasiness."[10] Two pages later, McQuhae's tone becomes less ominous: "The Same good sense & taste, which makes a man relish a piece of fine Composition in Poetry or musick, would if so directed—make him relish a beautiful Disposition of fields & plantations. And in such employmt. there is very great variety. Agriculture & Gardening are noble arts, they ought not to be neglected in any Gentleman's education" (C1883). The sympathetic voices of Bruce and McQuhae joined the more stern, paternal voice of Lord Auchinleck in urging Boswell to remember his duties to the family estate.

Boswell left London for Utrecht in August 1763. On 20 September 1763 he received a report from his father on his progress in landscaping the new house (*Boswell in Holland* 26). It also reminded his son of his responsibility to the estate. In two additional letters sent during October, Lord Auchinleck asked Boswell to study gardening and agriculture in Holland in order to advise him on improvements (53–54, 65). Boswell's "Inviolable Plan," written on 16 October 1763, reflects both internal and external pressures: "You can live quite independent and go to London every year; and you can pass some months at Auchinleck, doing good to your tenants and living hospitably with your neighbors, beautifying your estate, rearing a family, and piously preparing for immortal felicity" (389). On 2 April 1764 Lord Auchinleck recommended that Boswell would find it of the "greatest use . . . to acquire a taste for planting and gardening" (219). Boswell followed his father's directive immediately, at least to the extent of visiting the botanical gardens at Leiden on 19 April and the formal gardens at Huis ten Bosch (the "Prince's Place") at The Hague on 25 April 1764 (228, 232).

On Monday, 18 June 1764, after a very unhappy winter studying law and improving his French, Boswell set out for Germany with Lord Marischal and Madame de Froment on the first leg of his grand tour. The journal and letters he wrote in Germany and Switzerland show better than those written during any other part of the tour both Boswell's direct, emotional response to natural landscape and the enlightened response to "improved" landscape recently learned from Lord Kames. On July 30 Boswell wrote to Monsieur Diederik Jacob de Zuylen, father of Zélide, about the journey from Holland to Berlin: "I enjoyed the pretty countryside: the mountains which I love delighted me after having been almost a year in the level plains of Holland. Forgive, Sir, a good Scot born in a romantic land and nourished by prejudices for which he will always preserve an agreeable veneration" (*Boswell in Holland* 318). Boswell had made the trip from Holland to Berlin in the comfort of Lord Marischal's private coach; later in the German trip, when he was traveling in the open post wagon, usually at night, sometimes in the rain, his comments on the landscape were less enthusiastic.

The improved landscapes at some of the German courts also caught Boswell's attention. He spent the week of 24–30 September 1764 at the court of Anhalt-Dessau (*GT I* 106–16). Prince Leopold Friedrich Franz (who was not at home during Boswell's visit) had recently returned from England, where he had studied the English garden. He had just begun what was to be a fifty-year effort to improve his lands and develop the Gartenreich (Garden Kingdom), a garden which eventually exemplified the sort of improved estate that Lord Kames advocated in the "Gardening and Architecture" chapter of *Elements of Criticism.*[11]

Boswell enjoyed himself at Anhalt-Dessau. He admired the great oak forests, went on stag hunts through an improved, managed woods,[12] and rode out to see the Prince's cattle, which he found resembled "the Scots Highland beasts." He registered that he was "very well amused with these rural sights, and quite in the humour of being a clever farmer at Auchinleck. A Scots baron cannot do better than travel in Germany. . . . He may thus learn to support his character with dignity, and upon his paternal estate may have the felicity of a prince" (*GT I* 112–13). On the same day that he recorded this happy reflection on "these rural sights" (27 September), Boswell was reminded of his old mentor, Lord Kames, and wrote to him. He began the letter with an apology for not having written for over a year, and reported how much his manners had improved since he had been abroad. But he did not include a description of Dessau in the letter, reserving such details, as he said, "for the entertainment of those evenings which I hope to pass with your Lordship in Scotland, when I hope to be better company for you than you have formerly found me" (*GT I* 110).

Boswell spent October 23–27 1764 at Kassel, the town adjacent to Wilhelmshöhe, seat of the Landgraves of Hesse-Kassel.[13] He was somewhat disappointed with his reception at court, noting that it was not truly hospitable and that the landgrave, Friedrich II, seemed gloomy (*GT I* 158, 159). The journal entries for Wednesday and Thursday, the first two days of his visit, are more positive in tone and include the longest and most important comment on improved landscape made during the entire grand tour. He was fortunate to have an introduction at Kassel to Monsieur de la Porte, a resident French Protestant clergyman, whom he characterized as "a knowing, sagacious man, very plain, very obliging, and very deliberate" (*GT I* 153). On the morning of Boswell's first full day at Kassel, de La Porte, acting as guide, took him to see a diorama of the estate. Boswell wrote, "He carried me to see the Maison des Modèles, which is a singular thing. You have here models of all the buildings and gardens of the Prince, in particular, however, of the grand waterfall, which is not yet completely executed. But there are here many pieces yet unexecuted. The waterfall must be a work of prodigious expense" (*GT I* 153).

The model of the grand waterfall, a wooden structure measuring about 220 feet in length, was indeed "a singular thing," and an extremely important place for Boswell to begin his tour of Wilhelmshöhe.[14] The enormous wooden model, begun in the year 1709 by one Wachter, a "Modellist," was based on an engraving, "Idealprojekt für den Carlsberg bei Kassel," one of a series of plates depicting designs and plans for an elaborate baroque garden designed by the Italian architect Giovanni Francesco Guerniero. The engravings, *Delineatio Montis,* were published in Rome in 1705 and in Kassel in 1706. Guerniero had been engaged to draw the plans by Landgrave Karl I, grandfather of Friedrich II, after Karl had made the tour to Italy in 1699 and 1700 and seen the estates at Frascati, admiring especially the waterworks at Villa Aldobrandini.[15]

When Boswell stepped outside the Maison des Modèles and looked directly at the gardens on that morning in 1764, he would have seen a sharp contrast between the wooden model and the actual estate; hence his comment, "But there are here many pieces yet unexecuted." The giant statue of Hercules which Boswell describes in the journal and only about one-third of the cascade were completed before Guerniero left Kassel in 1715 (*The Oxford Companion to Gardens* 606). Boswell's observation in his journal that the waterfall was a work of prodigious expense identifies cost as one of the main reasons that the ambitious plan of Karl I remained largely unexecuted.[16]

The changing taste in garden design provides another reason that much of Guerniero's design was never realized. Hans-Christoph Dittscheid writes that "even before his accession [1760] Landgrave Friedrich II had already set new standards in European garden design by surrounding his Schloss Bellevue at Kassel with an Anglo-Chinese garden, the earliest example of this style on the continent. The English influence at Kassel came from Friedrich's wife Mary, daughter of King George II of England" (*The Architecture of Western Gardens* 318). Friedrich and Mary had been estranged for some years before Boswell arrived at Kassel, but he knew of Mary, and de La Porte must have pointed out her influence on the changing estate.[17] Boswell also noted in his journal entry for 25 October that as prince of Hesse, Friedrich had been in Scotland with his troops in 1745. Thus, Friedrich could have seen and been influenced by the new garden style in Scotland.

Boswell records other details of the gardens, including the *orangerie* (built 1709–11) and "some very pretty figures of white marble, which came from Italy a good time ago" (*GT I* 153). This explicit reference to the Italian statues suggests that Boswell knew something about Landgrave Karl's tour of Italy and the source of the model design. It seems probable that de La Porte, given his depth of knowledge about Wilhelmshöhe, would have known and related to Boswell the design source for the gardens. It also seems likely that the engravings from Guerniero's *Delineatio Montis* would have been displayed along with the wooden model, or at least mentioned in some explanatory material, in the Maison des Modèles. Near the end of the description of the gardens Boswell noted, "We then viewed some pretty walks on the side of the hill. They are done with taste" (*GT I* 153–54). Views and plans of the garden drawn at about the time of Boswell's visit show clearly that these walks "done with taste" are the curved, irregular walks that Kames and other Scots and English landscape designers favored rather than the straight, symmetrical *alleés* depicted in Guerniero's 1705 design.[18]

Although he left Kassel feeling somewhat disappointed by the court of Landgrave Friedrich, the garden at Wilhelmshöhe may have inspired the memoranda for October 26: "Is not *Britain* noble . . . Auchinleck and jaunts each year. Gardens" (*GT I* 157 n. 6). Reminded, somewhat guiltily, of his homeland, he resolves to reside at his family estate and cultivate gardens there, though he will make annual jaunts to London. The experience of Wilhelmshöhe was also instructive to Boswell because it showed a landscape in the process of change (the old design in the model and the new in the garden) and hinted at the baroque design he was to see in Italy. It may be more than coincidence that he spent part of a day at Villa Aldobrandini during the following April and made some rather interesting notes on that estate in his memoranda.

Later, when traveling in the Swiss Alps, Boswell several times associated the Swiss scene with specific, romantic locations in Scotland. On 3 December 1764, nearing Môtiers, he wrote, "We passed one place exactly like Killiecrankie and another where a group of broken rocks seems every moment ready to tumble down upon us" (*GT I* 216). Two days later, surrounded by a scene reminiscent of the rugged landscape in Scotland to which he and Johnston had responded so enthusiastically, Boswell wrote, "O Johnston! Wert thou but with me here! I am in a beautifull wild Valley surrounded by immense mountains" (*Corr: Grange* 148). On the same evening he quoted Home's *Douglas* in his journal to describe the wild night: "It was dark December; wind and rain / Had beat all night," and then added in his own words: "I was firm and bold and among the wild rocks had grand thought" (*GT I* 236). Ten days later, on 15 December Boswell wrote, "At seven in the morning I got on horseback and rode about a league to St. Sulpice, where I saw the source of the Reuse. . . . It was a prodigious romantic place. . . . All around here I saw mountains and rocks as at Hartfell in Annandale" (*GT I* 257). While Boswell associates these Swiss alpine scenes with very specific locations in Scotland, the emotional language is surely prompted, as Professor Pottle suggests, by having read Saint-Preux's effusions in *La Nouvelle Héloïse* in order to prepare for his interviews with Rousseau (*Earlier Years* 182).

If in Germany Boswell played the Scots Baron and recorded both direct, romantic responses to landscape and impressions of the "improved landscape," and in Switzerland became temporarily the disciple of Rousseau and noted the wild, romantic landscape which reminded him of the Scottish Highlands, in Italy Boswell responded to the landscape less subjectively. Here he was strongly influenced by the classics and by Addison's "Remarks on Several Parts of Italy" (1705). In a letter to John Johnston written on 24 July 1765 Boswell announces his debt: "Addison is my Classic while I travel in Italy, and the least expression of so favourite an Authour [is] valued by me like the least bits of the precious diamond" (*Corr: Grange* 178).[19] The journal on crossing the Alps into Italy on 6 January 1765 shows the shift to a classical emphasis. He describes the Alps machine, the chair in which people were transported over the mountains, and then in the compass of two sentences refers to both Juvenal and Virgil: "In this machine did four fellows (six I should say), changing two and two, carry me over the *saevas Alpes* [Juvenal's tenth satire]. I drank some of the snow, that I might say, 'I have climbed the rudest heights—and drunk the Alpine snow'" (Virgil's tenth Eclogue). Boswell then continued in his own words: "The prospect was horridly grand" (*GT II* 22). Professor Pottle, commenting on this passage, provides a key to the change in Boswell's response to landscape south of the Alps. "Boswell's response to Arthur's Seat may justly be called Romantic, but the feelings he had in the Mount Cenis pass—or at least the feelings of his transit that he chose afterwards to record—were mere Addisonian *clichés*." The main activities on Boswell's agenda for Italy were "to see with his own eyes the sites connected with the Roman poets, . . . to refresh his Christian faith, . . . and to form a correct taste by the systematic study of antique and modern art." Whereas during his tour in Germany and Switzerland Boswell usually traveled with only one manservant, but without either companion or "bear leader," and had to rely to a large extent on his own interests and tastes, in Italy, especially while in Rome, he depended on tour guides, including the Scots antiquary Colin Morison, to help him "form a correct taste." Pottle concludes the list of standard tourist activities by noting that "Every well born Englishman who went south of the Alps in that era seems to have assumed that a really complete tour included at least one Italian countess" (*Earlier Years* 198, 199, 211, 199–200).

A passage from a journal-letter to John Johnston of Grange, dated 25 January 1765, illustrates the first of the purposes Pottle identifies, to visit sites with classical Roman connections, and also shows the influence of Addison's "Remarks":

> You see from the date of this that I am now at Milan. Pleasing and curious are my ideas when I find myself for the first time in a City described by a Latin Classic. Milan is described by Ausonius as Mr. Addison has remarked. I have great satisfaction in comparing ancient and modern sentiments manners and Buildings. Let Ausonius be placed in Milan as it now is and it would appear more strange to him an old Italian than it does to me a distant Caledonian. (*Corr: Grange* 153–54)

Here, at the beginning of his tour of "classical" Italy, the dimension of time is added to that of distance. Not only is Boswell a "distant Caledonian," a traveller from a country separated by many miles from the contrasting climate and geography of Italy, but he also regards the scene through a triple time perspective: his own time, the time of Addison, and the time of the classics.

Boswell's journal manuscript for Italy ends on 30 January 1765. From this point on, the Italian section of the trade edition of *Boswell on the Grand Tour: Italy, Corsica, and France, 1765–1766* consists of selections from the memoranda, letters, and other documents. The editors write that the selection of memoranda "is somewhat misleading, since it omits Boswell's dutiful but uninspired notes on the visible wonders of Italy, its art and architecture." The editorial note also informs the reader that "the memoranda are supplemented by letters, especially a series of fifty-one which he addressed (but did not post) to John Johnston, keeping them to deliver on his return to Scotland" (*GT II* 48).

These two sources, the memoranda and Johnston letters, seem the logical places for Boswell to record his responses to the landscape, since the memoranda record his daily, first impressions of Italy, and the Johnston letters are intended for a friend with whom Boswell shared an interest in landscape and estate improvement. Indeed, at least four of the journal-letters to Johnston from Germany and Switzerland (2, 3, 11, and 12) contain references to these topics. But both memoranda and journal-letters reveal very few direct responses to the landscape of Italy. When Boswell does record a response in the 165 pages of manuscript notes covering the Italian tour from 1 January to 11 October 1765, the notes are usually very brief (two or three words) and in many cases influenced by Addison's "Remarks." While reading these notes on Italy, one can almost hear Boswell's own prophetic words written in September 1764 at the court of Anhalt-Dessau: "A Scots baron cannot do better than travel in Germany. When he goes to Italy and France, he lives with artificial men cooped up in towns and formed in such a manner that Nature is quite destroyed" (*GT I* 112).

In only one of the journal-letters to Johnston (no. 24), does Boswell record an emotional response to the Italian landscape, and even here it is a classical, intellectual association that evokes it. The letter is dated "Horace's Farm, May 24 1765":

> My Dear Johnston: Can you read the date of this letter without being rapt into Classical enthusiasm by supposing yourself where I now am. Divine Horace whose Poetry has charmed my youthfull Soul I am now on the very spot which was your delightfull Retreat. Johnston beleive me I would give much to have you here at this moment. I am viewing the Villa of the Philosophic Bard with a pleasure allmost equal to what he has felt from it. I see the very Nature from which he drew. The Romantic Sabine Hills, the sacred fountains the verdant trees are full before me. (*Corr: Grange* 167–68)

Boswell had prepared himself for this classical experience. As Robert Warnock explains in his essay, "Boswell and Andrew Lumisden," "The young Scot contemplated this pilgrimage to the shrines of Horace with appropriate awe, and gave his feelings elaborate instructions before setting out." Warnock quotes from Boswell's "Horace Jaunt" memorandum for 24 May: "At Villa, be in enthusiasm. . . . Swear firm tone, Devotion, Ambition, every noble and manly Pursuit."[20]

Boswell had been preparing intellectually for such a visit since his schooldays by identifying the rustic scenes of classical Roman literature with "romantic" Auchinleck. In the closing lines of this letter to Johnston he makes the sentimental association: "Adieu My Dear Freind. May the day yet come when we shall fancy this Villa at Grange or at Auchinleck and enjoy the superiour felicity of refined taste and true freindship" (*Corr: Grange* 169).

In a letter to John Wilkes, Boswell responded similarly to the village where Virgil was born. He imagines that "beings of finer substance than we inhabit such delicious scenes," and again he links the classical experience with his parental estate: "I do assure you that when I am at Auchinleck in a sweet summer season, my imagination is fully persuaded that the rocks and woods of my ancestors abound in rural genii. . . . I shall not be deprived of my romantic dreams." He writes hardly a word about the landscape before him, and imagines himself a few lines later as "really existing in the age of Virgil" (*GT II* 109).

These letters to Johnston and Wilkes include two of the rare cases where Boswell uses "romantic" to refer to the Italian landscape. The word appears again in the memorandum for Sunday, 3 March 1765, which includes a description of his first night's sleep in Naples, a city rich in classical associations. "Yesterday after fine night's rest lulled by romantic Italian sea rose drest went to

W. Hamilton."[21] The shift in Boswell's *denotation* of "romantic" paralleled his shift in perspective as he entered Italy. When he used "romantic" to describe scenery in Scotland, Germany, and Switzerland, he denoted rugged, even wild, scenery. South of the Alps, the word denotes not the real landscape before him but the idealized landscape associated with classical authors. The *connotation* of "romantic," a feeling of nostalgia for locations, either real or imaginary, remains the same in all cases when Boswell applies the word to landscape.

The few brief entries in the memoranda on the Italian landscape are worthy of attention. The memorandum for Thursday, 28 February, made during the journey from Rome to Naples, includes one of the rare and one of the longest notes on landscape. Here is the full note: "Yesterday rude mountains but such weather they smil'd disputed peevish wt. Servants fee at night went to Garden of oranges & lemons walked among them as among Apples and Pears at Auchinleck—mounted one & pulled what luxury was immed[iately] in fine frame & full of good Resolves." Boswell's tone and vocabulary take on a new, "Italian" flavor in this note. The nostalgic association of the citrus orchard in Italy with an apple and pear orchard at Auchinleck is more sentimental than accurate. Neither the landscapes nor the trees would have had much in common with each other. It is the act of walking among the trees and climbing to pick his own fruit that triggers nostalgic thoughts of his youth at Auchinleck and puts Boswell in a good mood. In Italy "*rude* mountains . . . smiled" in response to the fine weather; in Germany and Switzerland rocks in the *romantic* mountains "seemed every moment ready to tumble down upon us" [emphasis added]. The personified, smiling mountains seem appropriate for classical, sunny Italy.

Addison's "Remarks" probably influenced Boswell's tone and word choice here. Although on the second page of his book Addison applies the word "romantic" to the mountains around Cassis in France,[22] he never uses the word again, referring to similar scenes as "*rude* prospects of rocks and precipices (259) or "a very *noble* prospect" (257; emphasis added). Elsewhere in the memoranda Boswell describes mountains and prospects in classical Italy as *noble* (6 February, 10 and 12 April) or *fine* (20 June and 5 October; emphasis added). But Addison's observations when describing Verona, "I have not yet seen any gardens in Italy worth taking note of" ("Remarks" 168), may also explain the lack of references to gardens or improved landscape in Boswell's "Memoranda and Notes for Italy." Addison's developing taste for "natural" gardens during the first decade of the eighteenth century probably also accounts for his indifference to the formal Italian garden. He devotes the ten pages on Florence in his "Remarks" almost exclusively to a description of architecture and artworks, much of this devoted to works in the Uffizi Gallery. He thought the "new Palace" (Palazzo Pitti) "a very noble pile" (322), but says not a word about the elaborate, baroque Boboli Gardens on the hill behind the palace.[23] Like a dutiful tourist, Boswell carried Addison's "guidebook" with him on 16 August 1765 as he visited the Uffizi Gallery with the Marquis Venturi, an Italian from Parma who was living in Florence and probably conducted him to the Bobili Gardens (*Earlier Years* 237). Later in the day they crossed the Arno to the Pitti. The next day Boswell wrote, "Yesterday morning Marquis came & you went to Gallery consulted Addison was quite well. Then Boboli wild birds. Marquis *quite virtuous.* Din'd well." The memorandum is cryptic, and features only a rather odd detail, "wild birds." Boswell was more interested in the aviary in the garden than in the grand, baroque design.

This very brief note on the Boboli Gardens is typical. The memoranda for April and May, recorded when Boswell was making the tourist rounds in Rome and Frascati, usually contain a brief comment on the exterior of a villa and the garden, and then list the major artworks found within the villa. The memorandum written on Tuesday, 9 April, begins, for example, "Yesterday wt. Moris & Hamilt. to Villa Borghese—Good garden—Bas reliefs curious without—Palace crowd of Pictures—copies. Fawn carrying Bachus fine—called Silenus." More "dutiful notes" on artworks follow. The emphasis is understandable: Boswell's companions and guides at the Villa Borghese in Rome and for the two following days at Frascati were Colin Morison, the "Scottish antiquary," whom Boswell had engaged as a guide to show him classical Rome,[24] and Gavin Hamilton, a part-time resident of Frascati and a painter and art dealer whose tastes favored the classical, rather than the baroque.[25] From the minimal observation, "Good garden," one might deduce that Boswell approved the design at the Villa Borghese because it was neither strictly mannerist nor baroque but included characteristics of the landscape style favored by Lord Kames.[26]

Boswell, Morison, and Hamilton set out from Rome for Frascati on the morning of 9 April 1765 and for the next two days maintained a busy schedule visiting several of the baroque villas of Frascati and viewing the ruins of Cicero's Tusculum. While it is clear from letters Boswell wrote to Johnston on 9 April and to Temple on 22 April that a visit to ancient Tusculum was the main reason for the expedition, the memoranda for the jaunt contain a few interesting responses to the baroque villas and their gardens. The party stopped first at Aldobrandini, one of the most splendid of the villas, known especially for its "water theatre."[27] Boswell wrote, "Villa Aldobrandini waterworks & in house Parnass—& Mount Helicon—the Muses played on their tibiae—& Apollo on his Lyre—even Pegasus was made to Neigh." The memorandum refers to two related aspects of the complex water features at Aldobrandini. Patrick Goode describes in *The Oxford Companion to Gardens* what Boswell called the "waterworks": "A large semicircular retaining wall, far outflanking the villa, is cut into the hillside, forming a water theatre. This consists of five niches containing statues, with water-jets rising in front of them; in the central one Atlas carries the globe. Above the theatre the water falls down a staircase of eight steps, disappears, and then flows through the Aldobrandini emblem, the Star, to fall as a veil on to the Atlas figure" (6–7).

The next part of the memo, beginning "in house Parnass," describes one feature of the garden salon, a room located behind the south arm of the semicircular retaining wall. Franck explains the contents and function of this room in *The Villas of Frascati.*

> This room was the climax for the delight of the visitors of the seventeenth and eighteenth centuries. A whole bedlam of water was let loose in it. It gurgled, murmured, whistled and shrieked in all pitches and keys. Air jets produced by water pressure caused fifes and organs to sound, and wooden globes to dance over the floor. From the *Fontana del Monte Parnasso* Aeolian music was heard. At every step one was in danger of being assailed by hidden water jets. (122)

Apparently Boswell escaped the hidden water jets, allowing him to concentrate on the Fontana del Monte Parnasso or Mount Parnassus, a standard feature in many Italian Mannerist and Baroque gardens. A "Mount Parnassus" consisted of an artificial mound upon which were placed figures of Apollo, the Muses, and Pegasus, the latter usually in the form of a fountain, suggesting the creation of the Hippocrene spring. Sometimes, as at Aldobrandini, these figures were animated and produced music and other sounds.[28]

For a group of tourists whose tastes and interests focused on classical antiquity, this animated, musical Mount Parnassus must have seemed bizarre. One wonders what adjective Boswell's mentor, Lord Kames, who considered the "Statues of wild beasts vomiting water" at Versailles to be "unnatural" and "absurd," would have applied to this scene. Boswell's choice of the Latin *tibiae* for the Muses' flutes or pipes is surely more formal than the circus atmosphere merits, and the anticlimactic parallel series, "the Muses played on their tibiae—& Apollo on his Lyre—*even* Pegasus was made to Neigh" [emphasis added], suggests irony.[29] That Boswell was amused, but not impressed, might be substantiated by noting that his journal-letter written to Johnston later that same day contains not a word about Aldobrandini or the Parnassus (*Corr: Grange* 160).

The group stopped next at the Villa Conti, then dined, and after dining moved on to what Boswell in the memoranda called the "Jesuits new pretty place" (Villa Ruffinella), where the group enjoyed "noble views."[30] Franck's description of the Villa Ruffinella in *The Villas of Frascati* explains that comment: "For the fullest enjoyment of this view [from the facade facing the Campagna], a separate salon was formed above the middle of the main front. From the height of nearly 1800 feet above sea level, it gives a truly unique view over the Campagna and on the Eternal City" (160). The group then apparently climbed higher on the hill behind Villa Ruffinella, from which vantage point they saw at a distance of about half a mile what Boswell refers to in the memoranda as the "great ruins of Tuscul," the ruins of Cicero's Tusculum. The "noble views" of Rome and Tusculum which ended the day's touring activities placed Boswell literally in the classical Roman landscape, prompting him to write that same evening in his journal-letter to Johnston that he felt "the enthusiasm of the Place" (*Corr: Grange* 161).

After spending the night at Hamilton's country house at Frascati (*Corr: Grange* 161), Boswell, Morison, and Hamilton began the next day by viewing what Boswell recorded in the memoranda for Thursday, 11 April, as the "fine frescos by Domenichino" in the Chapel of St. Nilus at Grottoferrata,[31] and spent the remainder of the morning at Cicero's Tusculum, which Boswell characterizes in his note with the single word, "rich."

The stop after dinner on the second day, at Cardinal Passionei's villa on the grounds of the Camaldoli Monastery at Frascati, also gave Boswell pleasure. But his sigh, "at last most elegant Villa," seems to have been prompted not by the landscape, garden, or view but by the collections of books, manuscripts, and antiquities assembled by the late Cardinal (d. 1761), and by the hermitic lifestyle of the Camaldoli Monks.[32] Gavin Hamilton, himself a dealer in antiquities, probably pointed out to Boswell the "antiques, curious inscriptions, & etc." that he recorded in the memorandum. Boswell also remarked of the Camaldoli Hermitage, however, "Camaldolesi each cell garden do all," thus indicating the solitary, contemplative practice of the order.

Perhaps some of the friars offered the visitors wine, for in the memorandum immediately following "each cell garden do all," Boswell wrote, "drank wine—Then one or two more Villas—rested." Any tourist who has tried to see too much in a short time knows this feeling. After a glass of wine in the middle of the afternoon, one loses focus, remembers having seen "one or two more Villas," and then needs to rest. Boswell's rapid loss of interest is not surprising, moreover, because the highlight of the excursion, the visit to Cicero's Tusculum, had taken place on the morning of the second day. Writing to Temple from Rome twelve days later, Boswell summarized the Frascati experience thus: "I went lately and passed two days at Frascati, the Tusculum of old. The weather was delicious. I felt the genius of the place, and was supremely happy" (*GT II* 68). He wrote not one word about the five or six villas he had visited.

The most tantalizing of the brief notes on gardens Boswell made during his three-month stay in Rome appears in the memoranda for Saturday, 11 May. The entry reads in part: "Yesterday morning Picture. At 3 wt. Abbé. Winkelman at Card. Alex. Albani's Villa. house elegant *neg. & bianc* Porphry vases—gallery all kinds of marb.—Apollo & Muses [Minx}[30]—Garden like spread periwig—Night Lord Mountstuart's easy Wild stories." And then upside down at the top of the entry over the date, "In all this day & write. . . ." Boswell clearly visited the Villa Albani on Friday, 10 May, and spent Saturday writing letters, one of them a long letter to Johnston which he actually sent. He summarized his tour to this point, described his mood, wrote nostalgically about Arthur's Seat, Grange, and Auchinleck, and confided that "on Monday I am to kiss the Pope's toe." But he said nothing about the "garden like spread periwig" which he had seen the day before and had just written about in his memorandum (*Corr: Grange* 162–67).

What does this odd note mean? Professor Pottle suggests, plausibly, that Boswell may have been thinking of a passage in Voyage I, chapter 2, of *Gulliver's Travels*: "The country round appeared like a continued garden. . . . The ladies and courtiers were all most magnificently clad, so that the spot they stood upon seemed to resemble a petticoat spread on the ground, embroidered with figures of gold and silver" (cited in *Earlier Years* 511). But I would suggest a more immediate source of the simile. The Villa Albani and its French-style garden had been completed in 1757, only eight years before Boswell saw them. Germain Bazin describes the garden in *Paradeisos*: "The garden was laid out in the French style between two buildings; following a strict geometrical plan, there are four *broderie* parterres between the villa and the *Kaffeehaus*, which still retain the same design shown in engravings of the first years of the garden" (167, 170). A modern photograph, looking across the garden from the elevated terrace of the villa toward the *Kaffeehaus*, shows parterres with intricate, curved lines which look rather like a periwig, and to someone looking at the garden in 1765 the very regular design would have been exaggerated by the immature plantings (*Paradeisos* 166). It is possible that on this occasion, when he had no "Addisonian cliché" to fall back on, Boswell looked directly at the garden and described, in his own words, what he saw.

If the "periwig" comment on the Villa Albani garden is direct and original, it is one of the few such responses during the Italian tour. Boswell spent the first week of October 1765 in Lucca and visited the Villa Garzoni at Collodi, near Lucca, as a guest of Romano Garzoni, a "knowing sensible polite Man" (*Corr: Grange* 188). Boswell's papers include his notes on a collection of Gurcino paintings at the villa (M101.16), but, so far as we know, he wrote nothing about the most spectacular visual aspect of the Villa Garzoni, the great baroque garden which lies on a steep hillside immediately in front and to the left of the Villa. The notes for the duration of his stay in the Lucca area, 30 September through

5 October, include the usual topics: opera, churches, pictures, and women. But on the last day of his visit to Lucca, Boswell recorded in the memoranda an uncharacteristically direct response to the landscape, as seen from the city walls: "You walk'd vigorous on ramparts & saw fine fresh hills around."

Boswell probably failed to respond to Italian baroque gardens because he had no visual point of reference or vocabulary to guide him. These gardens were very different from the landscape-type that Boswell had seen and described during his "harvest jaunt" in Scotland in 1762 and during his tour in Germany. In addition, they were exactly the type of intricate, highly ornamented garden that Lord Kames ridiculed in the *Elements of Criticism.* Unfamiliarity also explains Boswell's lack of response to the unimproved landscape in Italy. He had no visual frame of reference except the guidebooks and the classics. He saw largely what they directed him to see, and thus rarely ventured an original impression.

A less conjectural, more clearly documented reason for the relatively limited direct observations on the Italian landscape in Boswell's journals, letters, and memoranda is the limited landscape of the bedroom. Boswell traveled to Italy to see classical sights and to pursue an amorous conquest. On this latter effort he spent much time and energy with little success until he stopped in Siena. His encounters with Porzia Sansedoni and Girolama Piccolomini (whom he called "Moma") are reported in detail in *Boswell on the Grand Tour: Italy, Corsica, and France.* His intrigues with them prompted Boswell to confess in his "Sienese Reflection" for 2 September, "I have been a week in Siena and have not as yet seen any *maraviglia,* as the Italians say. I should not be able to say why to any one who demanded a proper reason, but I can explain it very well to myself: it is because I have been so busy with women that I have felt no curiosity about inanimate objects" (*GT II* 120).

It seems appropriate to close with Boswell around 20 September 1765. He is not traveling through beautiful Tuscany, or even looking out the window, but in a bedroom, "ornamented with a great number of paintings," including landscapes and seascapes, and "five mirrors, arranged with admirable skill over my bed." In this setting, Boswell thinks of home and writes another "Sienese Reflection," fusing his aesthetic responses to the two places he then loves best.

> I must say that I am very happy today, for my soul is serene, my heart filled with gentle sweetness, my spirit bold, my imagination vivid. All that I lack is my native soil for which, as Virgil says, one always entertains loving thoughts. If I were now in the romantic woods of Auchinleck my happiness would be complete. I would see myself in the very place where Providence has established my residence, where I can honour the memory of my worthy ancestors, live happily cultivating my lands, doing good to my tenants, and showing a cordial hospitality to my neighbours. This is how I wish to live when my travels are over. In winter I shall go to London or Edinburgh, and in summer I shall stay in my country-house and think many, many times of beautiful Italy. (*GT II* 134–35)

Notes

1. Here and in all subsequent quotations from Boswell's MSS his spelling, abbreviations, and punctuation are followed exactly.

2. Text for *The Seasons* is quoted from James Thomson, *The Seasons*, ed. James Sambrook (Oxford: Clarendon Press, 1981).

3. Ferdinand Baldensperger includes Thomson's uses of "romantic" in his chronological list, "'Romantique,' ses Analogues et ses Equivalents: Tableau Synoptique de 1650 à 1810," *Harvard Studies and Notes in Philology and Literature* 19 (1937): 13–105. He cites about twenty occurrences of "romantic" in English as applied to "fanciful" landscape between 1654 and 1759 (only about half of which would have been available to Boswell).

George B. Parks, in his essay "The Turn to the Romantic in the Travel Literature of the Eighteenth Century," *Modern Language Quarterly* 25 (1964): 22–33, makes some interesting points about romantic responses to landscape, but unfamiliarity with Boswell's manuscript materials leads to his statement on p. 24, "James Boswell could journey in Switzerland, Italy and Corsica in the 1760's with not the slightest attention to nature."

4. Ian Simpson Ross, *Lord Kames and the Scotland of His Day* (Oxford: Clarendon Press, 1972). See chapter 13, "Boswell in Search of a Father? Or a Subject?"

5. William C. Lehmann, *Henry Home, Lord Kames, and the Scottish Enlightenment: A Study in National Character and in the History of Ideas* (The Hague: Martinus Nijhoff, 1971). See chapter 6, "'I Fly to My Farm': A Gentleman Farmer in Overalls."

6. James Truscott, *Private Gardens of Scotland* (New York: Harmony Books, 1988), 13, 14. The influences of climate, topography and economics in shaping the unique characteristics of the Scottish landscape garden are discussed in more detail by W.A. Brogden in the "Scotland"

entry in *The Oxford Companion to Gardens* (Oxford: Oxford University Press, 1986), where he notes that "pastoral qualities" of Lancelot Brown's landscape garden were not well-suited to conditions in Scotland. Brogden identifies Blair Atholl, Perthshire, the estate of the Duke of Atholl, as an example of the Scottish landscape style. This is the estate which prompted Boswell's emotional description, "the most wild romantic Spot imaginable," in the unpublished "Journal of North Circuit."

7. Henry Home, Lord Kames, *Elements of Criticism*, 3 vols. (Edinburgh, 1762; rpt. New York: Johnson Reprint Corporation, 1967), 3: 294. Iam Simpson Ross presents a good analysis of *Elements of Criticism* and the critical reception of the work in chapter 14 of *Lord Kames and the Scotland of his Day*, cited in n. 4, above.

8. James Boswell, "Journal of My Jaunt Harvest 1762" (hereafter cited as "Harvest Jaunt"), *Malahide* 1: 90. Boswell refers to Kames's *Elements* on p. 66 of the "Harvest Jaunt."

9. Boswell was probably thinking of Lord Chalkstone's speech in lines 105–9 of *Lethe*: "Ay, Styx—why 'tis as strait as Fleet-ditch—You should have given it a Serpentine Sweep, and slope the banks of it.—The place, indeed, has very fine capabilities; but you should clear the wood to the left, and clump the trees upon the right: In short, the whole wants variety, extent, contrast, and inequality" (*The Plays of David Garrick*, ed. Harry William Pedicord and Frederick Louis Bergmann, 2 vols. [Carbondale and Edwardsville: Southern Illinois University Press, 1980], 1: 1–34, 377–84). The Lord Chalkstone character first appeared in *Lethe* in 1756. Boswell may have read the 1760 Edinburgh edition of the play.

10. McQuhae occasionally begins complete sentences, as he does here, with lowercase letters.

11. Harri Günther, "Anhalt-Dessau," in *The Oxford Companion to Gardens* 19. For a discussion of the English influence on Wörlitz, one portion of the Gartenreich, see the "Wörlitz" entry, 613–14.

12. Describing these hunts at Anhalt-Dessau, Boswell reports of the September 25 chase, "I was mounted on a trusty old white, very quiet, very sure-footed, and by no means slow. . . . It was the first time that I saw this sport, and a most noble one it is" (*GT I* 107). In reporting this chase as "the first time that I saw this sport," Boswell either forgets an earlier hunt or indulges in a bit of revisionist autobiography. Just two years earlier, on 22 September 1762, during his tour with Lord Kames, Boswell had gone "a-hunting" with less "glorious" results, finding himself and his mare at one point during the chase in a muddy ditch ("Harvest Jaunt" 71).

13. Boswell doesn't name the estate in his journal. When he visited in 1764, it would have been called "Weissenstein," for Schloss Weissenstein, a hunting lodge built by Landgrave Moritz the Wise halfway up the

slope of the Karlsberg at the beginning of the seventeenth century. Since 1798 the estate has been called "Wilhelmshöhe," for Landgrave Wilhelm IX, son of Friedrich II (Hans-Christoph Dittscheid, "The Park of Wilhelmshöhe: From the Baroque *Delineatio Montis* to the Heroic Landscape," in *The Architecture of Western Gardens*, eds. Monique Mosser and Georges Teyssot [Cambridge, Mass.: The MIT Press, 1991], 317, 318). For a complete history of the estate see Paul Heidelbach, *Die Geschichte der Wilhelmshöhe* (Leipzig: Klinkhardt and Biermann, 1909).

14. The wooden waterfall model was moved twice on the estate before meeting an ignoble end. It was first located in the Kunsthaus. When it was completed it was moved to its own Modellhaus (the Maison des Modèles where Boswell saw it in 1764) near the racetrack on the little Fulda River, and during the reign of William IX it was moved once more into a new Modellhaus at the Holländische Tor (Dutch Gate). It was sold, along with the other models from Karl's time, during the reign of Jerome Bonaparte (1807–13). Hans Reuther suggests that all the models were sold for firewood, "Brennmaterial" ("Der Carlsberg bei Kassel: Ein Idealprojekt barocker Gartenarchitektur," *Architectura* 6 [1976]: 56). This information is a loose paraphrase of translations of passages from Reuther's essay and Heidelbach's *Die Geschichte der Wilhelmshöhe* 94. Special thanks to my colleagues at Ursinus College, Associate Dean Annette Lucas and Professor Derk Visser, for their translations.

15. Hans Reuther notes the connection between Guerniero's engraving and the wooden model in "Der Carlsberg bei Kassel" 56.

16. Ursula, Gräfin zu Dohna writes in the *Oxford Companion to Gardens* (1986 ed.) of the cascade at Wilhelmshöhe, "The idea came from the villas at Frascati (see Villa Aldobrandini) which the Landgrave saw while visiting Italy in 1699–1700, but it was translated into gigantic proportions at Weissenstein" (606). The waterworks at Aldobrandini had in turn been modeled on those at Villa Lante at Bagnaia. (Claudia Lazzaro, *The Italian Renaissance Garden: From the Conventions of Planting, Design, and Ornament to the Grand Gardens of Sixteenth-Century Central Italy* [New Haven: Yale University Press, 1990], 243). Landgrave Karl enlarged the Aldobrandini design, which had been enlarged from the Villa Lante design. Ironically, the expense of executing the twice-enlarged plan was so great that the design was completed at Wilhelmshöhe only in the form of the enormous wooden model.

17. De La Porte provided Boswell with court gossip concerning Friedrich's personality and his family problems following his conversion to Roman Catholicism (*GT I* 154–56). Although he didn't mention Mary in his journal while visiting Kassel, Boswell certainly knew who she was and tried (unsuccessfully) to see her only a few days later at Hanau (*GT I* 163–64).

18. For the contrast see *The Architecture of Western Gardens*, p. 318 for the 1705 Guerniero plan, and p. 317 for a plan drawn in 1780. An engraved view of the cascade and hillside by W.C. von Mahr done in 1760, only four years before Boswell's visit, is reproduced in Heidelbach, *Die Geschichte der Wilhelmshöhe* 124.

19. Pottle underscores Boswell's respect for Addison's "Remarks" when he notes that Boswell used Addison's book as a guide not only in the field but also as a model for *An Account of Corsica* (*Earlier Years* 358).

20. "Boswell and Andrew Lumisden," *Modern Language Quarterly* 2 (1941): 605.

21. James Boswell, "Memoranda and Notes for Italy" (J7). All quotations of memoranda in Italy are from this manuscript. William Hamilton was the English plenipotentiary at Naples (*Earlier Years* 207).

22. Joseph Addison, "Remarks on Several Parts of Italy, Etc., in the Years 1701, 1702, 1703," in vol. 2 of *The Works of Joseph Addison*, 6 vols., ed. George Washington Greene (Philadelphia: J.B. Lippincott & Co., 1867), 140.

23. To avoid possible confusion in defining garden types, I have used in this essay the terminology presented by Germain Bazin in *Paradeisos: The Art of the Garden* (Boston: Little, Brown, 1990). Bazin defines four types of gardens in modern times in the West: "the Mannerist (Italian), the Classical (French), . . . the Landscape (English), . . . [and] the Baroque." He writes that the Italian Baroque garden "was the natural outcome of the Mannerist style," and lists these distinguishing characteristics: "the grandiose scale of its design, the taste for shock effects, expressed in a multiplicity of other overblown and monstrous forms, and an exaggerated love for rocaille and for ornamental expressions of power and strength" (163). A visitor to the Boboli today, like Boswell, sees the baroque garden that had taken its form by the end of the seventeenth century.

24. Boswell describes Morison as a "Scottish antiquary" at the beginning of the "Course in Antiquities and Arts in Rome" (*GT II* 60). Pottle points out that "Morison appears to have been his daily companion for a month or more" (*Earlier Years* 211). Memoranda disclose that the daily companionship caused some friction (April 1, 6, 7, 12, and 18), but for the three days that they and Hamilton were together in Rome and at Frascati (April 8–10), they were congenial.

25. Hamilton's strong classical tastes and his knowledge of both modern and classical art in Rome and at Frascati certainly influenced Boswell's notes on the artwork at Villa Borghese and the baroque villas at Frascati. For further details on Hamilton's taste and activities as a dealer in classical antiquities, see David Irwin's *English Neoclassical Art: Studies in Inspiration and Taste* (Greenwich, Conn.: New York Graphic Society, 1966), 31–38.

26. Lazzaro, in *The Italian Renaissance Garden*, says that "Villa-parks . . . begun in the seventeenth century, such as the Villa Borghese in Rome, continued the design principles of the sixteenth-century park, but in the treatment of vegetation and above all in their vast size, they reflect northern European trends as well" (272–73). Sir Geoffrey Jellicoe and Pamela Coote write of the garden at the Villa Borghese: "There was no overall symmetrical plan of the French type and the design consisted of extensive plantings of trees of many varieties, intersected by *allées* with statues, fountains, grottoes, and lakes interspersed at intervals" ("Villa Borghese," *Oxford Companion*, 63).

27. C.L. Franck, *The Villas of Frascati: 1550–1750* (New York: Transatlantic Arts, 1966), 120. Franck provides an excellent general introduction to this group of eleven villas and an individual account, with drawings and photographs, of the architecture and history of each villa and its garden.

28. For a detailed discussion of this feature and a 1604 drawing of the Mount Parnassus at Villa Medici, Pratolino, see Lazarro, *The Italian Renaissance Garden*, 131–34. Bazin describes the Aldobrandini Parnassus in *Paradeisos*: "Behind the façade [of the retaining wall] are a chamber to Apollo [Franck's "garden salon"], several cool rooms and a chapel dedicated to Saint Sebastian. The ceiling of the Apollo room is decorated with a ravishing pergola of roses, orange trees and vines, while the walls bear 20 frescoes by Dominiquin telling the history of the god. The principal attraction of the room, however, was a Mount Parnassus, in the Mannerist style, but the stuccoed wood figures of Apollo, the Muses and Pegasus, which decorated it, have not survived" (166–67).

29. In contrast to Boswell's reaction, John Evelyn, who visited Aldobrandini on 5 May 1645, had written a detailed description of the estate, which he found, "for its elegance, situation & accommodation of plentifull water, Groves, Ascents & prospect, surpassing in my opinion the most delicious places that my eyes ever beheld" (*The Diary of John Evelyn*, ed. E.S. DeBeer, 6 vols. [Oxford: Clarendon Press, 1955], 2: 392).

30. The Jesuits had bought the property in 1740 and dedicated the rebuilt villa in 1746, which explains Boswell's calling it the "Jesuits new . . . place" (Franck, *The Villas of Frascati*, 160–62).

31. Boswell's comment on the frescoes, "Possest child perfect," may be explained, in part, by consulting Baedeker's *Central Italy and Rome: Handbook for Travellers*, 15th ed. (Leipzig: Karl Baedeker, 1909): "Chapel of St. Nilus, decorated with Frescoes from the lives of SS. Nilus and Bartholomew, one of the chief works of *Domenichino*. . . . To the left of the altar, St. Nilus heals a boy possessed by an evil spirit with oil from a lamp of the Madonna" (461–62).

32. Cardinal Domenico Passionei (1682–1761) had assembled a

large personal library of rare books and manuscripts. The entry in the *New Catholic Encyclopedia* (New York: McGraw-Hill, 1967) notes, "G.V. Vella calls him [Passionei] a bibliophile with 'library kleptomania,' who used his position as papal nuncio to visit monasteries with the intent of finding and receiving as gifts precious MSS and rare books" (10: 1065). Although the Cardinal died in 1761, some of his collection must have remained at Frascati in 1765 at the time of Boswell's visit.

33. "Apollo & Muses" refers to a fresco of Parnassus by Raphael Mengs (*Paradeisos* 167). The famous Johann Joachim Winckelmann, Cardinal Albani's librarian (*Earlier Years* 218), acting as Boswell's guide, probably pointed out this fresco of Parnassus, a more sedate treatment of the myth than the animated version seen by Boswell in April at Aldobrandini. The word after "Muses" in the MS looks like "Minx." I propose that this is Boswell's spelling of *Mengs* as pronounced by Winckelmann.

"Something that Put Me in Mind of My Father": Boswell and Lord Kames

RICHARD B. SHER

> BOSWELL: 'But, Sir, we have Lord Kames.' JOHNSON: 'You *have* Lord Kames. Keep him; ha, ha, ha! We don't envy you him.'
>
> *Life of Johnson*, conversation on the merits of Scottish literature, 1768

Except for occasional jaunts, a brief period of schooling in Glasgow, and a youthful grand tour of the Continent during the early 1760s, the geography of James Boswell's life took the form of a downward-pointing, elongated isosceles triangle. The southern point of the triangle was London, where Boswell most liked to be, but where he actually spent a relatively small proportion of his life. The other two points were situated far to the north, in Scotland. To the west was his family's estate at Auchinleck in Ayrshire, where he passed part of his childhood and later returned as the landowner or laird; to the east was Edinburgh, where he spent some of his time as a student and nearly all of his legal career as an advocate.

This triangular spatial structure complemented, and helped to define, the dynamic character of Boswell's life. Not only was he rarely in any one place for very long, but his life had no single geographical center. Instead, each point of the triangle represented a different kind of "home": London, literary; Auchinleck, ancestral; Edinburgh, professional. Boswell's multiple personalities, or if one prefers, variant identities within the same personality,[1] were nurtured by this unusual degree of geographical diversity. Each point of the triangle had its own set of opportunities, limitations, and associations; each was both appealing and disconcerting in particular ways that Boswell was constantly pointing out in his journals—which may, in this respect, be fruitfully considered as exercises in the comparative geography of his soul.

Taking this analysis further, it is possible to argue that Boswell associated each of his geographical "homes" with particular people whose support and guidance he frequently sought while resident there. In regard to Auchinleck and London, respectively, Boswell's spatial identity was structured around a single, considerably older man who functioned as a powerful authority or father-figure. The contrasts between his actual father, Alexander Boswell, Lord Auchinleck of the Court of Session, and his famous surrogate father in London, Samuel Johnson, are as obvious as they are significant: Whig versus Tory, Presbyterian versus Anglican, Scottish versus English, law versus letters. One lived and breathed literature to a degree matched by few people before or since; the other believed that literature had its place but should not get in the way of the primary business of making a living and achieving respectability as a member of the gentry. For Boswell, the spirit of London *was* Johnson, just as Auchinleck-the-place was permeated by the spirit of Auchinleck-the-man.

All this is well enough understood by students of Boswell's life and work. But what of the third point in the Boswellian triangle? If Boswell's experiences at Auchinleck were clearly defined by the theme of the rebellious young gentleman struggling to become "a worthy Scots laird" like his father, and if his London experiences were just as clearly centered around the theme of the young Scot coming to literary manhood under the tutelage of his English intellectual "father," what sense is to be made of Boswell's Edinburgh days? Elsewhere I have suggested that one part of the answer lies in understanding Boswell's place among fellow members of the Scottish-Presbyterian legal gentry such as Andrew Crosbie and John Maclaurin, who shared Boswell's propensity for social justice, heavy drinking, melancholia, irreverent wit, and support for the Popular party in the Church of Scotland. These were his big brothers.[2] This essay will explore Boswell's relationship with the man who came closest to filling the role of his Edinburgh father-figure: Henry Home, Lord Kames.

Just as Edinburgh was in some respects a middle ground between the bustle and excitement of London and the isolated serenity of Auchinleck, so did Kames represent for Boswell a kind of compromise between his father and Dr. Johnson. Like the senior

Boswell, Kames achieved considerable respectability and success as a Scottish laird, judge, and Presbyterian elder. Like Johnson, on the other hand, Kames lived a very full life of letters, associating prominently with the Edinburgh literati and becoming well known throughout Britain and Europe as an author on diverse literary and philosophical topics. When young Boswell contemplated the possible advantages of a legal career in Edinburgh, he consoled himself privately with the thought that "I might write books like Lord Kames" (24 February 1763, *London Journal* 200). Kames was living proof that one man could bridge the sizable chasm between Lord Auchinleck and Dr. Johnson, and his life showed how Boswell might possibly have won the approval of his real father, as well as Johnson, by becoming both an independent laird with eminence in the legal profession and a famous man of letters.

Moreover, Kames achieved success in spite of particular shortcomings and disadvantages with which Boswell almost certainly identified. He had a lively and sometimes impertinent wit and a well-earned reputation for buffoonery, as well as a vain and sometimes arrogant personality that rubbed many people the wrong way. As a young man Kames had shown a tendency toward wild and mischievous behavior. By means of a good marriage and an unexpected inheritance through his wife, Agatha Drummond, Lady Kames, he had gone from a social and economic position at the bottom of the gentry to considerable wealth and high social standing. From being a young man with a strong Episcopalian affiliation and apparent Jacobite sympathies, he had become a pillar of the Whig-Presbyterian establishment in Scotland. The passions of youth, including an urge (not unlike Boswell's) to become an officer in the "tall regiment" of the Prussian army, had been tamed by reason and maturity. Yet respectability never completely overcame the irreverent, clownish component in Kames's personality, and his reputation for impulsive, inappropriate behavior survived his promotion to the Scottish bench. After Boswell published a signed letter of an impudent nature in the *London Chronicle* in 1767, his brother David warned him that "the people of Edinburgh in general are now beginning to look upon you as a man like Lord Kames, who does the most extravagant things without thought or reflexion" (28 April 1767, C492).

Perhaps the similarity of Boswell's and Kames's personalities was responsible for the close bonds that developed between them, despite an age difference of some forty-four years.[3] As will be seen, Kames functioned as a father-figure to Boswell both by offering him guidance and direction and by serving as a model for emulation and biographical research.

"Like the Prodigal Son Restored"

It was in the first of these senses that Kames started playing a significant role in Boswell's life in 1761 and 1762. Boswell was then in his early twenties and suffering from a youthful crisis concerning his career and identity. Relations with his father were at a low point. Faced with his father's insistence that he pursue a legal career in Scotland, Boswell rebelled at every opportunity. His father, in turn, forced him to sign a document relinquishing his birthright as laird of Auchinleck. We do not know exactly how Kames began to assume an advisory role over Boswell during this critical time, but it seems probable that Alexander Boswell asked him to intervene because he understood that his friend had a much better rapport with his son than he did. As discussed below, Kames later remembered (though Boswell did not) being charged with making sure that James did not go off to London during one restless winter. Kames's willingness to comply with this request from Boswell's father is not surprising, for besides being a close friend and colleague of Alexander Boswell, he owed his greatest debt to Alexander's father, James (Boswell's paternal grandfather), who had assisted him when he was a struggling young advocate. "I was more obliged to your Grandfather than to any man," Kames told Boswell in 1778, to which he added, "and I never shall forget it as to any of his descendants."[4]

For his part, Boswell never forgot the help he received during this youthful crisis, which one of Kames's letters termed "the most ticklish time of your life" (5 December 1762, C1650). In a journal entry of 27 September 1764, Boswell noted gratefully that "while I was on bad terms with my worthy father, I was treated with great kindness by Lord Kames. His Lordship's house was a home to me" (*GT I* 109). Thirteen years later he took pleasure at entertaining in his own home Kames "and his lady, who had been very good to me in my dissipated days, as appears from my journal in 1762 and is gratefully remembered by me" (*Boswell in Extremes* 82). Certainly Boswell was treated graciously by Lord and Lady Kames, who entertained him regularly at their homes in town and country and in 1762 invited him to accompany them on a harvest jaunt through southern Scotland. It was then that Kames gave Boswell the idea of trying his hand at writing "lively periodical papers" as a suitable outlet for his talents and energies ("Journal of My Jaunt Harvest 1762," *Malahide* 1:101). Yet it is unlikely that Boswell would have been brought to feel such deep and enduring gratitude if Kames had done no more than provide some hospitality and a useful piece of literary advice. Nor is it likely that Boswell would have felt this way if Kames had maintained merely "a cynical interest" in him, as Geoffrey Scott believed ("Introduction to the Harvest Jaunt," *Malahide* 1:41).

What, then, did Kames do to earn Boswell's lifelong thanks? Circumstantial evidence suggests that Kames was involved in bringing about the parental agreement that enabled Boswell to make his famous London jaunt of 1762–63. We know that the period of Boswell's greatest debt to Kames occurred in the several months before his departure for London, when Kames was advising him on various personal matters, such as Boswell's schemes to secure the patronage of Eglinton and Queensberry in July 1762 and ways to curb Boswell's "too great avidity of Pleasure" (*Earlier Years* 85; 14 Oct. 1762, *Malahide* 1:99–100). A letter that Kames sent Boswell in London on 16 July 1763 says much and implies even more about the services he was providing for his young friend: "You have always taken my advices so well that I am tempted to go on with them. Supposing you to be tired with London or that you soon will be, I would not have you, however fond of your company, to return directly home. It is my sedate opinion that you should take a view of the neighbouring parts of the continent, were it but to satisfy your curiosity and to convince yourself that it is still better to be at home among friend[s] who honour you than among strangers who take no concern in you" (C1651). This passage not only hints, in the very first line, that Kames was the force behind Boswell's London jaunt, but also implies that Kames was in the general habit of giving Boswell advice about the proper conduct of his life—and that Boswell was in the habit of following it. Kames's plan was evidently to encourage his young charge to be exposed to other places in order to demonstrate to him that Scotland was more desirable. Earlier in the same letter, Kames hammered away at the conclusion he expected Boswell to reach: "Be candid and own fairly to me that at London you are out of your place, that you are beginning to be fatigued with a perpetual repetition of the same circle of idle amusements and that you are better at home improving your mind, gaining daily more knowledge, respected by your friends and contributing to their happiness."

It is not difficult to imagine Kames using this same argument in order to convince Alexander Boswell that he should give his son an opportunity to get travel out of his system. Very likely such arguments were used in combination with a concession, such as an understanding that Boswell would have to pass the private examination in civil law (which he did in late July 1762), but one suspects that passing this examination alone may not have been enough to cause the stubborn Alexander Boswell to reverse himself on the matter of travel, as Frederick Pottle believed (*Earlier Years* 85). The counsel of his respected colleague Lord Kames also helped. Kames's letter of 16 July 1763 provides still more circumstantial evidence on this point, for immediately after the long passage recommending a tour of the Continent he writes: "If this proposal [you] relish, I hope it will not be difficult to perswade your Father to give you scope; for I never yet found him averse to any measure that was rational and for your good. He always loved you even in the midst of your distractions. No human event will give him more happiness than to find you like the prodigal son restored to yourself and to your Country after much wandering." Once again Kames discusses a projected Boswellian adventure in a manner that implies his involvement with previous adventures, and once again he expresses himself as if Boswell's travels are part of his master plan. It is Kames's hope that Boswell will see London and Europe, grow tired of them, and return home to Scotland to live happily as a lawyer and laird, fully reconciled with his father. It is entirely possible that Kames had earlier articulated this plan to Auchinleck, who had recently granted his son permission to "go abroad for a while" in exchange for his giving up his scheme for a career in the Footguards.[5]

The letters that Kames sent to Boswell in London in late 1762 and 1763 should be read with this master plan in mind. These letters are filled with fatherly advice about the need for Boswell to temper his enthusiasm about London and its pleasures. Some six months before his historic meeting with Johnson, Boswell described London in glowing terms that brought forth the following reply from Kames: "It gave me . . . satisfaction to find you in such a delirium about the pleasures of London, which you express in a most rhapsodical strain. Doth not this approbation please you? but be not over heasty, lest there be a Snake in the grass. . . . Consult the Elements of Criticism and you will find there that violent passions never lest long: how happy the prospect for your friends here, after all your superfluous flame is spent, to have you here again among them gay but not giddy, pleasant but not dissolute, rational and yet entertaining" (5 December 1762, C1649).[6] Comparing Boswell first to Hotspur and then to Ulysses, dodging the respective dangers of spears and sirens, Kames concludes this letter with more fatherly advice: "If you always keep in view the old seat of Auchinleck, you will never deviate far from your course."

In London, Boswell was in constant danger of deviating from the "course" that Kames had in mind. In his next extant letter to Boswell, dated 27 March 1763, Kames noted that "Friendship has its honey month as well as marriage; and the ticklish time is in passing from the warm enthusiastic feelings of the passion to the calm habitual affection; for there both love and friendship must land, or neither of them will be lasting. I appeal to yourself for the truth of this reflection" (C1650). Another constant theme in Kames's letters was that "business is the chief purpose of life, and imagination is given us for recreation only" (5 December 1762, C1649); "gaiety and good humour," "mirth and jollity" are fine in their proper place, but "man was intended for more important occupations than to pass his time merely in amusement, which ought to be subservient to business and never to encroach upon it" (27 March and 16 July 1763). Boswell did his best to appease his "sage," assuring him in a letter from Germany of 27 September 1764 that he was "acting with perfect propriety," "fulfilling every duty that my station requires," and "every day becoming more temperate in mind [and] more convinced that imagination forms false views of life, and that in all human affairs there is not so much mystery as a young man is apt to think. Is not this true, my Lord?" (*GT I* 110–11).

In spite of Boswell's well-known restlessness as an Edinburgh advocate and lifelong tension with his father, Kames's master plan was not a complete failure. After he left home in 1762, and especially after he gave up his scheme to enter the Footguards toward the end of his stay in London in May 1763, Boswell's relations with his father improved somewhat, enabling him to use the past tense in the sentence of September 1764, quoted earlier, that thanked Kames for helping him "while I was on bad terms with my worthy Father." Certainly Kames had not fully anticipated the depth and durability of Boswell's love for London, "for which," Boswell confided to his friend Erskine on 4 May 1762, "I have as violent an affection as the most romantic lover ever had for his mistress" (*Erskine Letters* 101). But Kames's plan unquestionably relieved some of the restlessness, reduced some of the tension, and helped to save Boswell from doing something rash with his life during his "ticklish time." Boswell seems to have grasped the point, and it is therefore worth reconsidering in a fuller context Boswell's expression of gratitude in the journal for 1777, partially quoted earlier: "I was happy to have Lord Kames, aged about eighty yet in lively frame, at my table; and it was comfortable that he and his lady, who had been very good to me in my dissipated days, as appears from my journal in 1762 and is gratefully remembered by me, would now be in my home, when I am a settled advocate in good practice, with a wife and four children" (*Boswell in Extremes* 82). At this time Boswell apparently realized that the stability of his mature adult life, such as it was, owed much to the mediation of Kames with his father, as well as Kames's ability to persuade Boswell himself of the need to put gaiety, mirth, and imagination in perspective and to chart his proper "course."

"Determined . . . to be Plutarch"

The payment that Kames received for his trouble was not always pretty. Before his departure for London in November 1762, Boswell is believed to have had a love affair with Kames's married daughter, Jean, whose husband would divorce her a decade later on grounds of adultery with a naval officer (*Applause* 26–28). In the sketch of his early life that he prepared for Rousseau in 1764, Boswell indicated that he was ravaged with guilt for having an affair with the daughter of "a man of the first distinction in Scotland" who "had heaped kindnesses on me." "I was seized with the bitterest remorse. I was unhappy. I was almost in despair," he wrote of this episode ("Sketch," in *Earlier Years* 5). To put a psychoanalytic twist on this account (always tempting in Boswell's case), one might say that what Boswell experienced on this occasion was not simply the guilt generated by his first affair with a well-bred, married, Scottish woman, compounded by his friendship with her husband and father; the guilt he experienced went deeper because at the time of this affair his lover's father was serving as his own surrogate father. In this sense, what Boswell called "my criminal amour" was an instance of spiritual incest, and the psychological torment he experienced was appropriately hellish.

Fortunately for Boswell, Kames never learned of this affair, and relations between the two men were cordial after Boswell's return to Edinburgh in 1766. Still, there is nothing particularly affectionate about the "Song in the Character of Lord Kames" that Boswell penned in that year: it mocks Kames's celebrated harshness in capital cases in the irreverent style that was characteristic of the boisterous drinking songs which circulated among the Maclaurin-Crosbie circle of Edinburgh advocates.[7] It was only during the late 1770s that Boswell's relationship with Kames regained the intimacy of the early 1760s. The catalyst for this development was an arrangement empowering Boswell to gather biographical materials from Kames. According to the journal for 19 February 1775, it was Boswell who first requested permission to obtain "notes" of Kames's life. Kames agreed to the request on condition that his biography be written "before his death" and in a "flattering manner," but Boswell would say only that he "would do it fairly." At this time Boswell still had some doubts about whether Kames had "eminence enough to merit that his life should be written," and he therefore concluded this journal entry on an uncertain note ("Perhaps I may do it"). Four months later, however, Boswell recorded in the journal that he had dined with Kames and "got from him particulars of his life with design to write it," and the following day he told William Johnson Temple about his plans with scarcely a hint of his doubt about Kames's worthiness as a subject: "I think he has eminence enough to merit this" (*Ominous Years* 68, 160; Boswell to Temple, 19 June 1775, *Letters JB* 1: 234).

Although Boswell never completed his projected life of Kames, there is ample evidence that he took the matter quite seriously. For the duration of Kames's life, Boswell continually sought out biographical materials when the two men were together. Often he came up empty or did not preserve the accounts of their conversations. But the substantial body of biographical notes that has survived, drawn from interviews during Kames's last five years, from early 1778 until late 1782, suggests that Boswell meant to complete the project and might have done so if Kames's son, George Home Drummond, had not effectively terminated it in 1786 by demanding that Boswell pledge not to publish the book unless the text had Drummond's prior approval (Drummond to Boswell, 26 December 1786, C1113; *Later Years* 322–23, 549). Drummond's concern about how his father would be portrayed by Boswell is understandable, considering that in the *Journal of a Tour to the Hebrides* of 1785 Boswell had characterized Kames as "no profound scholar" (362). But there is evidence that his anxiety even predated the publication of the Hebrides *Tour*. Lady Kames wrote to Boswell on her son's behalf around 20 January 1783, less than a month after her husband's death: "As my Son seems anxious for a reading of your Manuscript with regard to his worthy Father I hope you are good enough to now endulge us. I shall be happy to carry a Copy of it to his Son" (C1647). The Home family, then, had no doubt that Boswell was actually engaged in writing a biography of Kames. The fact that in 1780 Boswell sent his "biographical anecdotes" to Kames's old friend Sir Alexander Dick, who responded with four pages of his own "Anecdotes . . . for Mr. Boswell's use relative to Lord Kaims" (C974), is further evidence of Boswell's seriousness about this undertaking.

In the first interview among his biographical notes, dated 31 January 1778, Boswell expresses his determination and ambition as Kames's biographer: "I said, 'My Lord, we have neglected our scheme of writing your life. I am determined to do it; to be Plutarch'" (*Malahide* 15: 267). When Kames raises the issue of the proper style of biography, Boswell's response reveals not only his theory of the biographical art but also his skill at applying it, for he deliberately shifts the conversation to the subject of Kames's life: "I agreed it should be dramatick. The great Art of Biography is to keep the person whose life we are giving allways in the Reader's view. I then at once brought My Lord to tell his own life" (15: 268).

These observations remind us that Boswell's passion for writing biography was not simply the result of his fascination with Samuel Johnson. From the mid-1770s he was attempting to write the lives of Sir Alexander Dick and Alexander Lockhart, Lord Covington, as well as Kames. "Biography is my favourite study," he announced in his journal for 11 January 1780, when reiterating his intention to write the life of Covington (*Laird* 165). Besides the fact that none of these schemes was ever completed, the unifying factor among them was that his chosen subjects were all Scottish gentlemen who had achieved eminence in Edinburgh as members of one or another of the liberal professions. Dick was for some years president of the Royal College of Physicians of Edinburgh; Covington was a renowned lawyer and judge, considered by Boswell to be the leading advocate "that ever practised in the Court of Session" (*Ominous Years* 69); Kames was both a distinguished judge and jurist and a polyglot author with an international reputation. Ambitious "to be Plutarch" and confined to Edinburgh by his profession as advocate, Boswell looked around him for local figures worthy of his emerging biographical talents and found them in these men.

Boswell made his biographical intentions clear to Kames, Dick, and Covington, got their approval in one way or another, and spent a considerable amount of time gathering anecdotes and other materials from them. All three were men of Lord Auchinleck's generation and social class, and it is quite possible that Boswell's wish to write their lives was rooted in his search for an alternative pattern of Scottish success or for an alternative father-figure.[8] Whatever his motives, these three schemes should be viewed as serious biographical projects, despite the fact that they were never completed. The life of Kames is certainly the most important of them, not only because substantial amounts of materials for it have survived but also because it apparently came closer than the others to being executed. But Boswell's journals and letters also provide ample evidence of sustained involvement with the Covington and Dick projects,[9] and in both cases this evidence is corroborated by material from other sources. In Covington's case, John Ramsay of Ochtertyre stated in his memoirs that Boswell "hovered like a vulture above the dying judge, in quest of anecdotes,"[10] and it is thought that Boswell wrote the sketch of Covington's life in the *London Magazine* for March 1775 (*Ominous Years* 69 n. 2). Dick recorded in his diary for 12 January 1777: "Last week Mr James Boswell my friend expressed a desire to make a Biographical account of my life to my 74th year. . . . I looked over many jottings . . . of past times and we had some droll interviews and it becomes he says very interesting"; and in an entry of 25 November 1782 he wrote of giving a letter "to my worthy friend Mr James Boswell of Auchinleck that he may after my Decease have the perusal of my great collection of Letters from my friends for many years past—for the purpose of his making out a Memory of my Life, he is desirous to collect together."[11]

In addition, Boswell casually or whimsically contemplated writing numerous biographies of other Scots, both living and dead. Such contemplations (they cannot be called projects) usually received no more than one or two passing references in journals or letters, with little or no indication of serious intent over a significant period of time. Examples include the Edinburgh classicist Thomas Ruddiman (11 April 1773), the seventeenth-century Edinburgh virtuoso Sir Robert Sibbald (18 August 1776), Boswell's great-great-uncle Sir David Hamilton (21 October 1776), the physician and moral philosopher Sir John Pringle (2 February [1777], L1081), Boswell's libertarian patron Lord Eglinton (13 March 1777), and Boswell's uncle, the Reverend Alexander Webster of the Tolbooth Church, Edinburgh (6 March 1784). Boswell's supposed plan to write the life of David Hume should also be put into this category, because the only evidence for it is a single speculative remark in his private journal for 17 December 1775: "I had a really good chat with him this afternoon. I thought also of writing his life" (*Ominous Years* 201).[12]

Thus, the life of Kames may be situated near the high end of a Boswellian biographical spectrum that stretched from whimsical urges to sustained, if unfinished, projects, and finally to the *Life of Johnson.* Considering that Boswell had a deep personal rapport with Kames, it is not surprising that the interviews with him are characterized by the highly subjective method that is the trademark of the Boswellian biographical style. Though scorned by critics who see biography and autobiography as contradictory, rather than compatible and, in some respects, complementary features of Boswell's writing,[13] the method deserves more sympathetic consideration. At his best, Boswell was able to turn his subjectivist bent to good advantage by identifying, empathizing, debating, and disagreeing with his subjects so as to bring them out and set them off. In such cases—and the *Life of Johnson* is filled with them—subjects spring to life because the reader is able to see them through Boswell's eyes or to see them responding to Boswell, in a manner that is certainly personalized and engaged but not necessarily distorted or false. If some portions of the notes on Kames are of limited biographical value because of autobiographical excesses, other portions reveal interesting biographical facts that might not have been attained through other means and suggest the outlines of a distinctive, penetrating portrait of Kames. Perhaps it is significant that after Boswell showed the manuscript of his notes to Sir Alexander Dick, Dick replied in a letter of 12 February 1780 that he found "in several parts a striking picture of that uncommon old man" (C973).

A discussion of three themes in Boswell's biographical notes on Kames will serve to elucidate this interpretation. First, Boswell made every effort to elicit and record information about aspects of Kames's past that might be considered unorthodox or deviant when judged by the conventional standards of Presbyterian Scotland in the eighteenth century. "I had come to Edinburgh a zealous Jacobite," Kames told him (*Malahide* 15: 270). He was also a nonjuring Episcopalian, indeed "a Deacon at the door of a Nonjurant meeting house in Edinburgh" (15: 282). When Boswell wondered how Kames could have later become a Presbyterian elder, "for that was acknowledging presbytery to be the best religion," Kames replied that it "was only acknowledging it to be the established religion in this country" (15: 285–86). In his youth he joined the Rankenian Club in order "to puzzle and make mischief" with two wild friends, "and they succeeded but too well with many, making them Deists" (15: 284). Kames told him that as a young man he "got into a pretty riotous and expensive society" with the same two friends and soon found himself £300 in debt, after which he suddenly "withdrew from that society" and settled accounts (15: 272). Since his family could not afford to send him to university, he received a rather inferior education from private tutors, an Edinburgh writer (solicitor) by whom he was employed, and some dull lectures on civil law given by Professor James Craig (15: 270).

Considering Boswell's attention to these biographical details, it would seem that Frank Brady missed the mark when he concluded that Boswell's biographical notes on Kames "illustrate clearly his desire to see into the mystery of the eminent and enviably stable" (*Later Years* 233). More likely, they illustrate Boswell's very personal interest in seeing how a young Scot of good birth but modest means could manage to overcome various obstacles of character and circumstance and achieve success and respectability in spite of an incurable tendency toward irreverence. They include at least one anecdote illustrating Kames's legendary buffoonery: at the trial of Mungo Campbell, Boswell was so "shocked" at Kames's "diverting himself, by playing Monkey tricks to Thomas Earl of Cassillis," that he sent the judge a note scolding him for the "levity" of his behavior, after which Kames stopped causing mischief and fell asleep (M135). If this was "stability," it was a kind quite different from that of his father. Boswell was fascinated by the paradoxical nature of Kames's personality, which nearly matched his own in its juxtaposition of seemingly contradictory traits. His personal or subjective bias led him to discover interesting and unconventional information that a more "detached" biographer might have missed.[14]

A second theme of the biographical notes on Kames is the triumph of philosophical reflection and moderation over superficial learning and unreflective passion. Boswell more than once records Kames talking about his movement from rote or mechanical learning to philosophical understanding. His first boyhood tutor, who does him "little good," makes him learn Latin grammar "by heart," without "the least notion of what the rules meant"; but three years later he begins to study the same grammar book "philosophically" (*Malahide* 15: 269). Similarly, when he starts to study the law he is "just a mechanical Student & got law by rote"; later, however, he begins "to consider law a little more intelligibly" and carries this "higher kind of study" so far that he nearly fails his legal trials for having "neglected the common mechanical preparation" (15: 270–71).

Kames's story of being unable to understand books one and two of Hume's *Treatise of Human Nature* the first time he encountered them is a variation on this theme. Some time later he picked up the *Treatise* and read it "to his astonishment with the clearest understanding" (15: 273–74). Kames viewed this incident as proof that "thoughts ripen in the Mind imperceptibly," and in his conversation with Boswell he expanded this idea into a primitive theory of the unconscious (15: 267). Whether or not Boswell accepted this theory, he would certainly have identified with Kames's experience, for his first childhood tutor, John Dun, was an enthusiastic devotee of rote learning; Boswell's complaint at age twenty-three that "I was not trained to think about what I was reading," and therefore "acquired a habit of skimming through a book without extracting any ideas from it,"[15] seems to betray a regret that he never developed the capacity for philosophical comprehension and analysis.

Still another variation on this theme is a story that Kames told Boswell about his rival, Alexander Lockhart, later Lord Covington, then a flamboyant Scottish trial lawyer whom Kames had once bested in a particular court case "by letting Lockhart have all the violence [i.e., passionate rhetoric] without opposition & then shewing that it was not warranted by the proof." Boswell helps to prepare the reader for the lesson of the story—that reason and moderation win out over passion—by beginning his account with the words "He said Lockhart never studied law as a science" (15: 280–82), the very thing for which Kames was famous. A similar lesson was directed to Boswell himself at an interview with Kames on 18 November 1782. Boswell has just told him about "a wonderful change," "an extraordinary metamorphosis," the acquisition of "a new sense" in his own life as a result of his suddenly experiencing "a high relish of the country, of actual farming." "'I am glad of it,'" Kames replies. "'But take care lest, like a fit of enthusiasm in religion, it go off and leave you as you were'" (*Applause* 19). Did Boswell realize that this conversation paralleled an epistolary exchange that had occurred between them twenty years earlier, when Kames, in a previously cited letter of 5 December 1762, tried to temper Boswell's "delirium" over London by warning him about the dangers of excessive enthusiasm? Once again, Boswell's character of Kames is shaped by his own experience, or his own wish to emulate Kames's generally successful transformation from youthful buffoonery to mature respectability, but his account is no less acute for all that.

To a large extent, Boswell's attempt to gather notes for a biography of Kames was grounded in the fatherly role that Kames had played in his life. In a conversation of 17 February 1782 this point was touched upon, not long after Kames had joked about Boswell's being his biographer ("as you are to write my life"):

> He said he was obliged to me for my attention. I said it would be very strange if I were not grateful for his goodness to me. He said there was a time when he had more opportunity of being good to me (alluding to my days of dissipation when he took much care of me). He said one winter he was Guarantee for my not going off to London. I grew impatient & came to him one afternoon & walked up & down

> his room & told him I was to set out next day. He said, What are you going & just gave me a serious look. I went away, & sent him word I was not to go. I do not remember this. But I suppose it is true. (M135)

This revealing passage leads to the most pervasive and profound, as well as the most autobiographical, theme in Boswell's notes on Kames, that of fathers and sons. In the only study to consider seriously Kames's role as a Boswellian father-figure, Ian Simpson Ross perceptively suggested that "part of Boswell's impulse as a biographer was a desire to form, through artistic re-creation, an image of the truly acceptable father to replace the one which nature had given him."[16] I would add that biographical projects like these provided Boswell with valuable opportunities for "paternal" intimacy, quite apart from their function as art. Had the *Life of Johnson* never been written, the project itself would still have enabled Boswell to spend more time with his subject, and establish a closer relationship with him, than would otherwise have been possible. When Boswell approached Kames in February 1775 with the idea of taking notes on his life, he was, among other things, trying to reestablish the father-son relationship they had enjoyed during the early 1760s. Collecting notes for a biography was not only a way of maintaining continual contact (mainly in the form of dinners at Kames's home in the Edinburgh New Town) but also a device for assuring a degree of familiarity that Boswell craved. As a biographer, Boswell could attend Kames's chambers as he lay dying, much as a son might do; once there, he could ask probing personal questions, and expect honest answers. This privilege extended to Lady Kames, who revealed to Boswell remarkably personal details about herself and her family on evenings when Kames himself was indisposed.[17] The project of biography, then, constituted in part a literary pretense for intimacy.

It so happened that in 1782 the health of Lord Auchinleck, Lord Kames, and Samuel Johnson deteriorated; Johnson struggled on for two more years, but Auchinleck died on 29 August and Kames followed on 27 December. Throughout the second half of 1782, therefore, Boswell was forced to think particularly hard about death and dying and about his relationships with his two Scottish "fathers." As the elderly Kames was slowly "fading into insubstantiality," Boswell passed the time one July evening by reading aloud numbers 45 and 46 of his *Hypochondriack*, with which Kames declared himself "much pleased." His ostensible reason for doing so was to "put [Kames] in mind" of the fact that in 1762 he had "recommended to me to write essays of that kind" (*Laird* 463). The particular numbers that he chose to read, however, suggest another, deeper motive, whether conscious or not. Both of those numbers, published in the summer of 1781, deal with the theme of "parents and children." Both contain remarkable passages of a transparently autobiographical nature, the first on the autonomy of sons in general, and the second on their special need for financial independence and paternal love.

In *Hypochondriack* number 45, Boswell lashes out against "fathers who very injudiciously, and in my opinion very unjustly, attempt to keep their sons even when well advanced in life, in such a state of subjection as must either reduce them to unfeeling stupidity, or keep them in perpetual uneasiness and vexation." In number 46, he steadfastly confronts, and defends, his patricidal fantasies: "There is nothing so ill judged in the conduct of a father, as to keep his heir in such scanty circumstances that it is impossible for him not to view his father's death as an event upon which he is to make a transition from indulgence and difficulties to opulence and enjoyment." Besides a "kindly partition" of the family fortune, he continues, "there must be a communication of kindness; there must be *love*."[18] If publishing these words in an anonymous magazine article served a therapeutic function for Boswell, the same must have been true of his reading them to Kames, his Scottish alter-superego. Without ever discussing his personal feelings directly, he was able to communicate them with great precision; and without ever letting on that he understood what Boswell was really doing, Kames could give him the approval he so desperately needed simply by declaring that he was "much pleased" with these essays.

Almost half of Boswell's biographical notes date from the last six weeks of Kames's life, when the discussion often turned to the subjects of death and the afterlife. On these occasions, the recent death of his father was weighing heavily upon Boswell's mind, and the notes sometimes grow intensely autobiographical. The most unsettling instance of this tendency occurs at an interview of 20 December 1782. Although Kames is just a week away from death and "very spiritless from bodily weakness," Boswell is a model of insensitivity and selfishness: "I wished much to hear him say something as a dying man. It was unsatisfactory to be with a very old man, and a judge, and perceive nothing venerable, nothing edifying, nothing solemnly pious at the close of life" (*Applause* 43). He then begins to speak of his father's death. Other instances are less insensitive but equally personal. On 18 November Boswell "talked of my father's easy death" and later raised the issue of a "future state," contrasting the dying Auchinleck's confidence on that point with the anxiety of his recently deceased friend, Sir John Pringle. Kames gives him the reassurance he so desperately needs: "Your father had never doubted of Christianity and as he was conscious he had done his duty to GOD and man, he was sure he would be well in another world" (*Applause* 17).

Eleven days later Boswell is once again receiving solace from his dying friend: "He said very well that a man of a vigorous mind has many degrees of failure to pass through before he is worse than a man of ordinary understanding. I took down the words from his dictating, for I made him repeat them again. . . . I thought the remark applied well to my father. I said this was a comfortable night when I had him just alone. He said I was very kind to him" (*Applause* 25). On 10 December, just after Boswell has contrived to raise again the subject of a future state, "I told him my father's death had relieved me of the horror I used to have at the act of dying, yet there was something discouraging that one could see no appearance of transition in death. 'None to our senses,' said he. He seemed to be firm in his belief of future existence."[19] Moments later, this extraordinary passage: "There was in his appearance tonight something that put me in mind of my father when in a calm, serious frame. He quieted me somehow. I told him I frequently could not help thinking my father was alive and that I might go and consult him; and when I was taking care of his improvements at Auchinleck I thought I was doing what he approved; and I wished always to preserve the notion of his seeing what I was about. My Grandfather was introduced into the conversation" (*Applause* 37).

Having wished for his father's death when Lord Auchinleck was alive, Boswell appears in these passages to be seeking to relieve his guilt feelings in the aftermath of his passing. He needed to know that his father had died peacefully, full of hope in an afterlife and confident that his estate was in good hands. Kames could best fulfill this need, both because he was the strongest living link between Boswell and his father and grandfather, and because he was in some respects like a father to Boswell himself. When Boswell relishes "a comfortable night when I had him just alone," is he savoring the kind of evening he never had with his real father? When he seizes upon a resemblance between Kames and Auchinleck which has a soothing effect upon him, is he compensating for the fact that his real father usually agitated him? Boswell's last meeting with his father, nearly a month before the latter's death, had been thoroughly unpleasant (*Later Years* 225–26). With Kames, he had a chance to relive his father's dying days the way he would have wished them to be: the dutiful son constantly at his father's bedside, the father kind, intimate, and ever willing to provide guidance and voice his approval. Kames appears to have understood his role, as in the following bit of dialogue that Boswell failed to record: "'Lord Kames, you are wellcome from the other world, what news?' 'The only news that I have is that your father is coming back to see how you are behaving yourself.'"[20] Although these lines are spoken in jest, the humor cuts deep: the dying Kames is teased for his nearness to "the other world," while Boswell is threatened with the ghost of his father (in the body of Kames?), returning for the sole purpose of passing judgment on his behavior. At moments like these, Boswell's interviews have less to do with a biography of Kames than with the belated return and reformation of the prodigal son and the approval he hopes to win from his father, real or surrogate.

Though Boswell never realized his dream "to be Plutarch" by writing the life of Lord Kames, we must not on that account fail to appreciate the significance for him of the attempt to do so. It is surely not coincidence that the two men whose biographies Boswell tries hardest to write were the two most important surrogate fathers in his life, one in London and the other in Edinburgh. Like his real father, each of these men represented to him a particular way of relating to the world, associated chiefly with a particular geographical location. Of the three, Kames was clearly the most like Boswell in personality and temperament, and the balance he had worked out between an active life of letters and a successful legal career in Edinburgh probably constituted the most promising model for Boswell to emulate in his quest for happiness. It was the middle course between what Boswell considered the austere, oppressive provincialism of Presbyterian Scotland and the beguiling, liberating lifestyle of the literary metropolis—between Alexander Boswell's Auchinleck and Samuel Johnson's London.

Notes

A briefer, preliminary version of this essay, now superseded, was read at the Université Stendhal in Grenoble, France, in March 1991 and published in the conference proceedings as "Between Johnson and Auchinleck: Boswell's Lord Kames," *Etudes écossaises*, vol. 1: *Ecosse-Regards d'Histoire* (Grenoble: Université Stendhal, 1992), 93–104. Another version was presented at the Enlightenment Congress in Bristol, England, in July 1991. The author wishes to thank William Zachs and the Boswell Office at Yale University Library for helpful source references and materials and Irma Lustig for valuable comments and criticisms. Unpublished Boswell manuscripts at Yale are quoted with original spelling and punctuation and identified throughout this essay by catalogue number.

1. On this point, see Kenneth Simpson, *The Protean Scot: The Crisis of Identity in Eighteenth Century Scottish Literature* (Aberdeen: Aberdeen University Press, 1988), chap. 5.

2. Richard B. Sher, "Scottish Divines and Legal Lairds: Boswell's Scots Presbyterian Identity," in *New Light on Boswell* 28–55.

3. Born in 1696, Kames was eleven years older than Alexander Boswell and thirteen years older than Johnson, though he died in the same year as the former (1782) and only two years before the latter.

4. James Boswell, "Materials for Writing the Life of Lord Kames." In citing this source, I have used *Applause* 16–46, whenever material is contained there; otherwise *Malahide* 15: 267–302, which is quoted at 15: 279 in this instance. The little that has not been published in either of these places is among the Boswell Papers at Yale University, M135. A complete text of the "Materials" is being prepared for inclusion in a forthcoming volume of Boswell's correspondence with Kames and other Scottish literati that William Zachs and I are editing for the Yale Editions of the Private Papers of James Boswell.

5. Auchinleck to Boswell, 30 May 1763, *London Journal* 342. At the time of the letter of 16 July, Kames either did not know or pretended not to know that Boswell's trip to the Continent had already been fixed. Another, considerably younger Edinburgh laird who had been abroad for part of his legal education, Sir David Dalrymple (later Lord Hailes of the

Court of Session), was corresponding more frequently with Boswell at this time (e.g., C1414–C1420), and it is therefore not surprising that Boswell and Auchinleck turned to him rather than Kames for advice and support on this matter (C1421–C1428).

6. Kames's tendency to give personal advice by repeatedly citing one of his own books, in this case the recently published *Elements of Criticism*, is an instance of his vanity. For Kames's argument that "no passion hath any long uninterrupted existence," see *Elements*, vol. 1, chap. 2, pt. 3, and vol. 2, chap. 17. When Boswell visited Kames in October 1762 he read the *Elements* and defended it vigorously against Andrew Erskine's suggestion that the book was "obscure," though privately he remarked that it "has genius but is abstrues." See *Letters between the Honourable Andrew Erskine and James Boswell, Esq.* (London, 1762), 149, 151 (hereafter cited as *Erskine Letters*), and "Harvest Jaunt," *Malahide* 1: 129.

7. The poem begins and ends, for example, with this stanza:

> Of all the judges in the land
> I surely must be held the chief,
> For, none so *cleverly* can hang
> A bloody murderer or thief.
> Tweedle, tweedle, tweedle didum,
> Up with the Justiciary Court!

Reproduced, along with "An Epistle to Miss Home" (Kames's daughter Jean), in the aptly titled *Boswell's Book of Bad Verse*, ed. Jack Werner (London: White Lion Publishers, 1974), 38–39.

8. Boswell was having recurring dreams of his father's death around the time that he was most strenuously pursuing these biographical projects: "Either last night or the night before I had again dreamt that my father was dead" (15 February 1776, *Ominous Years* 234–35).

9. The Covingon (C) and Dick (D) projects may be summarized from the trade edition of the journals as follows. Covington: JB resolves to write C's life (20 February 1775); JB interviews C for more than an hour and takes notes (26 February); C "more willing than formerly that I should write his life" (12 February 1776); JB proposes "to mark his life," but C replies evasively (2 August 1777); JB renews the scheme and writes up notes based on past conversations, feeling anxious about the project (11–12 January 1780); JB takes notes at tea with C (20 July 1780). Nothing further is mentioned, and JB's notes have not survived. Dick: JB writes a note to D revealing his design to write his life (13 December 1775); JB asks D, who declines to be recorded (16 December 1775); JB begins to interview D, who agrees to provide materials for a biography (31 December 1776); JB conducts another interview (6 January 1777); JB conducts an all-morning interview, "continuing his life" (2 February 1777); "Read over the sketch

of his life to him so far as done" (3 September 1777); JB looks over some of D's letters (5 May 1782); in a letter to his wife JB alludes to the project (18 May 1786).

10. John Ramsay of Ochtertyre, *Scotland and Scotsmen in the Eighteenth Century,* ed. Alexander Allardyce, 2 vols. (Edinburgh: W. Blackwood and Sons, 1888), 1: 138 n. 1.

11. *Curiosities of a Scots Charta Chest, 1600–1800,* ed. [Margaret] Forbes (Edinburgh: William Brown, 1897), 257, 303.

12. Boswell's famous deathbed interview with Hume occurred on 7 July 1776, more than six months after this whimsical remark in the journal, and there is no reason to believe that at the time of that interview Boswell was actually engaged in writing a biography of Hume or even in gathering materials for one. In a letter of 2 February [1777] (L1081), Boswell informed Sir John Pringle that he had begun to write the life of Sir Alexander Dick and might also be Pringle's Plutarch, but when he mentioned Hume's death in the same letter, he said nothing of any intention to be Hume's biographer.

13. See, for example, Richard B. Schwartz's remark in "Epilogue: The Boswell Problem," in *New Questions, New Answers*: "I would approach his work as great autobiography *rather than* great biography" (254, emphasis added). Similarly, in "Boswell and Hume: The Deathbed Interview," in *New Light on Boswell* (116–25), Schwartz claims that Boswell's approach was too "subjective," "personalized," "solipsistic," and devoid of "detachment" to convey an understanding of his supposed subject. "The extent to which he turns experience into highly subjective autobiography is an ongoing shortcoming," he writes. "He looks out at others but often sees only the self" (121).

14. Kames's biographer, Alexander Fraser Tytler, Lord Woodhouselee, relied heavily on Boswell's unpublished notes for this kind of information about his subject's early life. See *Memoirs of the Life and Writings of Henry Home of Kames,* 2d ed., 3 vols. (Edinburgh, 1814), 1: 14 n., 19–20 n., 61 n., 65 n., and 82 n.

15. *Boswell in Holland* 128. On John Dun's philosophy of education, see Sher, "Scottish Divines and Legal Lairds," in *New Light on Boswell,* 33.

16. *Lord Kames and the Scotland of His Day* (Oxford: Clarendon Press, 1972), chap. 13: "Boswell in Search of a Father? Or a Subject?" 248.

17. She told him, for example, that she would probably not have married Kames if she had known she would inherit the Blair-Drummond estate, and she made Boswell uncomfortable by speaking with great candor about the disgrace of her daughter, Jean. See *Applause* 26, 39 and n. 7.

18. *The Hypochondriack,* ed. Margery Bailey, 2 vols. (Stanford: Stanford University Press, 1928), 2: 89, 100.

19. The editors of *Applause* have transcribed the passage this way, but it is also possible that the phrase "None to our senses" was spoken by

Boswell, and that the last part of the passage should read: "Said he [Kames], 'He [Alexander Boswell] seemed to be firm in his belief of future existence.'" The original manuscript reads ". . . transition in death—None to our senses—said he—He seemed to be firm in his beleif of future existence."

20. Recorded by Sir David Dalrymple, Lord Hailes, in a manuscript notebook from the 1790s, National Library of Scotland, MS 25429, fol. 50. Hailes places the incident in the Court of Session within a week of Kames's death, which is to say the third or fourth week of December 1782. Cf. *Applause* 17: "Boswell. '*Cogito, ergo sum.* I am sure you are here, for I've shaken hands with you. Well, what news from the other world?' Kames. 'They told me it was not time for me yet.' Boswell, 'We're much obliged to them. We shall take as good care of you as we can.' I talked of my father's easy death."

James Boswell, Henry Dundas, and Enlightened Politics

MICHAEL FRY

James Boswell's obsession with the father-figure is familiar enough. Less heed has been paid to the role in his life of that other visitant from the depths of the Calvinist psyche, the Doppelganger, the alter ego who appears ever and anon as reproach and warning for things done or not done.

The man who most nearly fulfilled this role was Henry Dundas. A contemporary, professional colleague, and—within limits—a friend of Boswell's, he was also in their own time reckoned much the more successful of the two. He became the first home-based Scot since his country's union with England in 1707 to rise to and stay at the top of British politics, as chief lieutenant to the greatest prime minister of the age, William Pitt the Younger. On his behalf, Dundas ruled Scotland and India, besides running the war against revolutionary France.[1] To state these bare biographical facts draws the contrast with Boswell's failure to distinguish himself, as he dearly wished, in a public career. In this respect Dundas represented everything that Boswell might have aspired to be and in his own eyes ought to have been, though obviously never (any objective observer must surely say) had the least chance of being.

Yet personal circumstance had seemed to mark them for a similar course in life. Dundas was born in April 1742, eighteen months after Boswell. Both were scions of old but far from wealthy families in the Scottish Lowlands. Both their fathers, if possessed of middling landed estates, had to make their living in the law, and ended up sitting on the bench as Lords Arniston and Auchinleck, respectively. In professional ability, Arniston was superior. Recognized as the outstanding judge of his generation, at the climax of his career he reached the presidency of the Court of Session, the highest Scottish civil instance. It was Arniston who recommended Auchinleck for a gown, and they became friends. They shared a keen and subtle intellect, as well as some if by no means all their interests. Though Auchinleck scorned modern literature, he was well versed in the classics and loved Anacreon and Horace, manifesting, in other words, a cultured taste which communicated itself in altered form to his son. Arniston, on the other hand, was a philistine. He thought books and pictures a waste of money and time, warning a third colleague on the Bench, Lord Kames, that concerts were bad for him. Still, Arniston lived, like Auchinleck, amid the splendor (rather precariously supported by income) of a great house built in stately Palladian style. Each adopted the same terrifying judicial demeanor in front of their households as they exhibited in presiding over the courts.

It was expected that the two sons would follow in their fathers' footsteps. Though no evidence confirms it, they may well have known each other as boys. They at any rate found themselves as classmates studying law at the University of Edinburgh, whence they qualified as advocates, Boswell in 1762, Dundas the next year. Boswell formed the impression, which he never lost, that he had the better mind, an impression which from his side largely determined their relationship. Dundas could never indeed have counted as a profound or original thinker, but he would show himself intelligent and receptive enough. He joined Edinburgh's Select Society, a temple of the Enlightenment, where he could mix with intellectuals, learn to enjoy their company, and build a stock of ideas that proved useful in his political career.

The similar background was yet to work differently on the two young men. It was perhaps of advantage to Dundas that Arniston had died in 1753, leaving him to develop free of parental approval or disapproval. His true father-figure was his stepbrother, his senior by thirty years, who also in due course became Lord President of the Court of Session with the judicial title of Arniston. Dundas's relations with him were less fraught than they might have been with a real father, if we can judge from the example of Auchinleck and Boswell. The Dundases stood on the best of terms, the elder colluding in the professional advancement of the younger. Dundas could thus count on a degree of support from his family that Boswell (though largely by his own fault) could not.

This gives us the first clue why Dundas would rise in public life while Boswell scarcely got off the ground. Unlike Boswell, he fulfilled his family's expectations. Scotland was certainly in the throes of headlong intellectual and material change, but it had started out as a traditional, close-knit society where the extended family was the primary political and economic unit. Scots clannishness not only often dictated that sons and brothers should follow in their choice of career a path laid down before them, but also demanded of them a deliberate exertion along its course to advance the interest of the family as a whole. This was, in particular, an unspoken assumption of legal practice. Legal families existed because familial connections offered a way to professional success. For an advocate, it helped most of all to have a relative on the bench, solicitors being eager to ply such a man with work. Boswell would later notice with amusement how he prospered when his father was sitting, though their relations could by then hardly have been worse. But that only shows how he undervalued adherence to the social discipline that formed and bound together the Scottish landed and legal class. In this rather closed and somewhat stern society, such adherence was reckoned a vital qualification for public life, even amid the new freedom offered by enlightened thinking.[2]

Dundas, in contrast to Boswell, had set straight to work at the bar and proved quite a prodigy there. Contemporaries amply testified to his sound though never extravagant eloquence, to the pains he took to master his clients' briefs, to the concision and competence of his pleading. Soon he was handling sensational murders and other major cases. Reward came quickly too. In 1766, only three years after finishing his studies, Dundas was appointed Solicitor-General, the second highest post in the Crown's legal service in Scotland. He had to go regularly now to plead Scottish appeals before the House of Lords in London. Here his solid ability at once attracted the favorable notice of the Lord Chief Justice, Lord Mansfield, a Scot who had spent his career in England and there built up an extensive political influence. Before another year passed, Dundas was involved in Scotland's greatest civil lawsuit of the century, the Douglas Cause, as counsel for Archibald Douglas, successful claimant to the vast patrimony of his uncle, the Duke of Douglas. Eventually, in 1775, Dundas was promoted to Lord Advocate, the highest nonjudicial post in his profession, and also in effect the chief officer of government in Scotland.

Boswell lagged well behind. Soon the despair of his father, he would have it marked by fellow-Scots (to his disadvantage) that after his studies he went swanning round the Continent to hobnob with Rousseau and Voltaire: this was unbecoming a steady man. It did not especially bother Boswell, but even he was struck on his visits home by the widening professional gap between himself and Dundas. He wrote, on the latter's first official promotion, to another friend from college, William Temple: "Do you remember what you and I used to think of Dundas? He has been making £700 a year as an advocate, has married a very genteel girl with £10,000 fortune and is now appointed his Majesty's Solicitor General for Scotland." Temple agreed that "we used to think little of Dundas" (*In Search of a Wife* 10). Yet Boswell would not exert himself enough to close the gap, even after his father had insisted on his pursuing a legal career. For example, the Douglas Cause, which lasted through the 1760s, offered rich pickings for advocates, and Boswell himself made a little out of a subsidiary case arising from it some years later. But during its main phase his contribution was only literary, in *Dorando* and some ballads, or else scandalous, when he capered with the yelling, gesticulating mob that stoned his father's windows after the austere old judge disdained to join in popular celebrations of Douglas's victory. Boswell was still not markedly progressing in his profession by the time of Dundas's second and greater step up in 1775. "Harry Dundas is going to be made King's Advocate—Lord Advocate at 33!" Boswell howled to Temple. "I cannot help being angry and somewhat fretful at this. He has, to be sure, strong parts, But he is a coarse, unlettered, unfanciful dog. Why is he so lucky?" (*Ominous Years* 160)

His rise in politics would prove, however, that there was more than luck to Dundas's success. Both he and Boswell had seen their careers to date as in part a preparation for public life. Legal practice provides this in many societies, in none more so than the Scotland of the eighteenth century. Since membership of the landed class was the sole basis of political influence, the social position of both Dundas and Boswell naturally led that way. Dundas did not feel it a degradation to write in advance to the prime minister, Lord North, explaining who he was and why he would be loyal to the government once elected to Parliament. With an array of professional feathers in his cap, he had little trouble in being chosen to represent his native Midlothian at the general election of 1774. From his official position he quickly extended his power in Scotland through skillful deployment of patronage, through the promotion of beneficial legislation, and above all through his mastery of the electoral system. Winning plaudits at Westminster too for his skill in administration and debate, he became a pillar of Scottish support to North, who needed every bit of it as he struggled to retain British sovereignty in America.

That struggle would be lost, but Dundas survived the resulting political turbulence. He served on as Lord Advocate in the rapid succession of weak governments following North's fall in March 1782. Only the latter's temporary junction with the Whigs under Charles James Fox during the summer of the next year brought dismissal and a brief eclipse, for Fox thought Dundas too cocky. He used the respite well to harry this new ministry from the opposition's benches, not without the help of Boswell, who published an attack on its attempted Indian reforms spirited enough to merit quotation by Dundas himself in the House of Commons.[3] The government was, in fact, a desperate expedient which lasted only six months. Dundas had already identified the younger Pitt as the man most likely to bring the period of distracted confusion to an end and restore the state's moral authority after its shattering defeat in America. He maneuvered ceaselessly to bring Pitt to office, and in December of that year he succeeded.

Almost at once, in March 1784, the young prime minister called an early general election in which he was triumphantly victorious. He would stay in power till 1801, with Dundas as his faithful factotum, ready for any degree of hard labor or dirty work. That guaranteed him over the whole period not only the dominant public position in Scotland but also a secure place in the leadership of Britain, with effective political control also of the growing empire in India. A few years later he would become one of his majesty's principal secretaries of state and, by his exertions in the French Wars, a savior of his country to many. He would remain at or near the summit of British politics for two decades, to be ennobled at the end of them as Viscount Melville. "How," Temple had already written in 1793, "has Dundas overtopt us all?"[4]

It was not just by lack of application that Boswell, weighed against this exacting standard of comparison, was found wanting. In his own pursuit of a career in politics, he too had first sought to associate himself with established public figures, though he seemed little able to separate serious political ambition from his yen for the glittering metropolitan life. He cultivated Lords Mansfield and Bute, the elder, then the younger Pitt, as well as John Wilkes and Edmund Burke. The last was his ideal—"Be Burke," he would tell himself.

Burke's appeal lay in his eloquence and in his reputation as an independent, even a rebel. Still, Boswell never had liked to be an outsider in quite the way Burke was, a parvenu without aristocratic connections from poverty-stricken, seditious Ireland. Given that, the choice of Wilkes for a companion was all the more unfortunate. An amiable rogue, he was viewed with the deepest suspicion by fellow politicians, and detested by Scots (these feelings being mutual). Boswell, however, allowed himself to be charmed by Wilkes's meretricious kind of success, or perhaps by the notoriety of his independence, especially as in his case it had seemed to offer a way round the drudgery, frustration, risk, compromise—in other words, the *discipline*—of politics.

In fact, Boswell never even cleared the first political hurdle of getting a parliamentary seat.[5] He started to think about it at the same time as Dundas, believing himself, as representative of an ancient and honorable family, no less deserving of public confidence. He was of a mind to stand for his own Ayrshire in the general election of 1774. Instead Dundas, already spreading his wings as an electoral manager, seized control of the county. Through a friend from the bar, Sir Adam Fergusson of Kilkerran, he organized a coalition of independent gentlemen to overthrow the aristocratic interest previously holding sway there. Boswell was aghast not just at the outcome but at the methods employed by Dundas. They were not, to be sure, very commendable, using loopholes in the electoral law to manufacture fictitious votes, though this was standard practice in much of Scotland. Boswell felt most outraged that Dundas and Arniston induced Auchinleck to take up the practice, for his father had publicly condemned it in judging a test case (as had, indeed, Arniston).

At the next general election, in 1780, Boswell was obliged to hold back because of his debts. But he did assiduously canvass for the aristocratic candidate, Hugh Montgomerie, heir to the Earl of Eglinton, with an eye to establishing himself as a coming man. Montgomerie won at the polls, only to see his victory overturned (on grounds of corruption!) in the courts, and Fergusson came in for a second term. By the general election of 1784, Boswell was hopeful of being chosen himself, following his succession as laird of Auchinleck on his father's death two years before. To his amazement and mortification, Dundas this time blithely formed an alliance with Eglinton, gave the seat to Montgomerie, and dispatched the complaisant Fergusson to a different one. In the general election of 1790 Boswell found himself again too laden with debt to contemplate a contest, after a last appeal to Dundas for support was never favored with an answer. He did not live to see another election.

Thus Boswell, to his chagrin, had been outmaneuvered and outstripped by Dundas as effortlessly in politics as in the law. It is easy just to put this down to his personal shortcomings, as the late Frank Brady persuasively did: "He made no pretense to political theory, or even to a large view of affairs, like Burke. As a practical politician, he was at best middling: occasionally, his tactics were sound, but anything like a general strategy hardly entered his head. All he wanted was to be one of the 558 members of the House of Commons, not because he particularly hoped to do something for his country . . . or even to be conspicuous there; but simply because being an M.P. was a respectable position, which would enhance the reputation of the Boswells of Auchinleck, and ensure that he spend part of each year in London (*Boswell's Political Career* 2).

Still, a glance at Sir Lewis Namier's standard works on the politics of the reign of George III reveals many men no more eccentric than Boswell who did get into Parliament and who even made a mark there.[6] Why was he so singularly unsuccessful? His personal shortcomings cannot be denied, but there was at the same time a more profound disjunction between the values that Boswell sought to bring to or to represent in politics and the actual political requirements of the age. This indeed mirrored a disjunction in Boswell's own life. By comparison, Dundas was, if not a less complex character, then certainly one more capable of integrating an angular Scottish inheritance with the acquired qualities necessary to smooth the path for a metropolitan career.

We have seen that in his youth Boswell ostentatiously spurned the traditional, personal bonds that in their own country held the

Scots together and outside it made them ready to help each other along. Yet he never fully outgrew those bonds, any more than he outgrew the rest of his legacy from family, nation, and religion. Once he had inherited Auchinleck, he could accept the bonds as to some extent compatible with the independence he claimed, and was eager to exploit them in essaying a political career. So he exerted himself to be a conscientious and popular laird, worthy of his fellows' confidence, and was active in the constituency, attending voters' meetings and joining in debates. But this access of public spirit seems to have come too late to save his reputation among his peers, who never showed any great disposition to trust him. As they saw it, in accepting their values only as it suited him, he wanted it both ways; on those terms they were not prepared to accept him.

For political advancement, the alternative to local support was patronage from on high. To Scots this meant going to Dundas, and to Boswell it meant not only swallowing his pride but also subjecting his independence to a real test. Still, the first step was not too hard for him: he had often been scathing about Dundas but soon, cheerfully inconsistent as ever, he was avowing again their youthful friendship. They remained on good enough terms to dine together from time to time in London, when in conversation they might break into Scots as a token of their old intimacy. Once in 1783, Dundas was not at all offended when Boswell goaded him with questions about his exercise of Scottish patronage, and asked him why he consented to be "a salesman for us, like cattle." The urbane reply came that "it was better for the country, better for individuals not. For when all could scramble, they would have a chance to get more for themselves and their friends without regard to merit. Whereas an agent for government must distribute to the best purpose. He has a trust" (*Applause* 144–45). Four years later, when a still unsatisfied Boswell asked again, even Dundas seemed to be tiring of the business. "He said that power was thought desirable on account of the patronage annexed to it; but that the uneasiness was much greater than the satisfaction for you had six or seven letters to write to people who were disappointed and probably had to give the office to one for whom you did not care, but that the government must be carried on" (*English Experiment* 152).

By any standards but Boswell's, this sort of contact stretched the concept of independence. Intimacy with a friend of his youth was fair enough, given that the friendship had anyway been far from proof against political accident. But heavy hints that a little patronage in Boswell's favor would not go amiss, soon followed by direct demands for it, were scarcely compatible with any degree of independence. Typically, Boswell, rather than exert himself to resolve the contradictions, sought to evade them by provoking a crisis in relations with Dundas in the hope of forcing some concession from him. But as so often he greatly overdid it, permitting himself statements which in no circumstances could have recommended him for official employment. The underlying fault lay in his inability to draw the same line between the public and the private as a professional politician would, and so to see what motivated any particular award of patronage. Dundas had made it plain enough that he was not at liberty to use his power for the sole purpose of gratifying old pals. With Boswell, this fell on deaf ears: if he could not get what he wanted, then he had somehow to shift the personal blame on to Dundas, make him admit that he was the one at fault and Boswell the injured party.[7]

This formed the real purpose of his *Letter to the People of Scotland* (1785), the ostensible occasion of which was a proposal from Dundas to improve the quality of the Scottish bench by cutting the number of judges and raising their salaries. Boswell affected to see here only an abuse of power and breach of the Treaty of Union: "Our country is at a miserable ebb, when its great and good families are totally indifferent about every public concern, and have so little spirit, even as to their private concerns, that they never advance, like men, to the fountainhead of government, but indolently or timidly suffer all to be done by some person who for the time is brought forward as a *minister for Scotland.*" He still could not resist carrying on a sarcastic argument ad hominem: "Yet I will do Mr Dundas the justice to declare, that, large as his power is, he has not much abused it. He has, indeed, taken very good care of his relations! He has, indeed, taken very good care of his relations! And why should he not? Though, to be sure, flesh and blood must feel his having put his young nephew over the heads of I know not how many of us, as Solicitor General. But I do not believe he has been cruel, oppressive or vindictive!"

Soon he was back on the political subject that really interested him: "And I trust to the generosity of his feelings, that, as he knows he once did me a severe injury, which I have from my heart forgiven, he will be anxious to make me full amends if ever it shall be in his power. The desire of elevation is as keen in me as in himself, though I am not so well fitted for party exploits."[8] All this was mild compared to what Boswell, getting cold feet at the last moment, deleted from the proofs: "Mr *Dundas* is not the *lion.* Ye lords and lairds and people of Scotland, attend!—Ye Lowland sheep, ye Highland deer, why do you startle and fly? Don't be frightened! Come near him! Look at him! He roars indeed, and he roars admirably: but I tell you he *is not the lion.* He is only the *jackal!*"[9] Even the toned down version, once published, left Boswell worried that he had gone too far and that Dundas would openly break with him. In fact, while it did nothing for the author's public reputation, the great man took it in remarkably good part. He could afford to. By now an old political hand, he was inured to the rough and tumble of public debate. About pamphlets he had only to worry if they caused lasting political damage, as this did not.

Dundas thus showed himself simply not vulnerable on the personal level where Boswell sought to attack him. No doubt he had grown the practiced politician's proverbial thick skin. But beyond that, the whole of politics in the Britain of the late eighteenth century was growing more impersonal in the sense that it was ceasing to hinge on the caprices of aristocratic faction and coming to depend instead on professional expertise, on the readiness of its public men to master their business and faithfully serve the state. Dundas himself, an outsider among the old ruling caste, represented this new spirit. How little he worried about the personal aspect of political squabbles is surely revealed by his eventually yielding to Boswell's pleas for patronage on behalf of his brother, David, to whom a modest post in the Navy Pay Office was awarded in 1791. What Dundas the politician wanted to know of James Boswell was whether he could rely on him. And whether he could may be judged from what Temple wrote to Boswell as late as 1791, after Boswell had in effect given up on Dundas and made his disastrous attempt to win the parliamentary patronage of the monstrous Earl of Lonsdale: "You want high place and office. But can you be useful, can you go all the lengths with your party? I fear there is no other way of succeeding, and is it worth while at such a price? You have had experience of one patron (it is true you made an ill choice) but where are better to be found? You must afford them inducement to seek you, and I fear they will not think your virtues and talents fit for their use" (Temple to Boswell, 3 Nov. 1794, C2976). It was an accurate assessment of Dundas's position also. To him, other politicians or aspirant politicians, indeed all who sought his favor, were just people he encountered sliding up or down the slippery pole. Except with Pitt the younger, to whom he was devoted, neither his enmity nor his friendship was fixed. He subordinated personal considerations to the great game of politics which gave substance to his life. And this Boswell could not do.

Dundas was not necessarily callous or unprincipled, as Boswell would have liked us to conclude. Let us see how he dealt with the most deviant ideology available to contemporary Scots, with Jacobitism, the belief that the once tragic, now pathetic house of Stewart should be recalled from exile to sit again on the throne of its ancestors. Boswell cultivated a romantic attachment to its cause. Dundas, though of a sternly Whig family, showed a degree of solicitude to Jacobites too. After their persecutions and forfeitures, they were scarcely capable of further treason. He reconciled them, first by dispensing patronage to formerly diehard rebel families. Then in 1784 he had all the forfeited estates returned to their previous owners as part of a deliberate plan to restore the shattered social fabric of the Highlands. And in 1799 he actually arranged for the British government to pay a secret pension to the Jacobite pretender, Henry Cardinal of York, rendered destitute by Napoleon's conquest of the Papal States. What gave Boswell a glow of glamorous nostalgia, therefore, was to Dundas a complex of political problems which he set out successfully to solve. It was no wonder that many former Jacobites henceforth gave their political support to him. He had healed up for good an old sore in Scottish society. And that was a pragmatic end worth pursuing in itself, regardless of the principles involved.

Even Boswell once recorded, presumably with pleasure, the remark on himself that "I was a Tory with Whig principles" (*Boswell in Extremes,* 252), and felt delighted when Burke told him that "you have the art of reconciling contradictions beyond any man" (*Great Biographer* 36–37). Yet both descriptions would have been better applied to Dundas. He has often been dubbed by posterity a Tory, for his conservative lack of idealism. But he probably regarded himself as a Whig, in the sense of subscribing to the principles of the Glorious Revolution of 1688 and the Union of 1707, and meaning to further the interests of the enlightened gentry propelled into power in Scotland by those events. The problem was that this new political class had never formed a coherent interest of its own, but lined up behind one or other factious figure from the old, and now usually absentee, feudal aristocracy, the sort of people Boswell professed to admire. Government had decayed in consequence, with legislation sluggish and patronage neglected. Scotland had obviously failed to reap all the potential benefits from the Union.

This was another problem that Dundas solved. By a combination of benevolent concern for his country's difficulties, geniality towards friends, and ruthlessness towards enemies, he united the factions behind himself. Consensus and unity in Scotland, so often lacking, were in a sense value-free, in that they did not demand assent to a particular set of principles. But again they had a political value of their own, one certainly transcending any possible benefit from the rigid adherence to an aristocratic code of conduct in which Boswell took such pride.

At any rate they helped Dundas fight his way up the slippery pole, offering Scottish votes to governments needing them. Once at the top, he could reveal purposes wider than personal ambition. For the first time it became accepted that someone avowedly Scottish in allegiance should sit in the Cabinet of the United Kingdom. For the first time it became accepted that he should appoint Scots to their fair share (Englishmen complained it was more than a fair share) of official posts in Britain and overseas. For the first time, in effect, Scotland was entitled as of right to those benefits of the Union, and her relationship with England changed from subordination to partnership. Objection might be taken to the means Dundas employed, though for his times they were nothing out of the ordinary, but the ends were indisputably positive, as most Scots appreciated. And those who, like Boswell, remained preoccupied with means, standing on their dignity and harping on about their ancient honor and rights, were simply ignored.

An enlightened age required enlightened rulers, qualified not by their blue blood or broad acres, nor yet by their intellectual virtuosity, but by efficiency and discipline in the pragmatic and impersonal exercise of power. This was the form that the emergence of enlightened politics took in Britain, rather different from what was produced by the Enlightenment in America or France, but enlightened all the same. The British ethos was more conservative, though still well short of Boswell's idealistic or emotional conservatism. He was therefore quite unfit for public service in such a system. In his own imagination at least, he belonged to an older, more stirring, and more estimable world. That world of the imagination was his proper one, just as this mundane but no less necessary world of calculating politics and rational administration was Dundas's. In 1794, towards the end of Boswell's life, Temple accurately told him that he had "aimed at uniting two characters that were incompatible. Had Dundas been ambitious of being a wit and an author, he never would have been Secretary of State" (Temple to Boswell, 21 Apr. 1794, C2965).

Notes

1. Michael Fry, *The Dundas Despotism* (Edinburgh: Edinburgh University Press, 1992), passim.

2. J.G. Lockhart, *Peter's Letters to his Kinsfolk,* 3d ed., 3 vols. (Edinburgh: W. Blackwood, 1819), 2: 67; Karl Miller, *Cockburn's Millennium* (London: Duckworth, 1975), 4; N.T. Phillipson, "Lawyers, Landowners and the Civic Leadership of Post-Union Scotland," *Juridical Review* (1976): 97–120; see also Fry, *Dundas Despotism* 14–18.

3. *A Letter to the People of Scotland on the Present State of the Nation* (London, 1783); *Parliamentary History of England* (London, 1783–84), xii, cols. 514–15.

4. Temple to Boswell, 7 Sept. 1793, C2940.

5. Frank Brady, *Boswell's Political Career* (New Haven and London: Yale University Press, 1965), 56–96, passim.

6. *The Structure of Politics at the Accession of George III* (London, 1929; 2d ed., New York: Macmillan, 1957); Namier and John Brooke, *The House of Commons, 1754–1790,* 3 vols. (London: HMSO, 1964).

7. Boswell's political career consisted to an unhealthy extent of public indiscretions. Examples which would have been particularly noted among the gentlemen of Ayrshire were his quite unwarranted attacks on Sir Adam Fergusson's lineage and his promotion of an address from the county praising the Prince of Wales's conduct on the Regency crisis of 1788, conduct which would have led to the fall of the government on

which they were all reliant for patronage. See Brady, *Boswell's Political Career* 64–65, 69, 158.

8. *A Letter to the People of Scotland* (London, 1785), 8, 60.

9. Irma S. Lustig, "The Manuscript as Biography: Boswell's *Letter to the People of Scotland* 1785," *Papers of the Bibliographical Society of America* 68 (1974): 250.

Politics in the Boswell-Temple Correspondence

THOMAS CRAWFORD

It is useful to remember the late Frank Brady's experience as a biographer of Boswell, continually hearing in the background "a persistent grey murmur of sound, which pours forth advice, remonstrances, cries for help, and expressions of deep, unchanging affection. It is, of course, Temple's voice, strident, monotonous, yet almost soothing in its repetitiousness over the years, like the sound of katydids in a New England August" (*Later Years* 85). The owner of the voice, William Johnson Temple, scion of one of the leading trading families of Berwick upon Tweed, was Boswell's "old and most intimate friend" (*Life* 2: 316), whom he had first met when they were students in Edinburgh in 1755–57. In 1757 Temple left to study at Trinity Hall, Cambridge, with a career at the English bar in mind, and thereafter the friends were in immediate contact for a total of only some eight months in all of thirty-eight years, the most important period being one of three months in London during Boswell's annus mirabilis of 1763. Money troubles following his father's bankruptcy forced Temple to switch to a clerical career, first in Devon, where he was rector of Mamhead near Exeter from 1766 to 1776, then in Cornwall, as vicar of St. Gluvias on the outskirts of Penryn from 1777 to his death in 1796.

The grey murmur is certainly there throughout his correspondence with Boswell; it occurs largely in his many laments about his personal condition, his lowly poverty as rector of Mamhead, his inability to proceed with scholarship because of lack of books, his marital problems, and his quiverful of children. But there are other sounds too, most notably the sounds of intellectual debate, theological, metaphysical,[1] and political. As regards the political, Temple's tones are far removed from a complaining whine, but modulate from the firmly principled to the gently ironical and sometimes to the fiercely denunciatory.

A reader of those masterpieces of literary biography, Frederick Pottle's *James Boswell: The Earlier Years* and its successor, Brady's *The Later Years,* would hardly suspect the prominence of metaphysical, ethical, and theological concerns in the letters between Boswell and his "old and most intimate friend," still less of the importance of the political dimension. But the letters—all 464 of them—form the largest single correspondence in the entire Boswell archive, recording one of the most remarkable friendships of the sentimental era; and politics had been a major concern from the very beginning. "Voltaire! Rousseau! immortal names" was the triumphant cry the friends, when only boys, had chanted on Arthur's Seat, that volcanic hill so rich in associations for Scottish literature and culture. For young Boswell two opposite sets of ideas and emotions—sentimental Jacobite toryism and Enlightenment libertarianism—coexisted at this time, and had a local habitation and a name in the Palace of Holyrood and the area immediately to the south and east of it. It seems to have been Temple who was the first to be affected by Hume's ideas, and Temple, not Boswell, who conceived the idea as early as the spring of 1759 that the two of them should go to Geneva and meet both Voltaire and Rousseau.[2]

The political dialogue in the correspondence is of two sorts: passing references and debate proper. The passing references may be to details of Boswell's several attempts to become an MP and reports and observations on what today we would call cabinet changes. "Debate proper" is more interesting. It is not carried on in a series of sequential formal arguments, such as we might find in letters between people like Bertrand Russell and Lord Keynes, but in a rather allusive manner when an apparently inconsequential phrase makes its point by the whole mass of associations it has for the writers.

Debate about republicanism versus monarchy started when Boswell was in Holland, some three months after he left England, and it began obliquely, with allusions to the Stuarts and the seventeenth century. "A sensible history of the reigns of James I and Charles I came out the other day," Temple wrote on 23 November 1763, "written by a Lady, Mrs Macaulay. . . . The stile is not good, but she defends the cause of Liberty better than any of our historians. This is the character Mr Gray gave me of it today, for I have not seen it myself. It will appear odd enough, if the most constitutional history of England should be written by a woman" (C2668). Boswell's response, on 4 December 1763, was to move directly from history to the topic of republicanism (again, without having read the work in question): "I revere Mr Gray: But I will not subscribe to all his tenets. . . . And does the pensive Bard realy commend Catherine Macaulay's History of England. . . . Beleive me Temple that an english Republican is either a weak or a wicked Politician. I thank God we have got a Monarchy, limited as much as a true Patriot and true lover of order could wish" (L1217).

Next, Boswell glances at the current situation and his hopes for the new reign. George III had come to the throne three years before, at the age of twenty-two, and earlier in the year he had dismissed Portland, Rockingham, and other leading Whigs and concluded peace with France and Spain. And, of course, proceedings against John Wilkes were underway for his role in the *North Briton* affair. In this same letter of 4 December 1763, Boswell continues: "I rejoyce to find that the King begins to show real firmness. I hope he will make it be remembered that *The Crown* is the head of our Constitution." The debate continues in the next letter, where Temple embarks upon a refutation of Boswell's Tory principles. He prefaces his rational argument by emotive references to his heroes—Helvidius Priscus, leader of the Stoic and republican opposition to Nero, and Algernon Sidney, the republican executed after the discovery of the Rye House Plot in 1683: "O! Sidney! thou friend to mankind, thou scourge of tyrants and guardian of liberty, citizen, philosopher, hero, what can attone for thy sufferings, what expiate thy blood? The souls of departed patriots still call aloud for justice on thy inhuman murderers. And they shall be revenged; some future historian shall record your virtues and their crimes." Then he turns on Boswell:

> Your notions of government surprise me. They are slavish and unworthy of an Englishman. All power is derived originally from the people, and kings are but the servants of the public. They are chosen to govern nations, not for their own private good, but for the general good of the governed. If they do their duty, if they shew themselves the first in virtue and ability as well as in station, they will be revered while living, and lamented when dead, their fame will live forever in the minds of a grateful people. But if otherwise, if they crush the

> subject race whom kings are born to serve, they shall be abhorred and punished by their much injured masters, they shall live in dishonour and die in infamy; their names shall be blotted out of the annals of their country.
>
> The English government is not a Monarchy; it is a mixed Republic, where the supreme power is equally divided amongst the three Estates. . . . I am as zealous for prerogative as you, but a king of England has no prerogative but to do good by supplying the deficiencies of the Laws, the most honourable and glorious of all prerogatives, which whenever he shall be found again to abuse, I trust there will not be wanting other Hampdens and other Sidneys to pull the tyrant down and trample him in the dust. (7 Feb. 1764, C2669)

Republicanism, then, is a key concept in the allusive political dialogue at this point. When Boswell said an English republican was either a weak or a wicked politician, he was getting at Temple himself, for he was well aware of his friend's views: in the letter just cited, Temple explicitly approves of one kind of republic—a mixed republic. Republicanism, for Temple, does not necessarily entail a state without someone called a king at the head of it, but could apply to a monarchy where the king had no more power than the doge of Venice. Tories of Boswell's generation were afraid that further limitation of the royal prerogative would push the country in the direction of Temple's ideal by overthrowing the balance of power between Lords and Commons and between Crown, Parliament, and People upon which liberty was taken to depend.[3]

By 23 July 1764, when Boswell was in Potsdam, the focus of confrontation shifted back to monarchy. When he saw Frederick the Great on parade he was overwhelmed:

> Imagine then the Prussian officers when their King walked majestic in the midst of them. To thee, thou Sidney of our times this would have been an unpleasing sight. Slaves! Slaves! would have burst from thy indignant Soul. But, to thy Monarchical freind whose blood is warm with ancient Loyalty it seemed a Spectacle fit for Heaven to behold with Joy. It was a perfect Example of grand Subordination. . . . I viewed with an enthusiasm of reverence this image of supreme dominion. (L1224)

For some reason this long enthusiastic letter did not reach Temple until 12 November. In the meantime, Boswell had had second thoughts. He had seen terror-stricken Prussian soldiers on exercise and been made physically sick by the spectacle of one poor wretch running the gauntlet. The king, he had later observed, was feared "like a wild beast," and he had been appalled at the ruins left by the Prussian bombardment of Dresden (J6 4 Sept., 22 Sept., 9 Oct. 1764). Boswell had written again, on 14 October, registering a strong swing from the royalist to the "liberal" point of view. "With true candour," he confessed, "let me now own that a short residence in his Prussian Majesty's dominions has given me other sentiments. I have seen my Royalty in full force, and I have seen its sad effects on Mankind. I am now the warmest Briton that ever adored Liberty" (L1225). In the interval, Temple had received the delayed letter from Berlin with its rapturous adoration of absolute monarchy, and had replied in ignorance of its sequel by castigating Frederick as "the tyrant of his people, and the enemy of mankind" (13 Nov. 1764, C2671).

By 1766 Boswell was writing his *Account of Corsica*, and Temple was commenting "don't regard what Johnson says; no man that loves the Stewarts can wish well to Corsica and Paoli" (20 Nov. 1766). A year later, after reading the first installment of the manuscript of the *Account of Corsica*, which Boswell had sent him for review, Temple gave vent to an allusive comment of great significance: "I would fain hope that this book will do you some credit. . . . I fancy you expect at least to be named with a Stanyan and a Molesworth" (19 Oct. 1767, C2694). Temple is here highlighting the libertarian import of Boswell's *Corsica* by putting it in the context of two earlier travel books of a highly progressive cast—Abraham Stanyan's *Account of Switzerland*, published in 1714, and Viscount Molesworth's *Account of Denmark as it was in the Year 1692*, published in 1694. Both these gentlemen had been diplomats. To Stanyan, the "commonwealths" of Switzerland were analogues of ancient Greece, and by merely mentioning his name Temple is comparing Corsica to Athens and Sparta. Molesworth is slightly earlier: he had been ambassador to Denmark in 1689–92, and his historical account of the Danish revolution of 1660, which transformed what he regarded as an ancient "Gothic" constitution into a New Model absolutism where "the people had been perswaded intirely to part with their Liberties,"[4] was meant as an awful warning to his age, a tract for the times. It had been reprinted in 1738, 1745, and 1752, and Horace Walpole had called it "one of our standard books."[5] It had a profound influence in shaping left-wing Whig and indeed republican thought in Britain, as Caroline Robbins pointed out long ago.[6] Thus, Temple was hoping that Boswell's *Corsica* would be not just a standard work, but libertarian in its effect.

How close Boswell's sentiments came to Temple's at this time can be illustrated by his hesitation over the choice of a motto for the volume. Boswell first thought of one from Temple's hero, Algernon Sidney: "This hand, hostile to tyrants, with the sword seeks peace and quiet under liberty" (cited in 17 May 1766, L1235). Then he veered, most significantly, to one from the Scottish declaration of independence of 1320, the letter of the Scottish barons to the Pope which is today known as the Declaration of Arbroath: "For it is not glory, it is not honour, but it is liberty alone that we fight and contend for, which no honest man will lose but with his life."[7] It seems clear, then, that strands of emotion from republican tradition, which Boswell perhaps got from Temple, blended with a Scottish-patriot strand and a Scottish-Jacobite-royalist strand to help form the political feeling-structure of the *Account of Corsica.*

In 1769 the dialogue moved on to the Wilkes affair and Parliamentary elections. On 22 September Temple announced his intention of signing a petition protesting against the violation of electoral rights in the matter of Wilkes's expulsion from the House of Commons after he had been duly elected for Middlesex. "You will think me a party man," he wrote, "but I am not; I hate corruption and oppression" (C2709). In his reply—unfortunately missing—Boswell must have lashed out at Wilkes's followers, the Society for the Defence of the Bill of Rights, and attacked their personal characters, for Temple countered as follows:

> If you look back into history you will find that improvements in Government are not always owing to the best man, much less to the men of greatest property. . . . They dread the consequences of civil dissentions, they feel themselves tolerably happy at present but know not what they may be in a new system. It is therefore from the enterprising, the restless and the desperate that we must expect salutary corrections and opposition to an unconstitutional and arbitrary administration. Such men have little to lose and they have every thing to hope. The present most infamous violation of the freedom of Elections calls loudly for redress, and if the Chathams, the Camb-

> dens and the Yorks have not the virtue nor the courage to vindicate our Rights, we may think ourselves happy to find Champions in a Wilkes a Sawbridge and a Glyn. (13 Oct. 1769, C2711)

In 1775 the American Revolution began to concern both Boswell and Temple. As was to be expected, Temple was pro-American from the first. On 26 March 1775 he wrote, somewhat slyly, that he hoped Boswell would take his information from Burke, rather than Johnson (C2759).

Yet five years later, despite his generally pro-American sentiments, Boswell could still glory in his toryism: "I distinguish between our *limited monarch* and a *despotick ministry*," he wrote on 3 September 1780 (*Letters JB* 2: 309). In the intervening period Temple had made repeated pro-American statements, including such a remark as "Can you forgive your friend [i.e., Samuel Johnson] for writing against the Genius of our Government and the Rights of Nations? O what a byas it is to receive a pension" (12 June 1777, C2778).

In a missing letter of 27 March 1778 Boswell had apparently referred to members of the House of Commons as "fine fashionable men." In his reply Temple highlighted this socio-political difference in class terms and in the context of an extreme antiluxury stance:

> You do our fine, fashionable men as you call them too much honour when you say they have reached so happy a composure as to be able to do whatever is to be done with equal readiness and deliberation. . . . What a reproach to these fine men that the American Congress and Militia composed of Planters and Labourers, in greasy, woollen nightcaps and but half armed and half disciplined should have acted with more wisdom, humanity, conduct and valour, than a polished British Senate and a regularly formed army. In short effeminacy, sensuality and prostitution can never unite with true discernment, magnanimity and ardour of mind. But enough of such worthless characters. (2 Apr. 1778, C2783)

It is a position enlarged upon in Temple's second publication, a work that encompasses all his political concerns at this time—his *Moral and Political Memoirs* of 1779, an octavo of 424 pages.[8] Boswell made some effort to get Dilly to publish it, yet it is clear that neither he nor the bookseller were at all keen. It seems they considered the essays not only unfashionable, but damnably dull. Temple's *Memoirs* are not brilliantly original, it is true, but though the style sometimes creaks and cranks along, they are full of rhetorically effective passages, and they are always deeply felt.

In a letter of 3–8 May 1779 Boswell sneers at "the college-like sentences your book contains," which give him "a fresh proof how very few even of those who have good parts are fit for the study, far less the practice, of government. You are an agreeable companion in a post chaise; but by no means fit to be a driver. We should cultivate the excellent principle of *submission for the Lord's sake*" (*Letters JB* 2: 288). It is worth observing the tone manipulation in that last sentence. Boswell is ironically turning against Temple a clergymanly phrase, which his friend might well have used to his congregation with a quite general meaning but which in certain political contexts could be made to encapsulate the whole Tory attitude to political authority. Boswell's comments in that 1779 letter show his contempt for political theory, especially Whig theory; and the book which has led him to depreciate, and even slight, his friend's solemn beliefs, shows up a contradiction in its author's position. As is clear from his dialogue with Boswell on religious topics, Temple is anti-theory when theology or "metaphysics" is in question, yet he approves of theory of a sort in the domain of political speculation.

There are eleven essays altogether in *Moral and Political Memoirs*, all of them raising matters repeatedly touched upon in the correspondence. Luxury is vehemently attacked, and the decline from the simplicity and frugality of the Roman republic to the effeminate decadence of the Empire is seen as paralleled today in the decay of the English country gentleman, "ever the faithful guardian of the rights of the nation." It is luxury that is responsible for the oppression of Ireland and the plunder of India, and Temple denounces those nabobs who "return to insult us with their absurd and sottish ostentation and vanity, and to supplant us, by the reward of their crimes and enormities, in our boroughs, counties, and thus in the very legislature itself" (293). Here the Old Testament Prophet pops up behind the normally flat prose to link the looting of India with another of Temple's long-term political concerns—Parliamentary corruption and the system of rotten boroughs that could be bought and sold. And when in an essay entitled "Of Unrestrained Power" he addresses the theme that absolute power corrupts absolutely, he is constantly aware of the contemporary relevance of the examples he piles up from the despots of antiquity and the Renaissance, expressing the fear that "the very scene, the very enormities we have been describing, may be again repeated, and even with aggravation," and that "the very legislature may be corrupted in its very source," that it "may be perverted into a tool of oppression and tenfold tyranny, and the restraints of law and controul, being sapped or thrown down, the princes of Europe may be inflamed into fiends and demons, their subjects degraded into the vilest slaves and beasts of burthen" (140). Unrestrained power is not to be trusted in mortal hands, he passionately believes, but must always be limited by checks and balances and the rule of law.

In the months before and after the publication of *Moral and Historical Memoirs,* there was once more a real confrontation in the correspondence. On 10 April 1779, just before the letter in which Boswell sneered at Temple's "college-like sentences," Temple wrote: "would to God I could gain you over to my Sentiments." "However unfashionable and *unmodern* my notions may be," he says, "they are certainly noble and generous and derived from a long familiarity with the greatest writers in the world" (C2795). In a missing letter—again written before the "sneering" letter—Boswell had called Temple a "Whig-parson." Temple replied on 24 April: "It would be honourable for Religion, had all Parsons always been so, for I am sure there is nothing in Scripture rightly interpreted that authorises those servile and destructive opinions that have been countenanced by too many of the Clergy. . . . We despised whigs are as great friends to subordination and good government as you insulting Tories but then we chuse to be subordinate to Virtue, to Talents,—to Law, not to Vice, to Ignorance, to Passion." And he proudly proclaimed himself a disciple of "the greatest men and most profound thinkers that modern ages have produced; I mean Machiavel, Montesquieu and Locke" (C2797).

In the 1780s the political focus of the correspondence shifts from general topics to Parliamentary reform; to Temple's helping with a petition for more equal representation in Cornwall, long notorious for the corruption and venality of its boroughs; to the minutiae of Boswell's attempts to become MP for Ayrshire and his dealings with Lord Lonsdale, as well as the political works he wrote during the decade the *Letters to the People of Scotland* of 1783 and the one of 1785. It was in the middle of 1785 that Boswell underwent a sudden and complete revolution in his attitude to Parliamentary reform.[9] He must have written about it in a missing letter, prompting Temple to ask in his reply, with the intimate irony which characterizes his writing at its best: "What new ray has enlightened you? And how is Reformation become so suddenly Innovation in your eyes?" (8 June 1785, C2834). Boswell answered this question in another missing letter, probably in the same terms as those he used in a letter to Thomas Barnard, Bishop of Killaloe, where he said he had been "fairly converted . . . by observing that Reformers can agree on no one Plan, and that all of them have an inordinate spirit of resistance to their Superiors coupled with a desire of power over their Inferiors" (Boswell to Barnard, 1 July 1785, L42). Temple's answer to this *argumentum ad hominem* was to affirm that "far from wishing to oppress," the desire of reformers "is to diffuse freedom and happiness." And, he asked: "Who have ever been the greatest oppressors? Courtiers, or friends to popular government? Your reasons may please and satisfy a Bishop [possibly a side-swipe at the Bishop of Killaloe], but not many unaspiring Rectors and Vicars" (31 Aug. 1785, C2835).

From 1789 the political dialogue moved to the revolution in France and its repercussions in Britain.[10] We have no record of Boswell's reaction to the fall of the Bastille on 14 July, but we do have an early response from Temple on 24 August that combined the euphoria of "Bliss was it in that dawn to be alive" with distress at the violence that had already begun to occur, and ended with the eternal question: "Yet why must Evils be, to produce Good? Say what we will, *This* will ever puzzle Philosophy" (C2875). Boswell's first surviving comment came in a letter to Temple of 28 November 1789, and it shows him already at this early stage a fierce opponent of the revolution. In the previous sentence he had used the word "hierarchy," which immediately led Boswell to think of its opposite: "That venerable sound brings to my mind the ruffians in France who are atempting to destroy all order ecclesiastical and civil. The present state of that country is an intellectual earthquake, a whirlwind, a mad insurrection without any immediate cause, and therefore we see to what a horrible anarchy it tends. I do not mean that the French ought not to have a *Habeas Corpus* Act. But I know nothing more they wanted" (*Letters JB* 2: 386). Temple did not reply till 21 February 1790, in mildly reasonable tones, hoping that "order and security may arise out of anarchy and alarm," and asserting "that no government was ever greatly improved without previous compulsion" (C2880).

If Temple was still prepared to hope for some political liberalization in France, he was nevertheless becoming quite reactionary in ecclesiastical politics, agreeing with Boswell's condemnation of the Dissenters, that "troublesome, discontented tribe." They should be granted no further concessions—they don't deserve any, he maintained in the same letter. Yet "Voltaire! Rousseau! immortal names" still cast their spell. When on a visit to Oxford, Temple wrote on 12 May 1790, "How the arts embellish the world! What a dreary scene would it be without them and inequality of property! Rousseau is an eloquent madman or he never could have written such divine nonsense. Yet what cannot his pen embellish!" (C2885). Here cultural politics and cultural ideology come together to underwrite the necessity of social subordination.

On 18 October 1790 Temple was still enthusiastic about the revolution itself, but was converted to the anti-French position two months later by reading Burke's *Reflections*, published on 1 November. He must have read the book immediately, for by 16 December he was writing: "What penetration, what argument, what eloquence, what sensibility. How finely has he trimmed those incendiaries and fanatics Price and Priestley" (C2895). Temple's increasing conservatism soon made him doubt even the principles of Parliamentary reform, and he came to feel that it should be opposed as the first step to a revolution in Britain (6 Dec. 1791, C2915). A month later, on 3 January 1792, he was writing that republics were "full as bad if not worse" than "Courts and Kings and Monarchy" (C2916).

The growth of the reform movement, with its Constitutional and Corresponding Societies, does not seem to have been much impeded by the imprisonment of the French royal family in August 1792 and the September massacres of imprisoned aristocrats. It was only natural, therefore, that the supporters of government should hit back by forming their own associations. Boswell had links with two of them, a private club (of which Burke, Windham, and Malone were members), and the public Crown and Anchor Association (*Great Biographer* 206, 210 n. 4). At about the time Boswell was joining these groups, Temple was reporting that disaffection was still rife in Cornwall. Paine's *Rights of*

Man was circulating everywhere, he lamented, even among what he called "the lowest of the people: their very children have got the *cant*" (1 Dec. 1792, C2929). And ten days later he was still writing about the "lowest of the people," saying that they "talk strangely here; but every body that has any thing dreads a Change and is firmly attached to the present Government."

> Mrs T[emple] went this afternoon to pay a trifle to an old woman who keeps a little shop—Well, madam, I will take it as long as they will let me. I have lived too long to see such times, and will pray for the king with my last breath. God bless him.—The children say to Octavius [Temple's schoolboy son] in Penryn, a civil war will be better for us poor folks, we shall get something. The maid at Laura's school says, my poor *fether* will get £20 or £30 a year. Even Tucker, my labourer whom you recollect says to the servants in the kitchen, my wages at least will be raised and I shall live better. . . . Great pains have been taken to circulate Pain[e']s Pamphlet which has done more harm than you can conceive among the rabble. (Temple to Boswell, 11 Dec. 1792, C2930)

In this same letter he reported the loyalist response. A local landowner, Sir Francis Basset, had "dispersed many hundred copies of the Paper from the association at the Crown and Anchor [that is, of the organization to which Boswell belonged]. I have reason to believe that association will be entered into here in every town and part of the County," Temple continued. "I have also caught the contagion of Loyalty and the end of this week shall send my circular printed letter to the Clergy of two hundred and fifteen parishes or Churches." The purpose of the printed letter was to "sell" the idea of the freshly founded County Library, a project close to Temple's heart; and what he did was to turn it into an anti-revolutionary and anti-reform propaganda piece which affirmed "our own present Government to be the wisest and the best that mankind in any age or any Country of the world, were ever blest with."

On 30 January 1793 Temple was seized with horror at the execution of the king— "Louis, the humane, the pious and the good," as he called him (C2932). A week later he was writing, "I can hardly look with complaisance, or even tranquillity, on a partisan of the French Convention; they are dangerous characters," and telling Boswell that he had "composed and preached three Political Sermons, which have made no small *sensation* here: I think it a duty at such a crisis as the present." And he ends with this despairing comment: "The French Revolution, which we hoped would be so beneficial to mankind, is likely to involve all Europe in the greatest miseries. So little do we foresee the issue of things, and so hazardous it is to disturb Regular Government of whatever kind" (6 Feb. 1793, C2933). By 18 July Temple was writing: "It is wonderful that any gentleman can now adhere to what they call the *people*," and he had moved so far against reform as to say "I begin now to doubt whether Parliament is not better constituted as it is" (C2938).

Six months later, on 30 January 1794, the anniversary of the execution of Charles I, Temple reflected further on the French regicide. He penned this comment immediately before going into his church to preach on the subject, in the spirit of all who have committed ideological genocide since the first ideology was made: "I am just going to deprecate the vengeance of the Almighty from the Posterity of the actors of the horrid deed of this day, and which ourselves have seen repeated with aggravated circumstances of savage manners in a Country whose inhabitors ought to be wiped from the face of the Earth" (C2954). On 29 May 1794, responding to news of the execution of Louis XVI's younger sister, Madame Elisabeth, his indignation modulated to a more theoretical plane: "Alas! My dear Boswell! how have we been deceived and how callous, how dreadful a tyrant is the Peuple Souvereign," he wrote. Then his lifelong reliance on the Roman historians came into his mind and he began to question even that inspiration. He continued, "I shall now begin to think with old Hobbes that the Roman historians serve only to mislead and make us discontented and seditious. Yet what do the Sans Culottes know of Livy and Sallust. Some of their leaders *abuse* what they know of them. O let us preserve tranquillity at home and not throw away happiness" (C2970).

It is unfortunate that practically all of Boswell's letters to Temple in 1794 are missing. In one of these Boswell must have reported that he had been reading Clarendon's *History of the Rebellion and Civil Wars in England* (1702–4; see *Great Biographer* 304–7). In his reply of 15–16 January 1795, Temple drew the parallel between seventeenth-century fanaticism and "modern" revolutionary excesses, and went on to say

> How opinions change! In early youth I rejoiced at the Fate of the unfortunate Charles. I now cannot read his sad story without tears and abhorrence of the fanatical and hypocritical miscreants who shed his sacred blood. If tyranny is unavoidable, let it be one of Gentlemen and not of the *Swinish* multitude: the expression, however exclaimed against by the factious and unexperienced shews Burkes thorough acquaintance with mankind. The *pious* and what some would call the superstitious turn of our noble historian is far more congenial with my sentiments than the Sceptical or Irreligious one that pollutes the pages of Modern *Dissertations* and would deprive us of all trust and confidence in the Almighty. (C2977)

Two months later, on 5 March 1795, Temple made his last statement of any theoretical import: "Burkes immortal Treatise [*Reflections on the French Revolution*] and the Cause of it [the historical events themselves] have indeed produced a great change in my sentiments. My former inclinations to the popular side were fostered and inflamed by the Greek and Roman historians which I continued to read: but we now see and feel that the Many are far worse and more detestable Tyrants than the Few" (C2979). After this, we have only two very brief letters from Temple to Boswell, and three dictated by Boswell during his last illness to his son, James the younger. By 19 May 1795 Boswell was dead; and so, by 13 August of the following year, was Temple. It is difficult not to see the final mood of their life's dialogue as a grey plateau—the mutual recognition of lost opportunities, repeated disappointments, the failure of worldly ambitions. The years had dispersed one sort of philosophic mind, the sort that speculates about the nature of perception and the origin of evil, and replaced it by another— "philosophic" in the everyday sense of "calmly and temperately resigned to what cannot be avoided."

When ideology is separated from total experience, each of the protagonists is seen to preserve a certain consistency within his inconsistencies. Boswell's religious vacillations were practically over by the end of his grand tour, though he continued to be plagued by occasional fits of horror that we might, after all, be condemned to perish on the shore, in spite of his intellectual conviction that there *is* a life after death. Politically, he underwent a "bouleversement" over Parliamentary reform in 1785 which was paralleled in Temple's retreat from the reform position some seven years later. Boswell's basic attitude, however, was exactly as Robert Warnock put it fifty years ago when he spoke of "the peculiar turn of Boswell's mind at whatever age . . . the same liberal point of view combined with conservative principles."[11] In 1789–90, however, this liberalism never allowed him to lend any support to the French Revolution.

Temple's reversals were in some ways more interesting than Boswell's. His early "Commonwealthman" position, traces of which remained until the 1780s, was hardly typical of his generation, and where he got it from (apart from reading the Roman historians) is one of the most puzzling features of the correspondence. When the revolution came along, it seemed at first to fit in with what remained of his republican whiggery, but by 1791 he was beginning to display the classic "god that failed" syndrome, which led him to renege completely on his early radicalism. Temple's political disillusion adds an extra twist to the strands of disappointment and failure that intertwine in the letters of the 1780s and '90s, and parallels the experience of millions of people in our own century.

A moment ago I used the phrase (or rather clause) "when ideology is separated from total experience." But of course it never is in real life, and it never is in this correspondence regarded as a whole. The letters are filled with references to persons whom the reader is tempted to treat as characters in an imaginative work. Some of them seem almost like figures of myth—Paoli, the heroic leader of the struggle for Corsican independence, or the mediocre villain Dundas, filling a place like Mime's in Wagner's *Siegfried*; while others seem to inhabit the worlds of romance or the novel: one thinks of the pastoral and low mimetic heroines of Boswell's wife-searching days (see *In Search of a Wife* xix–xx, and passim); of Margaret Caroline Rudd, the femme fatale; of the long-suffering wives, Penelopes patient and not so patient. It is the men of ideas, however, who have the truest mythic stature—Voltaire, Rousseau, Priestley, Price, Sidney, the republican figures of classical antiquity whom Temple revered, and two contemporaries above all others, David Hume and Samuel Johnson. But since it is as colossi of ethics and metaphysics rather than of politics that these last bestride the correspondence, their role lies outside the scope of this essay, whose purpose has been to bring out the importance of political debate in the prolonged, almost lifelong, epistolary converse of these two very different men. The Boswell-Temple correspondence is a fascinating example of what might be called the dialogism of the everyday, and the political strand intertwines with many others in its rich fabric—legal, literary, clerical, and familial, to mention only a few—to provide an extraordinarily comprehensive picture of eighteenth-century professional and intellectual life.

Notes

Ninety-seven of Boswell's letters to Temple are in the Pierpont Morgan Library, New York, and are printed in *Letters JB.* Twenty-nine (prefixed in the *Catalogue* of the Boswell Papers by the letter *L*) are at Yale University. All of Temple's 338 surviving letters to Boswell are in the Yale Boswell Collection, and are prefixed in the *Catalogue* by the letter *C.* The spelling and punctuation of the manuscripts are retained throughout.

1. See Thomas Crawford, "Enlightenment, Metaphysics and Religion in the Boswell-Temple Correspondence," *Studies in Scottish Literature* 25 (1990) 49–69.

2. Extract (in Boswell's hand) of a letter from Temple to Lord Auchinleck, c. 9 Aug. 1759, to which Boswell added the following note: "This letter talked of our having climbed the lofty Arthur Seat and exclaimed Voltaire! Rousseau! immortal names etc.—etc" (C2654).

3. I should like to thank Nicholas Phillipson for drawing my attention to the nature of eighteenth-century (English) republicanism.

4. Robert, Viscount Molesworth, *An Account of Denmark as it was in the Year 1692* (London, 1694), 44.

5. In Charles, Baron Whitworth, *An Account of Russia as it was in the Year 1710* ([Twickenham]: Strawberry-Hill, 1758), Advertisement, iii–iv.

6. Caroline Robbins, *The Eighteenth-Century Commonwealthman* (Cambridge, Mass.: Harvard University Press, 1959), 98–109, and passim.

7. *Scottish Historical Documents,* ed. Gordon Donaldson (New York: Barnes and Noble, 1970), 57.

8. [W.J. Temple] *Moral and Political Memoirs* (London: E. & C. Dilly, 1779). Temple's previous book was *An Essay on the Clergy; their Studies, Recreation, Decline of Influence,* etc. (London: E. & C. Dilly, 1774).

9. Frank Brady, *Boswell's Political Career* (New Haven and London: Yale University Press, 1965), 99, 175.

10. See Marlies K. Danziger, "Horrible Anarchy: James Boswell's View of the French Revolution," *Studies in Scottish Literature* 23 (1988) 64–76; and Thomas Crawford, *Boswell, Burns and the French Revolution* (Edinburgh: the Saltire Society, 1990), 31–50.

11. Robert Warnock, "Boswell on the Grand Tour," *Studies in Philology* 39 (1942) 661.

Master of Ulubrae: Boswell as Enlightened Laird

JOHN STRAWHORN

> As I am now Master of *Ulubrae*, of which we have often talked, I hope you will venture to pay it a visit.
>
> JB to John Wilkes, 14 Feb. 1783, *Letters JB*

On the front of the fine country mansion in Ayrshire which Alexander Boswell, Lord Auchinleck, erected in 1762, he had inscribed lines from Horace's First Epistle: "*Quod petis hic est, est Ulubris, animus si te non deficit aequus*," which may be rendered as "What thou seekest is here, it is in Ulubrae, unless equanimity is lacking." Ulubrae, a small town now known as Cisterna, lay some thirty miles from Rome. C.B. Tinker, veritable founder of Boswell studies, suggested that as "Ulubrae, a town near the Pontine marshes of Latium, had been a byword among the Latin authors for its remoteness from Rome," so James Boswell after succeeding to Auchinleck "referred sarcastically to himself, when writing to John Wilkes, as the 'Master of Ulubrae,' and he remained consistently unwilling to exile himself there" (*Letters JB* 2: 297). In fact there was no sarcasm in Boswell's reference to Ulubrae here or in his letter of 22 November 1779 to Samuel Johnson.[1] The two great scholars and biographers of Boswell have confirmed the importance of Auchinleck. Frederick A. Pottle emphasizes Boswell's expressed desire to be "a worthy Scots laird" (*Earlier Years* 7), while Frank Brady emphasizes that "Boswell's accession as Laird marked a new start in life," and that his "new lively interest in rural activities seemed to him like developing a sixth sense" (*Later Years* 230, 231). Yet the myth continues to be perpetuated that Auchinleck occupied a peripheral place in Boswell's life.

James Boswell, born in Edinburgh in 1740, spent his earliest years there. Until 1749, when his grandfather died, it does not seem likely that he was often at Auchinleck, but from the age of nine till he was twenty-two he was there for several months each summer. After his first visits to London (1760, 1762–63) and his extended continental tour (1763–66), he lived in Edinburgh for the greater part of the next sixteen years, practicing as an advocate. Though he visited London eight more times in that period, he actually spent more time altogether at Auchinleck. He proudly invited there as guests John Johnston of Grange (1761, 1782), William Johnson Temple (1767), General Pasquale de Paoli (1771), and Dr. Samuel Johnson (1773). After 1782, when he succeeded his father as laird, Boswell could spend more time in London, but for several years he was as often at Auchinleck and for as long. Then, in 1786, he chose to be called to the English bar, gave up his house in Edinburgh, and transported the family to London. For the next few years visits to Auchinleck were brief; but in 1794 he settled there for more than six months—his longest stay ever—returning in January 1795 to London, where he died on 19 May.

It is appropriate that writers have concentrated their attention on Boswell's life in London. But it is unfortunate that they have failed to appreciate how much time he spent at Auchinleck and how important it always was for him. After becoming laird he wrote, "My brother T.D. . . . pressed upon me my duty as head of our Family, entreating me to reside at Auchinleck. I was moved, and regretted much my feverish fancy for London" (*English Experiment* 17–18). After he set up house in London, the distant Scottish estate might have appeared to be a superfluous encumbrance. He did complain to his son that "the expense of living here [at Auchinleck] is much greater than in London" (Boswell to Jamie, 27 Oct. 1794, L148). But to abandon that family property was unthinkable. He never contemplated selling it, which was anyway not permissible under the terms of Lord Auchinleck's entail. To lease it, which might have seemed sensible, would entrust it to strangers, and "rather than let the house of Auchinleck I would set fire to it" (Reg. Let. 2 Dec. 1789).[2] For, as Brady concluded, "Auchinleck was central to JB's life."[3]

James Boswell when a youth was made aware of his heritage. He read, possibly in 1766, memoirs commenced by his grandfather and continued by his father (*Earlier Years* 288). These Auchinleck Memoirs (C338.7) include a history of the family from the grant of Auchinleck in 1504 by King James IV to Thomas Boswell from Balmuto in Fife, and lists those fortunate marriages of successive lairds which entitled James Boswell to boast of royal blood in his veins. So in 1773 he could describe himself as "a gentleman of ancient blood, the pride of which was his predominant passion" (*Hebrides* 32). In 1767 he had his brother Thomas David swear an oath at the old castle of Auchinleck for "the continuance and prosperity of the ancient Family of Auchinleck" (M22). In 1790 he reminded his eldest son to "Remember always our ancient Family, for *that* is the capital object" (Boswell to Sandy, 2 June 1790, L81).

For Boswell, Auchinleck was always "a most sweet, romantic place" (Boswell to Grange, 26 Sept. 1759, *Corr: Grange* 3), and "one of the most delightful places upon earth" (Boswell to Jamie, 14 Aug. 1793, L129). In the *Life of Johnson* he recalled that "the family-seat was rich in natural romantic beauties of rock, wood, and water: and that in my 'morn of life' I had appropriated the finest descriptions in the ancient Classicks to certain scenes there" (*Life* 3: 178). He especially enjoyed visiting the old castle, praying at the ruined chapel nearby, where the Dipple Burn emerged from its gorge to join the Lugar Water. But the chief attraction lay neither with scenery, nor with places, but rather with people, those who shared the land and its heritage with him. The Auchinleck Memoirs include a record of lands acquired and improvements initiated in the seventeenth century; the archives contain also a chartulary in twelve volumes (C232) and estate papers with rental books from 1661 (BFP 92.1687). These last records Boswell examined in 1778 to find "Names of tenants holding certain farms of the Estate of Auchinleck during the latter half of the Seventeenth Century" (M10). He was therefore able later to dispute a claim by the miller that the Samson family had been at Auchinleck longer than the Boswells (*Laird* 231–32). When served heir to his father he could choose a jury of fifteen from tenants whose families had been on the estate for generations (Boswell to Bruce, 4 Feb. 1784, L292). His journals reveal him often conversing with old men of the neighborhood and absorbing their oral histories.

There was ambivalence, of course, in his feelings for Auchinleck. Referring to the inscription on the front of the House, he admitted, "It is characteristic of the founder; but the *animus aequus* is, alas! not inheritable" (*Hebrides* 374). Boswell, brought up in

Edinburgh, remained fond of urban life. His affection for Auchinleck was at times inhibited because of the inevitably closer association when there with an antipathetic father. Visits often involved unpleasantness. One constant contact with the estate was through James Bruce, the overseer who knew Boswell from childhood, and whose correspondence with him is unique in its span of years. From 1762 till 1782 Bruce kept young Boswell informed of estate affairs. He also served as a confidant: on one occasion Boswell obtained from Bruce "a parcel of my letters to him at the most foolish time of my life" and "burnt all but one or two of the best" (*Laird* 237); and Boswell later informed Bruce "that I have burnt his last letter, and he must burn this" (Reg. Let., 9 July 1782). From 1782 until his death in 1790 Bruce continued as the new laird's overseer, but the correspondence still exhibited interest in his master's wider career. Whenever Boswell was at Auchinleck he enjoyed evening walks with Bruce, discussing farming, religion, and family history (see, for example, *Laird* 105–8). Bruce was a sort of substitute father, "a kind of friend and tutor" who "seemed in imagination to be an inseparable circumstance about the Place" (*Great Biographer* 105).

Boswell was quite well prepared for his role as laird. The allegation of "his father's selfish refusal to teach him how to manage the estate" would seem to be exaggerated (*Later Years* 228). As a youth Boswell learned much from Bruce, obviously with his father's acquiescence. He planted trees, as his father and grandfather had done when they were heirs. There are hints that he was allowed some small share in managing the estate (Bruce to Boswell, 19 July 1766, C604). As his father's health deteriorated he acquired more responsibilities; he exhibited initiative in suggesting new ideas—for this once earning denunciation as "a gowk," that is, a cuckoo, or fool (*Laird* 244). He struck up an acquaintance with Alexander Fairlie, the county's chief exponent on agricultural improvements, who "instructed me in country affairs" (*Boswell in Extremes* 93), and he would further prepare himself by taking lessons on tax collection and arithmetic (*Laird* 241; *Applause* 11). He had at one stage found it "strange that all the country gentlemen should talk so much about farming; that I would as soon talk of shoemaking" (*Boswell in Extremes* 94). But in three articles "On Living in the Country" (*London Magazine*, Sept.–Nov. 1780), he argued that though agriculture was "to a great proportion of people, a very indifferent, and a very dull topic," yet "there are better enjoyments in the country than he had supposed." True, there were "dull intervals," and these he would experience at Auchinleck as laird, especially when rents were slow in coming in. But he could rejoice that "I have the old *Lairdly* principle very strong in me, and would suffer much in such a cause" (Boswell to Robert Boswell, 15 Mar. 1791, L246).

There was reason for Boswell to have pride in Auchinleck. Within Ayrshire six earls had seats, their estates mostly larger than Auchinleck, some taking in rents of more than £10,000 a year. Of the other estates in the county, those possessed by Fergusson of Kilkerran and Boswell of Auchinleck were the largest, though admittedly not the most lucrative, among thirty held by commoners and yielding between £1,000 and £2,000 a year.[5] Boswell could boast that as laird he "could ride ten miles forward upon his own territories, upon which he had upwards of six hundred people attached to him" (*Life* 3: 178). This was certainly an underestimate, for the estate covered some twenty-seven thousand acres, impinged upon four parishes, and by the 1790s supported a population of almost a thousand persons. Lord Auchinleck cleared £1,500 annually from the estate, which he described as "sufficient for answering all the reasonable Expenses of a Gentleman's family" (Deed of Entail, BFP 132. 2400). His son, however, was burdened by annuities to be paid, and deprived of some of the best farms, which the widowed Lady Auchinleck had in life-rent. He was unfortunate also because the disastrous harvests of 1782–83 impoverished tenants in subsequent years. In 1787 Boswell cleared only £500 (Bruce's Rentals, BFP 169.2961). But by diligence and good management that amount was in course of time more than doubled (Boswell to Jamie, 3 Jan. 1795, L159), and there was prospect of another £500 annually if he outlived his stepmother (BFP 173.3050:2767). In process he had invested over £1,000 on improvements, as well as £5,000 in purchase of additional lands, outlays which contributed to, and must be set against, debts at his death of £9,000 (A52).

Boswell could not treat Auchinleck simply as a source of income: it was a business enterprise which required his constant involvement. When the overseer James Bruce became unfit, Boswell's cousin Bruce Campbell was brought in to assist; and when Bruce died, Boswell's brother Thomas David was sent to Auchinleck and engaged Andrew Gibb. Boswell required this new overseer to continue the regular correspondence he had initiated with Bruce: "I expect to receive a letter from you at least once a week, informing me what you and others employed by me have been doing. . . . I am very anxious that all things about Auchinleck should be kept in good repair, and not suffer by my absence" (Boswell to Gibb, 6 Nov. 1790, L581). In the subsequent six months, when Boswell was so busy preparing the *Life of Johnson* for the press, he wrote twenty-four letters to Gibb, an indication that neither absence nor other concerns could ever allow him to neglect his estate.

Boswell obviously scrutinized his overseers' letters carefully, and in replying to them supplied precise and detailed instructions which reveal an exact knowledge of estate matters and an intimate acquaintance with tenants and servants, as the following extracts illustrate.

> Much pleased with your abstract. Just what I wished. Let me have one such every Saturday. Only let the title be not Auchinleck House but Place of Auchinleck. Try to get Ja. Wilson to engage not to part with [the horse] Chance without telling me. You may sell or give Punch to any of the tenants who will keep him. . . . Let a roup [auction] of Dernlaw in grass for a year be advertised in print at Lapraik's on thursday 2 Janry. 1783. . . . It is a great comfort to me that I can have such dependance on your skill and fidelity and that all my directions will be executed. (Boswell to Bruce, 26 Nov. 1782, L274.1)

> All the things came safe by the Carrier. The House Book is returned signed by my Wife. The other is exceedingly neat. I only suggest that it would be better to have at the end of the Labourers an abstract or Summation of their wages to shew at one view it is exact with the Discharge which upon summing I have found it. As soon as the weather will permit, let fence be made to compleat enclosure of Stevenstown. I wish to see myself when I am out at Christmas the fence compleated along Woodside park. If you have not Hollies to plant on it as on other parts of the fences along old Avenus let them be bought. As I am anxious about renunciation of Liferents on Estate let you or your son take a ride to Hallglenmuir and search the drawers for it. Apply to Mr Gavin Hamilton and get the key or take him along. If Craigengillan has not sent for Apples, write to him. I hope to be home on the 26, 27, or 28. Let the family bedroom be well aired and do you see once a Week a fire at each end of the Library. The weather has been severer with you than here. You have done well to

> thresh out Corn that was wettish. Poor Meg Murdock has not lived long. I hope Jo. Colvin is comfortably settled in Tenshillingside. (Boswell to Bruce, 4 Dec. 1782, L275)

> You tell me in your letter that you were begun to cut hay on the 12. But, I do not observe it marked in your Journal. (Boswell to Bruce, 16 July 1783, L286)

> James Wilson in Clewhouse wants to have a mare and foal grazed by me for six months. Let him know the grassmail should be forty shillings but I shall charge only thirty. Let Alexander Pedin know that I wish him to have one of my parks near the Village for which let him apply to Mr. Bruce Campbell, and make me an offer as a creditable man as he is, should do. Let me know if the bills have been taken for the oats in tenshillingside west park, and send them to me. Let the carpet which is at the church and would be spoiled by the damp be brought down to the house. (Boswell to Gibb, 6 Nov. 1790, L581)

Early in his career Boswell confided in a letter to Lord Eglinton his four aims in life (*London Journal* 181). He was to realize only one of these, that "He improved and beautified his paternal estate of Auchinleck." In this he continued the family tradition. Planting of trees at Auchinleck was begun in the early seventeenth century by James Boswell, the fourth laird, and continued by his successors, including that namesake who became ninth laird in 1782. Some improvements in field cultivation were attempted early in the eighteenth century. Lord Auchinleck began making enclosures and improving the soil by liming from 1766, working coal and lime at Gasswater, with coal pits sunk at Birnieknowe to provide further fuel for the lime kilns. But the advances he made were limited. When Andrew Wight made his farming survey in 1778, he found that here "the ridges were so high as to leave the furrows bare of soil, and without a single stalk of corn."[6] James Boswell, as soon as he succeeded, introduced a scheme of major renovation.

He wisely sought the expert guidance of Alexander Fairlie. "He advised me to let all I could in grass for some years, then lime a third of each farm, and thus get a good rent" (*Applause* 12–13). Fairlie, as factor to the Earl of Eglinton, had worked out this successful formula: by a series of ploughings reduce the old raised ridges and rest the exhausted farmland; then crop one third of the farmland for three years before reversion to six years in grass.

Boswell introduced new tacks (leases) which required tenants to adhere to Fairlie's system. He reminded Gibb to "give me pointed information whether each tenant has laid on the quantity of lime which he is bound by his tack to do. This must be strictly attended to, and when they fail, an example must be made in terms of their tacks. Care must also be taken to have the houses and fences inspected; and if they be in disrepair the provision in the tacks must be followed without relaxation. In short no Estate can flourish where the tenants are not kept to steady order and regularity" (Boswell to Gibb, 13 Dec. 1793, photocopy in Boswell Office, Yale). The Fairlie rotation, with its emphasis on grassland—most appropriate for local soils and climate—became the basis of modern Ayrshire dairy farming. Boswell was innovative in bringing to the estate the new breed of Ayrshire dairy cattle, which were then becoming popular. "There is a cow of an excellent kind to be sent to Auchinleck with her calf from Stewarton by Dr. Deans. As the cow is very highpriced and valuable you will . . . take particular care of her and her calf" (Boswell to Bruce, 12 July 1783, L285). To obtain the massive quantities of lime which Fairlie recommended for the acidic local soils, Boswell extended the mineral operations, which from 1787 also supplied the new Muirkirk Iron Works with coal, limestone, and iron ore. Boswell's correspondence with his overseers provides an extended commentary on the transformation of the estate during his lairdship.

The new system of farming brought difficulties for many tenants. Of the eighty holdings from which James Boswell drew rents, three were very large hill farms devoted to sheep; thirty-three were between one and two hundred acres; the majority were smaller than a hundred acres, including half a dozen of less than ten acres. Tenants on small farms found it difficult to feed the family and pay the rent and were tempted to plough more than the new leases allowed. Hence Boswell instructed his overseer to "frequently visit the different farms upon the estate, and mark down whether the tenants have managed them according to their leases" (Boswell to Gibb, 6 Nov. 1790, L581). There are repeated admonitions like "James Farquhar in Dippleburn . . . must plow none during his agreement to have his farm in grass" (Boswell to Gibb, 4 Feb. 1791, L583). Some tenants inevitably failed to survive. Boswell advised Gibb, "I wish not to be a hard landlord. But I am clear that allowing them to run in arrear is ruinous to them"

(Boswell to Gibb, 10 Jan. 1794, *Letters JB* 2: 504). There is evidence of four tenants falling so deeply into debt as to be rouped, which involved being dispossessed by auction of their farms and all else they had. Many more must have gone, surrendering their tenancies, and taking away what few possessions they had. Analysis of various estate papers indicates that more than half of the farms had to be let to new tenants during the twelve-and-a-half years of James Boswell's lairdship.

The application of new methods sometimes clashed uncomfortably with a regressive desire to retain feudal practices. Boswell in 1784 revived the Barony Court of Auchinleck, an institution rendered obsolete by the Heritable Jurisdictions Act of 1747, but now providing a convenient means of pressing those in arrears of rent (Court Book, BFP 107.1944). Again, Boswell insisted upon the retention of thirlage, by which tenants were compelled to take their grain to a particular mill and pay multures (tolls) due to the miller. Boswell in 1793 found the "numerous and loud complaints of the thirlage" to be "unreasonable" (Turnerhill Tack, BFP 171.3008:470). He admitted "different opinions as to Multures in general, as to which, mine is some what singular; but I am nevertheless very firm in it" (Boswell to Claud Alexander, 4 Feb. 1794, L15.4). Yet Boswell could be generous. When one tenant was dispossessed, Boswell noted that "my heart is sore for the McKerrows of Carbellow" (Reg. Let., 8 Oct. 1787). Several times he found another farm to provide a second chance for an unfortunate tenant. This he did after having taken legal action against Andrew Dalrymple in Back Rogerton, who was "the first of my tenants that I ever imprisoned and I hope he will behave better in time to come" (L584.62). So often we find Boswell, after urging strictness, indicating that leniency must be allowed. As Irma Lustig has concluded, Boswell's concern for his tenants was "the noblest feature of his performance as laird" (*Applause* xii).

Boswell's feudal paternalism matched that of his father, who was praised by the parish minister for "his benignity to his tenants" and eulogised in verse by the schoolmaster as "The Honest Counsellor as all will own, And most indulgent Landlord ever known."[7] Three generations shared an inheritance of old Ayrshire tradition and new Edinburgh ideas. Grandfather James had attended Ochiltree school, then studied at Glasgow, Edinburgh, and Leyden before becoming an advocate in Edinburgh. Son and grandson had a different upbringing; their education, begun with private tutors, was based principally in Edinburgh, and continued also in the Netherlands. All revealed an unwillingness to submit to a father's wishes: the grandfather had "with great difficulty . . . obtained his father's assent to go over to Leyden to Study" (Auchinleck Memoirs C338.723), and Lord Auchinleck was beaten by his father for keeping bad company (*Earlier Years* 56–57). Yet each wished to be a dutiful heir. James Boswell on succeeding his father "thought I was doing what he approved; and I wished always to preserve the notion of his seeing what I was about" (*Applause* 37); and again, "was quite satisfied with my character and conduct at present. It was what would have pleased my father and grandfather. May I ever behave in like manner at the seat of my ancestors!" (Ibid. 50).

As laird, it pleased Boswell when he "received my village rents in the room off the aisle at the kirk and had the bellman for my attendant" (Ibid. 275). Possessing land in several parishes, he "thought it proper to go once after my succession to each parish church" where he sat in the family loft and "looked with satisfaction on my tenants ranged behind me" (Ibid. 9). After harvest the haymakers were entertained and "I with my own hand gave each of the rustick dancers a glass of Mountain Malaga" (Boswell to Jamie, 22 Aug. 1794, L138). Boswell not only regarded himself as responsible for the eighty farms from which he derived rent but also had appropriate concern for twenty-four others which his stepmother held in life-rent and which he regarded as part of his patrimony. He would not interfere in what he considered was Lady Auchinleck's business: he refused to help John Murdoch pay for a corn-drying kiln at Bellow Mill, which was one of her properties (Bruce to Boswell, 18 June 1783, C623; Boswell to Bruce, 24 June 1783, L283). But he insisted that the hedges and woodlands on her Trabboch lands be properly maintained. When a man from the Trabboch deserted from the army, Boswell went to considerable trouble to secure his discharge (*Applause* 41, 86).

As principal landowner in Auchinleck, the laird had responsibility, following the Patronage Act of 1712, for choosing a minister for that parish whenever the charge fell vacant. In 1752 Alexander Boswell, later Lord Auchinleck, presented John Dun, who was then his son's tutor. Unpopular presentations produced opposition in some Ayrshire parishes, and the local seceders gathered enough support to build their own church in 1756. When Dun died after serving the parish for forty years, James Boswell made a strenuous midwinter trip from London, for "the choice of a Minister to a worthy Parish is a matter of very great importance; and I cannot be sure of the real wishes of the People without being present" (Boswell to Temple, 26 Feb. 1793, *Letters JB* 2: 445). Eventually he settled on the Reverend John Lindsay, who had been unanimously recommended by the kirk session.[8] James Boswell's grandfather and father had each been ordained as elders to serve on Auchinleck kirk session—appropriately, since both were convinced Calvinists. Though James Boswell attended church at Auchinleck and took communion at the annual sacraments, he did not follow them as elders, presumably by choice.

Lord Auchinleck as chief heritor (landowner) had especial responsibility for the church itself. He renewed its fabric, added an aisle in 1754, and a new manse in 1756, "one of the most commodious neat houses to be met" (*OSA Ayrshire* 16). The minister was less fortunate in respect of money, for the stipend was, as the Reverend John Dun also noted in 1791, "the same that was settled by decreet in 1649, since which period no augmentation has taken place" (*OSA Ayrshire* 16). The heritors were also expected to cooperate in providing poor relief and schooling. But the Boswells were reluctant to exercise their statutory responsibilities, preferring paternalism to public provision. The Auchinleck heritors (like those in most Ayrshire parishes) failed to impose a tax upon themselves to support the poor. The poorfund was supplied by church collections, supplemented by baptismal, marriage, and burial fees. Lord Auchinleck augmented this by voluntary donations, and so did his son. James Boswell's generosity was further exemplified after the catastrophic harvest of 1782 when he contributed meal from his own stocks and purchased imported grain at Leith to be sold at a subsidized price, for the benefit of all the parishioners (*Applause* 47; Boswell to Bruce, 17, 24 June 1783, L282.3, L283; Bruce to Boswell, 21, 28 June, 5 July 1783, C624–26).

Boswell resistance to social improvement is evident in their failure to provide a parish school. A series of Acts from 1567 till 1696 resulted in many places being thus provided, including fifteen of the twenty-seven parishes within the presbytery of Ayr by 1735. But Auchinleck remained without a parish school until 1764. Only when a Dr. Charles Cochrane bequeathed a small sum to the kirk session "for the encouragement of a Schoolmaster" did

Lord Auchinleck belatedly agree with five minor heritors for an annual local assessment, and himself provided a site for the school. William Halbert was appointed schoolmaster, precentor, and session clerk.[9] At a drinking party in a local inn James Boswell "got in Halbert the schoolmaster and drank to the rising generation" (*In Search of a Wife* 69). But when he became laird he showed no particular interest in the school. Nor did he at any time exhibit enthusiasm for parishioners wishing to better themselves. When a local mason in 1766 wished to become an exciseman, Boswell recommended that the applicant be given a translation of Horace's First Satire, "How comes it, Maecenas, that no man lives contented with his lot?" (Boswell to Rev. George Reid, draft, L1097). Here, too, he was like his father. There is no evidence that Lord Auchinleck encouraged Gavin Gibb (1760–1831), who would become professor of Hebrew at Glasgow University and moderator of the General Assembly of the Church of Scotland (*Fasti Scot.* 3: 433–34). Nor did he advance the career of William Murdoch (1754–1839), who on his way to fame as an inventor would entertain Boswell at Redruth. Boswell felt "a curious sensation to find a tenant's son in so good a state" (*Great Biographer* 174, 178).

Boswell appears to have regarded learning and enlightenment as an aristocratic monopoly. His name does not appear among those who subscribed to the schoolmaster William Halbert's *Practical Figurer*; nor was he impressed when the Reverend John Dun published his two volumes of *Sermons*.[10] When John Ballantine of Ayr proposed in 1794 that an academy in that county town be established to cater for "the great bulk of the people in a commercial country," James Boswell refused a subscription (C63, C64). Though a good number of Ayrshire lairds joined the Ayr Library Society, which had been founded in 1762, neither Lord Auchinleck nor his son became members. Yet it is worth note that the minutes of this society list in 1786 purchase of copies of the recently published "Johnson & Boswell's last Tour" and also "Boswell's Account of Corsica"; in 1789 they gave an advance order for "Boswell's life of Johnson" though it was "not yet published."[11]

Thomas Crawford has written that "The men and women of the very families whom we regard as typical of the Enlightenment were familiar with popular song, and moved from the tea-table to the plebeian with equal facility as subject and occasion demanded. . . . James Boswell, in so many ways the embodiment of the contradictions in Scottish thought and behaviour during the second half of the century, produced verses from his earliest years and was familiar with both the English and Scottish popular traditions."[12] Popular song finds mention in one letter from James Bruce to young Boswell (22 November 1766, C606), and a generation later, on 26 February 1793 (BFP 174.3072), his successor Andrew Gibb would address in verse young Sandy Boswell, who became a votary. We discover the parish schoolmaster writing seventy-three lines of elegiac verse in praise of Lord Auchinleck (OPR 269–71), and the parish minister composing "The Deel's Answer to his Verra Friend R. Burns" (*Sermons* 1: 257–79). Yet Boswell's only recognition of the local versifiers was one shilling in 1783 "To Tibby Pagan the poetess" (*Applause* 163 n. 1).[13] When Robert Burns in 1788 expressed a desire to meet Boswell, he did not respond, save for endorsing the letter "Mr. Robert Burns the Poet expressing very high sentiments of me" (Burns to Bruce Campbell, 13 Nov. 1788, C709).

Boswell, seeking to impress Dr. Johnson with what Ayrshire had to offer, introduced him to several of his propertied and learned acquaintances. John, fourth earl of Loudoun, was full of "good-humour and benevolence," and his mother, the 95-year-old dowager countess, was "sensible and well-informed." John Campbell of Treesbank had "a numerous and excellent collection of books"; they missed meeting John Cuninghame of Caprington, "a very distinguished scholar" who "wrote Latin with great elegance." The dowager Countess of Eglinton had "manners high-bred, her reading extensive, and her conversation elegant." At Auchinleck, Boswell showed pride in his father, who had "the dignified courtesy of an old baron" and was also "a sound scholar" with a library which "in curious editions of the Greek and Roman classics, is, I suppose, not excelled by any private collection in Great Britain" (*Hebrides*, 377, 370). Had time allowed there were others whom he could have introduced to illustrate that Ulubrae was not a barbaric backwater. There was "Mr. Fairlie, who, with all his attention to agriculture, finds time both for the classics and his friends" (*Hebrides* 374). In the adjoining parish of Sorn were the country homes of two university men: Dugald Stewart, professor of moral philosophy at Edinburgh; and Alexander Stevenson, professor of medicine at Glasgow, with whom Johnson and Boswell breakfasted in that city. Among numerous Ayrshire lairds who had imbibed enlightened ideas were three near-neighbors who had been classmates of Boswell's at Edinburgh: John Hamilton of Sundrum, Hugh Logan of Logan, and Hugh Montgomerie of Coilsfield, later twelfth earl of Eglinton.

I have argued elsewhere that "the Enlightenment was a social phenomenon not restricted to Edinburgh or the universities, but something whose influence made itself felt through a wider area. New ideas were diffused by landowners, merchants, ministers, and teachers."[14] All of these, Boswell included, were committed to maintaining the existing social order. Typical examples were three parish ministers. The Reverend John Dun, chosen for Auchinleck by Lord Auchinleck, had previously tutored young James: "He began to form my mind. . . . He set me to reading *The Spectator*; and it was then that I acquired my first notions of taste for the fine arts" (*Earlier Years* 2). But after thirty dull years as parish minister he was condemned by Dr. Johnson as ignorant as a Hottentot because he scoffed at dignitaries of the Church of England (*Hebrides* 375). William McQuhae, a favorite pupil of Adam Smith, whom Lord Auchinleck appointed as tutor for his younger sons, proved to be an agreeable companion for James, the eldest son. Then ordained to St. Quivox, McQuhae chose to "live contented as a country clergyman," raising a large family and continuing his "pursuit of elegant literature" as committee member of the Ayr Library Society (Journal, 26 Feb. 1763; *Fasti Scot.* 3: 66). The Reverend William Auld, whose company James Boswell enjoyed, was the best qualified minister in Ayrshire, having been like Boswell educated at Glasgow, Edinburgh, and in the Netherlands; but for fifty years he presided as Burns's "Daddy Auld" over the narrow-minded kirk session of Mauchline (*Fasti Scot.* 3: 50).

The equanimity (or submission) of such ministers appears to have been shared even by parishioners who suffered from agrarian changes which involved the virtual elimination of the cottagers and dispossession of many tenant farmers. The only definite evidence of local resistance to agricultural improvements comes from the parishes of Stair and Kirkoswald, where early in the eighteenth century dykes were broken down and hedges uprooted (*OSA Ayrshire* 395, 574). The high price of meal inspired a disturbance at Stewarton in 1767, and another at Irvine in 1777, as described by John Galt in his novel, *The Provost* (1822); but no popular outbreaks are recorded following the calamitous harvest of 1782 and the subsequent dearth. Boswell, who won acquittal for the four Stewarton rioters who stood trial, would in 1783 secure sufficient meal for his own parishioners at that time of severe scarcity, an act typical of the feudal paternalism that quieted discontent. When in 1792 the spread of French revolutionary principles caused concern, Boswell sent Gibb from London copies of "two little sensible pamphlets . . . which may be posted up in the smithy's and lent about." Gibb reported that they were sufficient to "dispell the remaining Clouds that may overhang the minds of every Malcontent sooner than otherways might have happened especially from one of your popularity" (Boswell to Gibb, 18 Dec. 1792, *Letters JB* 2: 493; Gibb's undated reply on L1028.5). Shortly afterwards Alexander Fairlie assured Boswell that "the spirit of turbulence and discontent" had "got a severe check by the Associations that are almost universally entered into for the preservation of the peace and order of Society—You will see in the Papers a very strong one from Ayrshire" (Fairlie to Boswell, 12 Jan. 1793, C1234).

Boswell as a leading landowner in the county was inevitably involved in its affairs. He participated in its social life, visiting and entertaining guests, as detailed in his Book of Company. A year after he succeeded as laird he attended the Quarter Sessions and was elected chairman by the Justices of the Peace; a few days later the freeholders elected him chairman of the Commissioners of Supply. He also took his place among the Ayrshire Turnpike trustees and became quite heavily involved, along with John Loudon McAdam, in their practical work of supervising the building of new roads. Boswell was particularly gratified by his appointment as chairman of the Commissioners of Supply, even though only seventeen were present at the meeting. At a subsequent meeting he was successful in having various motions approved by packing the meeting with those nominal and fictitious voters to whose creation by Lord Auchinleck he had objected in 1774. On 17 March 1784 he won support from Ayrshire for his loyal Address to the King. "I never in my life felt myself better than I was today," he wrote. "I recalled to my mind all the ideas of the consequence of county meetings and of the credit of the family of Auchinleck which I had acquired from my father in my early years, and I superadded the monarchical principles which I had acquired from Dr. Johnson" (*Applause* 194).[15] At this point Boswell announced that he was willing to offer himself as parliamentary candidate for the county in the forthcoming election. Though the election of Ayrshire's MP was made by open vote of around 230 freeholders, in practice factional maneuvers by the Ayrshire peers determined the choice. Boswell, who had sufficient credentials and Eglinton connections, could realistically keep alive his aspirations. Had he survived until 1796 he might well have replaced Hugh Montgomerie of Coilsfield, who then had to relinquish the seat on succeeding as twelfth earl of Eglinton.

One particular responsibility Boswell assumed as laird was to prepare for his succession. He chose to provide his children with education in England. But he inculcated in them a love for Auchinleck, where they could share, as he himself had once observed, "the pursuit of elegant literature, and the enlivening pleasures of society, which, though not in profusion, are yet to be enjoyed in the country" (*LJ* 204). When Sandy was sixteen years of age Boswell sent instructions to Andrew Gibb "by my eldest son, to whom you will pay all proper attention" (Boswell to Gibb, 1 Aug. 1791, *Letters JB* 2: 483). Not long afterwards Sandy was appointed "to be my proxy at Auchinleck" (Boswell to Claud Alexander, 9 June 1792, *Letters JB* 2: 488). Subsequent letters show how much authority he delegated. Yet Boswell's attitude to his heir bore a striking similarity to the authoritarian style of his own father. He had earlier instructed Sandy to "compose yourself and apply to your studies and think and act like a gentleman, and not like a spoilt child" (Boswell to Sandy, 5 Nov. 1789, L78). In letters to his younger son, Jamie, he repeatedly criticized Sandy, in particular for indulgence in sports (Boswell to Jamie, 22 Aug. 1794, L138). He ultimately complained, "I am hurt by his loud and unpolished manners; and I find that he is accustomed to domineer over the country people who pay great court to him and talk of me as *the old man*" (Boswell to Jamie, 12 Sept. 1794, L142).

A year later, in 1795, the nineteen-year-old son succeeded his father and became tenth laird of Auchinleck. Alexander Boswell proved a worthy heir. He extended and enhanced the estate. He made notable contributions to literature. He became a member of Parliament. For loyalty and public service he was rewarded with a baronetcy. In 1822 he died needlessly, after a duel which he believed honor compelled him to fight. Like his father, he combined enlightened ideas with feudal pride.

Notes

1. C.B. Tinker, *Young Boswell* (London: Putnam; Boston: Atlantic Monthly Press, 1922), 9, 100.

2. Boswell Family Papers, JB's register of letters sent and received, M255. Boswell's other unpublished manuscripts at Yale are cited by *Catalogue* number or identified hereafter as BFP and by box number, folder number, and (sometimes) numbered item.

3. In a private letter to Nellie Hankins, 5 Sept. 1979; photocopy held by present writer.

4. This and later letters from "Correspondence of James Boswell with James Bruce and Andrew Gibb, Overseers of the Auchinleck Estate," ed. Nellie P. Hankins and J. Strawhorn, forthcoming volume in Yale Research Editions.

5. Introduction to *The [Old] Statistical Account of Scotland 1791–1799*, vol. 6, Ayrshire (Wakefield: EP Publishing, 1982; hereafter cited in the text as *OSA Ayrshire*). Also *Ayrshire at the Time of Burns*, ed. J. Strawhorn (Kilmarnock: Ayrshire Archaelogical and Natural History Society, 1959).

6. Andrew Wight, *The Present State of Husbandry in Scotland* (Edinburgh, 1778–84), 3 [1784]: 1, 263.

7. Rev. John Dun, *Sermons*, 2 vols. (Kilmarnock: John Wilson, 1790), 2: 122 (hereafter cited in text as *Sermons*). Old Parish Register, Parish of Auchinleck, in Scottish Record Office, 270 (hereafter cited in text as OPR).

8. *Fasti Ecclesiae Scoticanae*, ed. H. Scott, new edition, 9 vols. (Edinburgh: Oliver and Boyd, 1915–61; vol. 10, St. Andrew Press, 1981), 3 [1920]: 3, 4, 62.

9. William Boyd, *Education in Ayrshire through Seven Centuries* (University of London Press, 1961); Kirk Session Minutes, Auchinleck, 25 Apr. 1758, 27 May 1764.

10. William Halbert, *The Practical Figurer* (Paisley: John Neilson, 1789); "Poor John Dun will be a sad loser by his *Sermons*" (*Letters JB* 2: 387).

11. Minutes of Ayr Library Society (in Carnegie Library, Ayr), 45, 58, 60.

12. Thomas Crawford, *Society and the Lyric* (Edinburgh: Scottish Academic Press, 1979), 165, 168; also J. Strawhorn, "Burns and the Bardie Clan," *Scottish Literary Journal* 8 (Dec. 1981):2.

13. Isobel Pagan, *Collection of Songs and Poems* (Glasgow, 1803), included anonymously a satirical poem, "The Laird of Glenlee," which has been attributed to James Boswell (John Macintosh, *The Poets of Ayrshire*, [Dumfries, 1910], 29) though it may have been written for the Earl of Dumfries by a local versifier, William Gemmel, a tailor from Cumnock (*Andrew Crawfurd's Collection of Ballads and Songs*, ed. E.B. Lyle [Scottish Text Society, 1975] xlv–xlvii).

14. J. Strawhorn, "Ayrshire in the Enlightenment," in *A Sense of Place*, ed. G. Cruickshank (Edinburgh: Scotland's Cultural Heritage Unit, 1988), 199.

15. Strathclyde Regional Archives, Ayr, has Minute Books of Road Trustees (CO3.4.1) and of Commissioners of Supply (CO3.1.3) which supplement Journal references and Frank Brady, *Boswell's Political Career* (New Haven: Yale University Press, 1965).

PART II

The Life of Johnson

"The Journalist, With a View of Auchinleck—or the Land of Stones" from the first series of caricatures, *Picturesque Beauties of Boswell,* engraved by Thomas Rowlandson after original sketches by Samuel Collings, 1786. Boswell waves his journal and in the other arm holds "Materials for the Life of Sam. Johnson." The caption quotes *The Journal of a Tour to the Hebrides,* 1785: "I am I flatter myself compleatly a Citizen of the World." *Courtesy of the Print Collection of The Lewis Walpole Library, Yale University.*

Rhetoric and Runts: Boswell's Artistry

CAREY MCINTOSH

What proportion of the power of the *Life of Johnson* derives from its prose style? We assume that some literary masterpieces are more self-consciously crafted than others. We also assume (a slightly different thing) that style exerts itself more actively in some texts than in others—it plays a more varied and obtrusive role in *Ulysses*, for example, than in *Middlemarch*, in *Humphry Clinker* than in *Moll Flanders*. "Appropriateness" is one measure of the stylishness of a given work; variation and "foregroundedness" are others. Although Boswell's prose style has had intelligent attention (from Pottle, Passler, Lustig, and Brady, among others), the question of Boswell's artistry is still very much an open one.[1]

"Appropriateness": as a criterion, this is both old and new—it goes back to Aristotle and his directives for adjusting the rhetoric of different types of discourse to different subjects and audiences; it plays a central role in late Renaissance and neoclassical discussions of decorum. Although the precepts derived from doctrines of decorum can seem tautological ("proper words in proper places"), they nevertheless sanction wide stylistic variation; in this respect they differ in emphasis from expressive theories of style ("*the* style is *the* man" seems to imply that only one style is possible for that man), and anticipate contemporary sociolinguistic frames of reference. Sociolinguists point out that if language were solely and merely a means of communication, stylistic variation would be "dysfunctional"; that is, all those different "ways of speaking" would be confusing. On the other hand, if language is (among other things) a form of social behavior, it will reflect a variety of social relationships.[2]

The overlap between neoclassical ideals of decorum and sociolinguistic principles applying to "the ethnography of speaking" is, on reflection, quite understandable. Artistotle's premise, "to each class and habit there is an appropriate style," justified not only the separation of styles but also variety of styles, high and low, colloquial and learned, male and female. Compare John Gumperz (1982): "particular stretches of speech can legitimately be associated with speakers of certain ethnic or social backgrounds or with certain distinct speech events." *Variation* of this sort has convinced many linguists to abandon or crucially modify Chomsky's assumptions (1965) that "linguistic theory is concerned primarily with an ideal speaker-listener, in a completely homogeneous speech-community." On the contrary, as James McCawley put it (1988), "a language (or even an *idiolect*—the linguistic system of a single person) normally provides not a single way of speaking or writing but a number of styles and registers."[3]

There is plenty of evidence that Boswell had thought about prose style, carefully and at length. He wrote in some measure *archivally*, for posterity, with the thought that his writings would some day be "laid up among the archives of Auchinleck" (*LJ* 305): his own words tell us this, and so (more convincingly) do the ten thousand Boswellian documents actually deposited in those archives. When Boswell wrote about his own education (in 1791, in the *European Magazine*), the only subject of study that he chose to name explicitly was rhetoric. Prose style is a central concern of the lectures by Adam Smith that Boswell attended in Glasgow in 1759 and early 1760, and of Hugh Blair's lectures on rhetoric and belles lettres, "which I heard him [Blair] deliver at Edinburgh" (*Life* 3: 172). Quite early in his life as a writer, he journalizes self-consciously about his own journal style, reminding himself to be more "correct" and gloating a little that "words come skipping to me like lambs upon Moffat Hill" (*LJ* 187). He worried about non-standard locutions in his prose, and among the books he planned one day to write was a dictionary of Scotticisms. In Frederick Pottle's judgment, he wrote better light verse in Scots than in English—a measure of his "diglossic" capacities. Virtually every distinguished late eighteenth-century British writer on language and style was his friend or teacher or acquaintance: Johnson, Kames, Campbell, Blair, Monboddo, Harris, Jones, plus Rousseau on the Continent. He was tutored by Sheridan on pronunciation. He took the trouble of stitching together an imitation of Sterne's prose style (in the *Observations . . . by a Genius*, 1760). The *Life of*

Johnson and the journals are full of references to the style of one author or another, Addison, Temple, Martin, South, Dalrymple, and many others.[4]

We can therefore deduce confidently that Boswell was familiar with standard seventeenth- and eighteenth-century ideals of decorum. This principle governed not only the "suitability" of words but also their elegance or vulgarity; most educated writers of the time assume a radical separation between elevated or refined styles (or genres) and "low," popular styles (or genres). High styles were associated with high rank in society, with heroic enterprises and their traditional archetypes in history and poetry, with human nature in its most dignified guise. Low styles were associated with working-class people, barnyard animals (not lions and eagles), the physicality of everyday actions and things, grubby particulars, comedy and satire. All this is reasonably well known, though so far as I know it has not been used extensively in style-studies.[5] How does it affect the *Life of Johnson*?

It fosters craft: it allows Boswell an artful mix of several styles, high for celebration and praise, middle for narrative, and low for humor. Even though, as Geoffrey Scott put it sixty years ago, "Boswell's conscious effort seems to be fixed far less upon art than upon authenticity," and even though biography is not normally mentioned in eighteenth-century treatments of decorum, which concentrate on poetry, I cannot believe that Boswell did not know at some level just how various his styles are in the *Life*. Few critical issues were more widely debated in the eighteenth century than the "lowness" of Homer, Shakespeare, and Fielding, the "highness" of Milton and other "sublime" poets. Boswell himself observes that without big words as vehicle Johnson's "stately ideas" would have been "confined and cramped" (*Life* 1: 218).[6]

High and Low Styles in Boswell's Life

The opening and closing sections of the *Life* are written in high style. They are keyed to "admiration and reverence" (4: 430), filled with the sense of Johnson's "greatness," and inspired by Boswell's need to "worship" Johnson and to feel "awe" for him. The sentences are for the most part long, the diction formal, the structure frequently periodic. Boswell exploits here an almost Johnsonian "grandeur of generality": even though the last four paragraphs of the book are a portrait, they do not depend on particular details, on the "small specks" of pigment that give so much life to Flemish brushwork elsewhere in the biography. In composing this portrait, Boswell rewrote the portrait of Johnson that opens the *Tour to the Hebrides* (1786), and he excised a number of particularities, including Johnson's characteristic dress, his twitchings and "cramps."

Parallel and antithetical structures are a staple of the grand style in prose from Isocrates to Churchill. Boswell avoids the spectacular symmetries of Johnson's own prose, but achieves nicely balanced cadences of a comparatively unobtrusive sort:

1. when he walked, it was // when he rode, he had
2. He was prone to superstition // but not to credulity
3. impetuous and irritable in his temper, // but of a most humane and benevolent heart
4. obtrusive ignorance, // or presuming petulance
5. His moral precepts are practical, for they are drawn // His maxims carry conviction; for they are founded
6. a most logical head // a most fertile imagination

(4: 425–29)

Only two of these sets of balanced phrases belong to the description of Johnson in the *Tour to the Hebrides*, which consists of a single paragraph ending in "a good joke" (5: 19).

Classical rhetoric was still a staple of ordinary programs of higher education in 1760; Boswell encountered it at several stages. Its formal structures play a role in Boswell's high style. He uses the word "climax" in its rhetorical sense quite unself-consciously in the *Life*: "Johnson. 'Yes, Sir, I knew very well what I was undertaking,—and very well how to do it,—and have done it very well.' Boswell. 'An excellent climax!'" (3: 405). In this passage Boswell intends to compliment Johnson on his skillful use of the figure *gradatio*, or climax, a series of parallel phrases of increasing weight or intensity.[7] We can be pretty sure that Boswell was aware of using anaphora in citation (1) above, a chiasmic structure (antimetabole?) in (3), prosopopoeia in (4), and isocolon in (5). Such figures do not automatically create a high style, but they may enable a writer to adjust cadences, distribute emphasis, and form prose of dignity and power.

It is epideictic rhetoric that is being practiced here, the first of Aristotle's major kinds, and less exalted specimens of high epideictic rhetoric occur elsewhere in the *Life*, when Boswell is paying tribute to his friends or flattering "eminent" personages: "This hasty composition is also to be remarked as one of a thousand instances which evince the extraordinary promptitude of Mr. Burke; who while he is equal to the greatest things, can adorn the least; can, with equal facility, embrace the vast and complicated speculations of politicks, or the ingenious topicks of literary investigation" (3: 85). Note the hyperbole, "a thousand instances," "extraordinary promptitude"; note also the two carefully arranged antithetical structures. Taking advantage of his privileges as narrator, Boswell openly courts friends and important people mentioned in the *Life*. Many of these acknowledgments or tributes are written in the high style associated with elegant compliment: "I was fortunate enough to be found worthy of [Oglethorpe's] good opinion, insomuch, that I not only was invited to make one in the many respectable companies whom he entertained at his table, but had a cover at his hospitable board every day when I happened to be disengaged; and in his society I never failed to enjoy learned and animated conversation, seasoned with genuine sentiments of virtue and religion" (2: 350). The grammar of courtly compliment depends on "quantities of qualities": I had "enough" fortune to be worthy of Oglethorpe's good opinion, and "enough" of Oglethorpe's good opinion to be invited to his table.[8] Elevation of style here depends also on copiousness: almost redundant adjectives ("hospitable board," "respectable companies") and almost unnecessary doublets ("learned and animated," "virtue and religion").

Periodic sentences played a more prominent part in eighteenth-century rhetorics than did esoteric tropes and figures. Campbell found periodic sentences "more susceptible of vivacity and force" than loose sentences, which are "apt . . . to languish and grow tiresome." Blair recommended that the "members" of a sentence be arranged in order of importance, strongest last; concluding a sentence with "any inconsiderable word" like a preposition or an adverb is "always enfeebling and degrading."[9] The first three paragraphs of the *Life* depend heavily on periodic sentences for dignity and weight: "To write the Life of him who excelled all mankind in writing the lives of others, and who, whether we consider his extraordinary endowments, or his various works, has been equaled by few in any age, is an arduous, and may be reckoned in me a presumptuous task" (1: 25). By inserting relative clauses and a conditional-concessive clause between subject and verb, Boswell builds his opening around what Stanley Fish has called an "arc of suspension" that focuses on the magnitude of the work being introduced.[10] The artifice of periodicity is even more obvious in the first sentence of the third paragraph, where five "as" clauses are lined up in sequence, in a sentence 168 words long, to give increasing weight to the "advantages" Boswell is claiming (1: 25–26).

We recognize a low prose style by short sentences, colloquial language, and a homely vocabulary of "creaturely" (it is Auerbach's word) objects, animals, and physical vulgarities:

> *He*, (said Johnson) the little black dog! (1: 284)
>
> Who's for *poonsh*? (2: 464)
>
> They will spit upon any place . . . I e'en tasted Tom's fingers. (2: 403)
>
> an old coat with a new facing . . . the old dog in a new doublet (3: 329)
>
> "They talk of *runts*" [that is, young cows]. (3: 337)
>
> how is it that we hear the loudest *yelps* for liberty among the drivers of negroes? (3: 201)
>
> Nay, if you are to bring in gabble, I'll talk no more. I will not, upon my honour. (3: 350)

Most of these "low" words occur in conversation, not in Boswell's narrative or in the writings he quotes, and many of them occur when Johnson is driving home a point, perhaps by means of a homely analogy. Johnson seemed to take pleasure in the "shock value" (John Vance's phrase) of some of his statements. They play a key role in what Brady has called "conversation as performance." For example, a member of the Club had read aloud an ode full of "bold words" and "timorous meaning," and the conversation turns to Gray's odes:

> They are forced plants raised in a hot-bed; and they are poor plants; they are but cucumbers after all. [Someone proposes that they would have been "better things" as cucumbers than as odes.] Yes, Sir, (said Johnson), for a *hog*. (4: 13)

James Boswell (1740-1795) by George Willison, 1765, painted in Rome, where Willison, also a Scot, was then a student. Except for the breeches, Boswell is wearing the costume in which he first visited Rousseau. *Scottish National Portrait Gallery.*

Jean-Jacques Rousseau (1712-1778) by Allan Ramsay, painted in 1766 after Rousseau had fled to asylum with David Hume in England. *Scottish National Portrait Gallery.*

Henry Home, Lord Kames (1696-1782), Boswell's friend and mentor, from a posthumous painting by David Martin, 1794. Kames is wearing the brilliant red robe of a Lord of Justiciary. *Scottish National Portrait Gallery.*

The garden and Kaffeehaus at the Villa Albani, Rome, a recent photograph but still much as they appeared to Boswell in 1765. In his memoranda he described the parterre cryptically, but graphically, as "like spread periwig." *Photograph by Derk Visser.*

The garden at Villa Garzoni, Collodi, c. 1760. Boswell almost certainly saw this elaborate baroque garden when he visited Romano Garzoni in October 1765, but he recorded no description of it. *Encyclopedia of World Art.*

Margaret Montgomerie Boswell (?1738-1789), the only known portrait, artist and date unknown. *The Hyde Collection.*

Samuel Johnson (1709-1784) from a portrait by John Opie, 1783-1784.
By permission of the Houghton Library, Harvard University.

James Boswell by Sir Joshua Reynolds, 1785. Boswell asked Reynolds, his friend, to paint his portrait when he anticipated a call to the English bar (1786) and promised to pay the price (apparently £50, half the artist's usual fee) from his first fees as a barrister. The debt was still on Boswell's accounts in February 1791, but Reynolds forgave it shortly after the *Life of Johnson* was published (May 1791), bearing a dedication to him. *National Portrait Gallery.*

Or Johnson may simply be illustrating his opinions:

> A Judge may be a farmer; but he is not to geld his own pigs . . . he is not to play at marbles, or at chuck-farthing in the Piazza. (2: 344)

> You may have a reason why two and two should make five; but they will still make but four. (3: 375)

I include this last example for its plainness, its lack of the "metaphors, Grecisms, and circumlocutions" that (for Joseph Addison) give a text "greater pomp" and "preserve it from sinking into a plebeian style."[11]

Now it seems to me quite remarkable that low words in the *Life* are concentrated largely in Johnson's speech, rather than in other people's speech or in the narrative. (One apparent exception to this general rule in fact confirms it, the animals Johnson is compared to at various times in these thousand-plus pages: bear, ox, bull, dog, rhinoceros, elephant, lion, whale.) Hence the wide and wonderful distance between Johnson the sage and Johnson the jokester, the glutton, the bully. We know from general testimony that Johnson was in fact on occasion profane and bawdy, rough and harsh, and we know that Boswell edited most of this out of his sources and notes. As a rule, Marshall Waingrow points out, Boswell devoted himself to the "refinement" of language in his notes and sources, to "polishing an abbreviated or colloquial style." So the roughnesses that remain are surely intentional; they are included because they promote Boswell's overall artistic goals.[12]

It follows that both high style and low are necessary to Boswell's art. The high corresponds to his "worship" of Johnson, to his respect for Johnson's wisdom, and to his sense of Johnson as cultural hero. The low answers more obviously to his appreciation for Johnson as a human being (not a deity), a person more fully alive than most people are, more closely in touch with reality. Johnson's humanity, it seems to me, is Boswell's principal achievement as biographer. Among Johnson's most human acts in the *Life* are his attempts to deflate pomposity, to clear our minds of cant; and low words and commonplace idioms are proper instruments for this task. What we remember of Johnson in the *Life* is his passionate temper, capacity for affection, his pugnaciousness, disdain for pretensions, his tough-mindedness, his triumphant sense of humor; and low words are virtually indispensable for the expression of all these qualities. On the other hand, without the respect that Boswell feels for Johnson, this long, long life would dwindle to a string of anecdotes about "characters," a mere series of sayings. The *Life* draws power from both worship and affection.[13]

Decorum in the Age of Revolution

How seriously can we take this contrast between high language and low in the late eighteenth century? Boswell certainly knew what the principle of decorum decreed for the separation of styles, but was he writing at a time when those old-fashioned doctrines still had bite and meaning? Voltaire and Johnson could still get away with attacking Shakespeare for low or commonplace words in the tragedies, but Voltaire was a foreigner, and Johnson was famous, in part, for endorsing, now and again, extreme positions and lost causes.

My sample of critical writings of the period suggests that a substantial residue of high neoclassical doctrines of decorum lingered on in the late eighteenth century. Hugh Blair, whose lectures on rhetoric (open to the public in the 1760s and 1770s, published 1783) were extraordinarily influential, argued that "the familiarity of common words, to which our ears are much accustomed, tends to degrade Style." High ornament, on the other hand, can "bestow dignity"; it may "have a similar effect on Language, with what is produced by the rich and splendid dress of a person of rank" (*Lectures* 1: 285). Blair is, I think, echoing Pope: "Expression is the *Dress* of *Thought*, and still / Appears more *decent* as more *suitable* (*An Essay on Criticism*, ll. 318–19)." Such statements imply three closely related judgments of low style, two of them hostile.

Any text, especially a dignified one, is debased or degraded by low language. "In *Descriptions* a judicious *Author* will omit low and vulgar Circumstances," wrote Anthony Blackwall in 1719, and, more specifically, "Things capable of Heightening and Ornament [should not be] debas'd and vilify'd by low Expressions." Both these remarks are reprinted in the condensed version of Blackwall's *An Introduction to the Classics* that constitutes Part 5 of *The Preceptor*, Dodsley's popular school text, reprinted many times during the mid-eighteenth century. Addison had stated this position more uncompromisingly: any "phrase or saying in common talk" detracts from "solemnity" and adds "too great a turn of familiarity." To William Melmouth, whose *Letters . . . By the late Sir Thomas Fitzosborne* (1748) were a celebrated model of elegant prose, "*sharking shifts*" and "*thrusting* religion *by*" were "mean" expressions. Richard Hurd in 1749 warned against "too low, or vulgar expression, in the comic parts" of a poem. Thomas Warton in 1781 excused the gross impropriety with which Dante mixes satire and sublime poetry, "familiar and heroic manners," as "common to all early [i.e., medieval] compositions." Blair himself goes one step further: "We must beware of ever using such allusions as raise in the mind disagreeable, mean, vulgar, or dirty ideas" (*Lectures* 1: 302).[14]

Furthermore, low expressions were associated with low social class. On this subject Lord Kames (1762) offers another paraphrase of Pope, one that highlights the class-consciousness implicit in the lines from *An Essay on Criticism*: "Language may be considered as the dress of thought; and where one is not suited to the other, we are sensible of incongruity, in the same manner as where a judge is dressed like a fop, or a peasant like a man of quality." Olivia Smith has presented evidence that correctness and elegance of language were annexed by conservative thinkers in the late eighteenth century as aspects of a "Tory" style and used to disenfranchise political reformers; but here is Joseph Priestley on decorum in 1777: "every term . . . that hath ever had the least connexion with *mean subjects*, or even which hath been chiefly used by persons of a low and illiberal class of life, should be carefully avoided."[15]

Perhaps the most wide-ranging discussion of genteel vocabulary in the eighteenth century is Hester Thrale Piozzi's *British Synonymy; or, An Attempt at Regulating the Choice of Words in Familiar Conversation* (1794). Mrs. Piozzi wrote (at considerable length, with chatty digressions) for English-as-a-second-language learners trying to choose the right word among all the different English words with similar meanings. She points out that England, where reputation depends far less on rank than on talent and general behavior, is more self-conscious about language than Italy. The word "cute" is used only by "coarse people" and "low Londoners," and would "shock a polished circle" by its "grossness." Latinate words are more "genteel" than Saxon. "Nothing is so certain a brand of beggary in our country as coarse and vulgar language," including words like "brag," "brawl," "cash" or "chink" (meaning money). Perhaps it is worth noting here that the word "vulgarism" meaning "a colloquialism of a low or unrefined character" is not recorded by the *Oxford English Dictionary* before 1746 (in Walpole's letters).[16]

Boswell probably shared a third perspective on low language, one that recognizes and even welcomes vulgarity, in a backhanded way, as a source of comic vitality. For example, here is an anonymous reviewer discussing an anonymous book of humor published by F. Newbury in 1768: "His jokes are sometimes low, but his editor thinks that they bear strong marks of originality; and he confesses that they are sometimes indelicate, not to say indecent, and hopes that the reader will find he has carefully cleansed the Augaean stable." This passage appeared in the *Critical Review* in the same year as a long and enthusiastic review of Boswell's *Corsica,* in the same volume as "Kenrick's Epistle to James Boswell, Esq."[17] It expresses a point of view that we can find in almost any century, in Ned Ward and Till Eulenspiegel and Al Schock's *Jokes for All Occasions.* Politeness and refinement were certainly in vogue in the last half of the eighteenth century, but laughter, gross and raucous laughter not excepted, does not go out of style.

Generic Explanations for Stylistic Variety in the *Life*

An explanation of Boswell's use of high and low styles in the *Life* may perhaps be found in the gravitational pull of genres other than biography. This line of thinking confirms our sense of his artistry in some respects, and weakens it in others.

The *Life* is not only heroic biography but also Lucianic comedy. I am thinking of the *Dialogues of the Gods* (not the *Verae Historiae*), Lucian's uniquely ludicrous and irreverent fantasies featuring the gods as "just folks": Zeus the vulgar rake, Hera the shrew. Exactly how much divinity remains to the Zeus and the Hera thus humanized can be disputed, but the key characters of Lucianic comedy have to be extraordinary in some way because to portray just folks as just folks is not in itself comical or satirical. Boswell's genuine reverence for Johnson, and the high styles that express that reverence, guarantee that he is not writing "mere" satire here, and the low words that figure in Johnson's down-to-earth "clinchers" give some of the same feelings of release and freedom that Lucianic comedy does. Patricia Spacks remarks on the pleasure produced when we "challenge the moral grandeur of larger-than-lifesize public figures"—the pleasures of leveling and of realism.[18]

Just the kind of verbal (stylistic) play that most exuberantly flourishes in Lucianic comedy can be found in Boswell's classical quotations, when they are used to heighten disparities between high and low. The deadpan introduction to the Wilkes dinner episode includes a quotation from *The Aeneid* that gives away the game. This paragraph starts, "I am now to record a very curious incident" ("curious" in the eighteenth century, of course, often denoted the merely odd and singular) and goes on to characterize the incident to follow as one "of which *pars magna fui*": "I myself saw these sad things; I took large part in them," says Aeneas, acknowledging his own heroic part in the tragic war at Troy. Disparities between the majestic self-control of Boswell/ Aeneas and the sly slickness of Boswell the go-between, who "kept [himself] snug and silent" as Johnson mutters "'Too, too, too' (under his breath)" (3: 64, 68) in explosive consternation, are surely Lucianic. Boswell gets similar effects by applying lines from Addison's *Cato* to Johnson's apparently stoical indifference to the dinner invitation itself (3: 67–68). I wonder whether Boswell's excursions into philosophic diction (even including the dreadful "Ode to Mrs. Thrale, by Samuel Johnson": "*Cervisial coctor's viduate* dame," *Life* 4: 387) do not exploit some of the same disreputable energies.[19]

It is clear that Boswell is enjoying himself here, laughing at Johnson's discomfort, applauding his triumph, relishing discrepancies. The same kind of thing happens on a smaller scale at various points in the *Life*. Recall the dinner party of 1778 when a distinguished assemblage is discussing Johnson's manners and abilities before he arrives: these are not common folk but one of the three most famous historians of the eighteenth century (Robertson), the president of the Royal Academy (Reynolds), the Earl of Haddington, and the mother of a Viscount (the Hon. Mrs. Boscawen); but "No sooner did he, of whom we had been thus talking so easily, arrive, than we were all as quiet as a school upon the entrance of the head-master" (3: 332). The comparison is a tribute to Johnson's powers of domination and simultaneously a comic reduction of all these dignitaries to the condition of schoolchildren, smothering their laughter. The sympathetic reader somehow shares both Boswell's admiration for Johnson and his impudent (Lucianic) enjoyment of the awkwardness here.

Boswell was of course strongly attracted to "low" comedy, and the undignified prose styles of the *Life* have a potential context in genres lower than biography. He tells us himself that once "in a wild freak of youthful extravagance, I entertained the audience *prodigiously*, by imitating the lowing of a cow" (5: 396). Wimsatt reminds us of Boswell's fondness for bons mots and puns. One purpose of the journal was to record Boswell's best efforts along these lines (e.g., "I said I would rather see *Sir* George and the *goose*, than *St.* George and the *dragon*").[20] In places the *Life* reads like a joke book. Boswell tells the reader that his *Life* will collect not only Johnson's "*wisdom*" but also his "*wit*" (1: 9).

When Boswell thinks of biography he thinks of anecdotes. He is described at dinner by one contemporary as laying down "knife and fork . . . in order to register a good anecdote" (1: 6 n. 2). Anecdotes are amusing, that is, quite frequently, jokes. At one point in the journal Boswell "talked how much *bons mots* were relished by everybody" and named both Plutarch (biographer) and Ménage (anecdotalist). Ménage was a scholar, but the collection of curious facts and witty sayings associated with him (in *Ménagiana* [1693, 1713, 1729, etc.], archetype of the *ana* genre), though bookish in character, is not above ribald humor.[21]

The *Life*, then, is not a single genre, not biography undiluted. We can think of it as responding to seven or eight forms of generic pressure; each moves in and out of focus as we view the *Life* from this angle or that: biography + autobiography + confession/apology + comic drama + *ana* + journalism + journal + jokebook. Its "polygeneric" character justifies the fact that topics and opinions come up almost as often in response to Boswell's personal anxieties as they do in reference to Johnson. It justifies Boswell's claims on the title-page to having written a literary history of the age, "the Whole Exhibiting a View of Literature and literary Men in Great-Britain, for near half a Century." It explains why the *Life* is irrepressibly centripetal, leading outwards at all points to footnotes, endnotes, appendixes, letters, and associated texts that Boswell or someone else is talking about or alluding to. Walter Ong proposes that books of "massive and dense" structure like the *Life* are attempts "to construct on the printed page something that will substitute for the full context of the talking world"; hence the proliferation of texts about texts in the eighteenth century, as well as of personal narratives, novels, memoirs, diaries, letters.[22] Variety of style is certainly appropriate to a book governed as this one is by such a variety of generic conventions.

Boswell's Style? or Johnson's?

Except for quotations, the grand passages in the *Life* were not crafted by Johnson but by Boswell. One can assume that Boswell tried to reproduce in the conversations in the *Life* the full splendor of Johnson's eloquence, but even though Johnson was famous for talking in *Ramblers*, for magnificent sentences that sprang forth fully-formed extemporaneously during ordinary conversation, we do not get *Rambler* style in this biography. The closest we come is something like this: "Then, all censure of a man's self is oblique praise. It is in order to shew how much he can spare. It has all the invidiousness of self-praise, and all the reproach of falsehood" (3: 323–24). This pronouncement "surprises, pleases, and teaches," according to Ralph Rader, because of the "paradoxical and surprising" power of the first sentence and the "compelling analytic judgment" of the third. In style, however, in elegance and precision of language, it does not measure up to *The Rambler*. It has some balance, but nothing comparable to the multifoliate symmetries that Johnson was famous for. Wimsatt describes one of these as "two predicates each of three emphatic elements, each of these elements in the one exactly paralleled in syntax, and closely paralleled in substance, by each in the other."[23] The more formal sentences in *The Rambler* do not start with "Then [comma]." In his most dignified and eloquent prose Johnson chooses action verbs, not *to be* and *to have*. The second *is* in this passage is asked to bear more semantic weight than it should have to: if we substitute "subsists," or "derives from the need to shew," we raise the level of formality.

R.W. Chapman and many others believe that Boswell is responsible for the wording and phrasing of Johnson's conversations in the *Life*—that is, for its style. "Boswell was not a stenographer; and . . . what he gives us is not always—perhaps is not very often—*ipsissima verba*."[24] The notes that Boswell took, when he did take them, were seldom written down during conversations, and consisted not of full sentences or complete utterances but of topics and key fragments. When Boswell tested what he called "my way of taking notes" (that is, "writing half words, and leaving out some altogether, so as yet to keep the substance and language of any discourse"), it worked "very imperfectly"; it failed to duplicate the exact words and phrasing of a text that Johnson was reading aloud "slowly and distinctly" (3: 270). In every case when Boswell is dealing with a written account of what Johnson said, either a friend's memorandum or his own journal, he edits it: I take this as ipso facto admission that these are not Johnson's actual remarks but a version of them that can be improved or adjusted. Almost every variable that controls style in the *Life*—word order, actual words used, sentence length, discourse strategies—was controlled by Boswell (or Malone on Boswell's behalf).

We can find additional evidence for Boswell's authorship of the conversations by comparing the language of statements that Johnson dictated to Boswell with language in the conversations "recorded" by Boswell. On a number of occasions, when Boswell asked for Johnson's "official" opinion on a certain matter (such as the rights of a Scottish schoolmaster whom Boswell was defending in the House of Lords), Johnson agreed to speak in such a way that Boswell could write down *ipsissima verba,* and Boswell includes these dictated statements in the *Life* (e.g., 2: 183–85; 2: 242–46; 3: 59–62; 3: 202–3). They are noticeably more formal than the conversational speeches. The sentences are longer, the vocabulary more abstract and learned. In Johnson's dictation on the claim of lay-patrons to present ministers to parishes (2: 242–46), the reader encounters half a dozen striking features that are common in *The Rambler* but rare in the conversations: embedded propositions ("That justice would be violated by transferring to the people the right of patronage, is apparent to all who . . ."); inversion for end-focus ("Against the right of patrons is commonly opposed, by the inferiour judicatures, the plea of conscience"); nouns to be verbed ("something to be done, or something to be avoided"); passive voice (in seven out of nine sentences in the first paragraph); balanced phrases and clauses ("it is a conscience very ill informed that violates the rights of one man, for the convenience of another"); semi-allegorical personified abstractions ("That ignorance and perverseness should always obtain what they like . . .").

The converse is also true: the grammar and vocabulary of speeches attributed to Johnson in the *Life* are different from the grammar and vocabulary of Johnson's published writings. Some of these speeches depend very heavily on the verbs *to be* and *to have.* To demonstrate the semantic weakness and ordinariness of the verbs Boswell attributes to Johnson, let me list consecutively the verbs, verbals, and deverbal nouns in a sequence of remarks on writers: "has," "invention," "imagination," "conduct," "has had," "approbation," "believe," "have had," "sale," "is," "begins," "was," "translation," "wrote," "is," "to think," "read" (2:238). Contrast a section of *Rambler* No. 2: "search," "survey," "detected," "escape," "observation," "wantoning," "is," "tempting," "resign," "enables," "to shine," "to conquer." Six of Boswell's verbs are *have* or *be*, only one of Johnson's. Four of Boswell's deverbal nouns are *-ion* abstractions, only one of Johnson's. *The Rambler* does not use absolute constructions, or end sentences with non-restrictive relative clauses, or use *which* to refer to an idea rather than a substantive; Boswell causes Johnson to do all these things regularly in the *Life*. The narrative portions of the *Life* do them also.

A ruthless editor will find an appreciable number of "errors" and infelicities in Johnson's utterances in the *Life*, of kinds that almost never appear in Johnson's published writings: on the one hand, occasional violations of rules that prescriptive grammarians (e.g., Lowth, Kames, Campbell, Blair, and many others) had recently brought to the attention of the reading and writing public; and on the other, frequent passages where the style is flaccid and imprecise, where "Johnson" does not seem to take the trouble to express himself with elegance or power. "If he must always have somebody to drink with him, he should buy a slave, and then he would be sure to have it" (3: 329): pronoun reference in that sentence is ambiguous. "No more" in the following would have been censured by Lowth or Campbell as a misplaced modifier: "You had no more this opinion after Robertson said it, than before" (3: 350). Infelicities: five existential predicates ("there is," "there are") in six lines of prose (3: 42); four *that* clauses in three lines ("it is of so much more consequence that truth should be told, than that individuals should not be made uneasy, that it is much better that the law does not restrain writing freely concerning the characters of the dead" [3: 15]).[25]

Johnson's speeches in the *Life* are full of missed opportunities for periodicity, balance, elegance, precision, and power.

> "In the foreign Universities a professorship is a high thing. It is as much almost as a man can make by his learning; and therefore we find the most learned men abroad are in the Universities. It is not so with us. Our Universities are impoverished of learning, by the penury of their provisions. I wish there were many places of a

> thousand a-year at Oxford, to keep first-rate men of learning from quitting the University." (3: 14)

In his writings Johnson is a master of end-focus and end-weight, complementary principles that allow the reader to look forward to decisive, meaningful cadences at the end of clauses of sentences.[26] Would such a person, if he "had accustomed himself to such accuracy in his common conversation, that he at all times expressed his thoughts with great force, and an elegant choice of language" (4: 428)—would a speaker of such ready and habitual dexterity have allowed himself to end that first sentence with so paltry a word as "thing"? And then to confuse "professorships" with "salaries" in the next sentence? To omit a "that" needed to tell the reader that "men" is not the direct object of "find"? We must make allowances for the fact that Johnson is speaking informally here, at his ease. But there is a difference between informality and slovenliness.[27] (It will be apparent that I cannot agree with critics, though of the highest authority, who describe Boswell's style in general terms as "transparent," "plain," and "simple.")[28]

If it is Boswell who controls verbal nuances in the *Life*, that would help explain why such scholars as Donald Greene have felt that the *Life* does not explore Johnson's full intellectual depth. It is no derogation of Boswell's genius to say that moral profundity was not his strong suit. The penetrating seriousness of the remark quoted above on self-censure is unusual in the *Life*. If we wish to understand why Harold Bloom called Johnson "the greatest English writer of wisdom literature," we go to Johnson's writings, not to the *Life of Johnson*. If we wish to understand Johnson's reputation for grand and splendid prose, we go to *Rasselas* not to the *Life*.[29]

It should be clear that if appropriateness and variation may count as criteria for the artistry of a writer's style, Boswell gets very high marks on both counts. His other achievements as stylist in the *Life of Johnson* include prose of authentic grandeur in major celebrations of Johnson's character and genius. Prose style helps to convince us of Johnson's greatness. Likewise, prose style enables us to feel a degree of intimacy with the formidable subject of this biography, by descending sometimes to low, familiar, vulgar depths. Neither those heights nor those depths would have been possible without conscious craftsmanship, as Boswell's revisions and editings make abundantly clear. And the mixture of high and low styles is almost certainly responsible in part for Boswell's most extraordinary achievement in the *Life*, the profound humanity of this Johnson, the Johnson whom Boswell created. It enabled Boswell to dramatize and bring to life his complicated and wonderful relationship with Johnson, a relationship that embodies reverence and affection, gossip, profound understanding, mere impudence, and a gleeful enjoyment of character and comedy. Control of prose style also figures in Boswell's comic art, in a Lucianic counterpoint between respect and laughter. As author and as editor, Boswell is responsible for dramatic variation in the styles of all his speakers, as well as for skillful and unskillful prose in narrative and description. Without this range of styles, the *Life of Johnson* would fall very flat indeed.

Some critics have argued that the most memorable parts of the *Life* are not Boswell at all but Johnson, his comments and quips, on which Boswell was not required to exert artistry, just memory. (The "type" of such critics is of course Macaulay.) But this argument can be refuted by a careful comparison of style in Johnson's speeches in the *Life* with style in *The Rambler* or in passages recorded from dictation. In spite of Boswell's strenuous efforts to make his manuscript correct and elegant, the grammar and diction of a substantial number of passages in the *Life* would not have satisfied a rigorous scholar of his own time, Robert Lowth or George Campbell or Hugh Blair or Johnson himself. Twentieth-century readers seldom find these "errors" a liability. They probably contribute to the informal liveliness of the narrative. And they confirm the notion of Boswell's Johnson as an interpretation, an independent creation, not a replica of Samuel Johnson "as he really was" (*Life* 1: 30).

Notes

1. See Frederic V. Bogel, "'Did You Once See Johnson Plain?': Reflections on Boswell's *Life* and the State of Eighteenth-Century Studies," in *New Questions, New Answers*, 73–93. On Boswell's artistry, though not on his prose style, see Paul K. Alkon, "Boswell's Control of Aesthetic

Distance," *University of Toronto Quarterly* 38 (1969): 174–91; Alkon, "Boswellian Time," *Studies in Burke and His Time* 14 (1973): 239–56; Greg Clingham, "Truth and Artifice in Boswell's *Life of Johnson*," in *New Light on Boswell* 207–29.

2. See Suzanne Romaine, *Socio-Historical Linguistics: Its Status and Methodology* (Cambridge: Cambridge University Press, 1982), 1–19. For backgrounds to eighteenth-century notions of appropriateness, see Thomas Kranidas, *The Fierce Equation: A Study of Milton's Decorum* (The Hague: Mouton, 1965).

3. Aristotle, *The "Art" of Rhetoric*, trans. John H. Freese, Loeb Classical Library (Cambridge, Mass.: Harvard University Press, 1982), 379 (III, vii, 6); John J. Gumperz, *Discourse Strategies* (Cambridge: Cambridge University Press, 1982), 33–34; Noam Chomsky, *Aspects of the Theory of Syntax* (Cambridge, Mass.: The M.I.T. Press, 1965), 3; James D. McCawley, *The Syntactic Phenomena of English* (Chicago: University of Chicago Press, 1988), 1: 5.

4. Ten thousand documents: Irma S. Lustig, "Fact into Art: James Boswell's Notes, Journals, and the *Life of Johnson*," in *Biography in the 18th Century*, ed. John D. Browning (New York: Garland, 1980), 128–29; autobiographical sketch: Frederick A. Pottle, *The Literary Career of James Boswell, Esq.* (Oxford: Clarendon Press, 1929), xxx; Adam Smith, *Lectures on Rhetoric and Belles Lettres* [1762–63], ed. John M. Lothian (Carbondale: Southern Illinois University Press, 1971), see chaps. 2, 4–8, and 10–11; Scotticisms: *Boswell in Holland*, 158–64, and Pat Rogers, "Boswell and the Scotticism," in *New Light on Boswell*, 56–71; Sterne parody: *Earlier Years*, 328.

5. See Francis Gallaway, *Reason, Rule, and Revolt in English Classicism* [1940] (New York: Octagon Press, 1965), 161–65; Erich Auerbach, *Mimesis: The Representation of Reality in Western Literature* [1946], trans. Willard Trask (Garden City, N.Y.: Doubleday, 1957), chap. 13; Mikhail Mikhailovich Bakhtin, *The Dialogic Imagination: Four Essays*, trans. Michael Holquist (Austin: University of Texas Press, 1981), chap. 1; Carey McIntosh, "High Styles and Low in Pope," *The Eighteenth Century: Theory and Interpretation* 29 (1988): 208–24.

6. Geoffrey Scott, "The Making of the Life of Johnson as Shown in Boswell's First Notes" [1929], in *Twentieth Century Interpretations of Boswell's Life of Johnson*, ed. James L. Clifford (Englewood Cliffs, N.J.: Prentice-Hall, 1970), 27. Perhaps the best known discussions of lowness in Homer and Shakespeare were Alexander Pope's Preface and notes to his translation of the *Iliad* (1715), his Postscript to the *Odyssey* (1726), Voltaire's 18th *Lettre philosophique* (1734), and Johnson's *Rambler* No. 168 (1751).

7. Frederick A. Pottle, "Boswell's University Education," in *Johnson, Boswell and Their Circle: Essays Presented to L.F. Powell* (Oxford: Clarendon Press, 1965), 230–53. For "climax," see Hugh Blair, *Lectures on Rhetoric*

and Belles Lettres [1783], ed. Harold F. Harding, 2 vols. (Carbondale: Southern Illinois University Press, 1965), 1: 237 (subsequent references to Blair's *Lectures* will be to this edition).

8. See Carey McIntosh, "Quantities of Qualities: Nominal Style and the Novel," *Studies in Eighteenth-Century Culture* 4 (1975): 139–53, and *Common and Courtly Language* (Philadelphia: University of Pennsylvania Press, 1986), chap. 2.

9. George Campbell, *The Philosophy of Rhetoric* [1776], ed. Lloyd F. Bitzer and David Potter (Carbondale: Southern Illinois University Press, 1963), 369; Blair, *Lectures*, 1: 206, 237–40; see also John Ward, *A System of Oratory* [1759], 2 vols. (New York: Georg Olms Verlag, 1969), 1: 346–52.

10. Stanley E. Fish, *Self-Consuming Artifacts: The Experience of Seventeenth-Century Literature* (Berkeley: University of California Press, 1972), 62. See also Richard A. Lanham, *Analyzing Prose* (New York: Scribner's, 1983), chap. 3.

11. John A. Vance, "The Laughing Johnson and the Shaping of Boswell's *Life*," in *New Questions, New Answers*, 212; Brady, *Later Years*, 110–11; Joseph Addison, "An Essay on Virgil's *Georgics*" [1697], in *Eighteenth-Century Critical Essays*, ed. Scott Elledge, 2 vols. (Ithaca, N.Y.: Cornell University Press, 1961), 1: 5.

12. Waingrow, *Corr: Life*, xxx. William C. Dowling makes a "network of antithetical relationships," including one between the "slovenly particulars" of Johnson's physical appearance and the sublime eloquence of his conversation, a basis for his ground-breaking analysis of "a partial grammar of discontinuity" in the *Life*: see *Language and Logos in Boswell's Life of Johnson* (Princeton: Princeton University Press, 1981). Stanley Brodwin quotes a key passage from Dryden's Preface to the *Life of Plutarch* (1683) authorizing "various" styles in biography: "There are proper places in it, for the plainness and nakedness of narration, which is ascrib'd to Annals; there is also room reserv'd for the loftiness and gravity of general History, when the actions related shall require the [*sic*] manner of expression. But there is withal, a descent into minute circumstances, and trivial passages of life, which are natural to this way of writing, and which the dignity of the other two will not admit": "'Old Plutarch at Auchinleck': Boswell's Muse of Corsica," *Philological Quarterly* 62 (1983): 75.

13. For Johnson as culture hero, see William C. Dowling, *The Boswellian Hero* (Athens: University of Georgia Press, 1979), 2; for illuminating remarks on the affection that Boswell creates between the reader and his hero, see Ralph W. Rader, "Literary Form in Factual Narrative: The Example of Boswell's *Johnson*," in *Essays in Eighteenth-Century Biography*, ed. Philip B. Daghlien (Bloomington: Indiana University Press, 1968), 21–39.

14. See Anthony Blackwall, *An Introduction to the Classics* [1719] (New York: Garland, 1971), 239, 158; Robert Dodsley, *The Preceptor*, 5th ed., 2 vols. (London: for J. Dodsley, 1769), 1: 385, 356; Addison, "On Virgil's

Georgics," 1: 4–5; William Melmouth, *Letters on Several Subjects. By the late Sir Thomas Fitzosborne, Bart* (London: R. Dodsley, 1748), 110; Richard Hurd, *Q. Horatii Flacci Ars Poetica Epistola ad Pisones* [1749], in *The Works of Richard Hurd DD,* 8 vols. (London: T. Cadell & W. Davies, 1811), 1: 209; Thomas Warton, *The History of English Poetry* [1774–1781], 4 vols. (New York: Johnson Reprint Corp., 1968), 3: 255.

15. Henry Home, Lord Kames, *Elements of Criticism,* 6th ed., 3 vols. [1785] (New York: Garland, 1971), 2: 24; Olivia Smith, *The Politics of Language 1791–1819* (Oxford: Clarendon Press, 1984), vii–x; Joseph Priestley, *A Course of Lectures on Oratory and Criticism* [1777], ed. Vincent M. Bevilacqua and Richard Murphy (Carbondale: Southern Illinois University Press, 1965), 160.

16. Hester Thrale Piozzi, *British Synonymy; or, An Attempt at Regulating the Choice of Words in Familiar Conversation,* 2 vols. [1794] (Menston: Scolar Press, 1968), 1: 14, 54, 79; 2: 34, 37. I am grateful to Howard Weinbrot for drawing my attention to this work.

17. *The Critical Review: or, Annals of Literature* 17 (1768): 205.

18. Patricia Meyer Spacks, *Gossip* (Chicago: University of Chicago Press, 1986), 99.

19. *The Aeneid of Virgil,* trans. Allen Mandelbaum (New York: Bantam Books, 1972), 29. The comic effects of Boswell's contrasts between high and low are explored by Jo Allen Bradham, "Comic Fragments in the *Life of Johnson,*" *Biography* 3 (1980): 94–104; David L. Passler, *Time, Form, and Style in Boswell's Life of Johnson* (New Haven, Conn.: Yale University Press, 1971), 46–47; Felicity A. Nussbaum, "Boswell's Treatment of Johnson's Temper: 'A Warm West-Indian Climate,'" *Studies in English Literature* 14 (1974): 421–33; and Lustig ("Fact into Art," 44) for Boswell's use of *Hamlet* to heighten the high seriousness of his first meeting with Johnson.

20. See William K. Wimsatt Jr., "The Fact Imagined: James Boswell" [1959], in *Hateful Contraries* (Lexington: University of Kentucky Press, 1965), 171.

21. See *Ménagiana ou Les Bons Mots et Remarques Critiques, Historiques, morales & d'erudition, de Monsieur Ménage,* 4 vols. (Paris: Chez la Veuve Del Aulne, 1729), 1: 318, 321. Volume 2 of the Columbia University copy has two pages 3–4, one including a decidedly off-color joke that is replaced in the other. For *-ana* as a genre, see *Thraliana: The Diary of Mrs. Hester Lynch Thrale,* ed. Katharine C. Balderston, 2d ed., 2 vols. (Oxford: Clarendon Press, 1951), 1: xi, 467; *Later Years,* 340; and Joseph Spence, *Observations, Anecdotes, and Characters of Books and Men,* ed. James M. Osborn, 2 vols. (Oxford: Clarendon Press, 1966), 1: xvii–xxi. For Plutarch as a collector of bons mots, see *In Search of a Wife,* 271.

22. Walter J. Ong, "Reading, Technology, and the Nature of Man," *Yearbook of English Studies* 10 (1980), cited in Alvin B. Kernan, *Printing*

Technology, Letters and Samuel Johnson (Princeton: Princeton University Press, 1987), 225.

23. Rader, "Literary Form," 21; William K. Wimsatt Jr., *The Prose Style of Samuel Johnson* (New Haven, Conn.: Yale University Press, 1941), 28.

24. R.W. Chapman, *Boswell's Note Book 1776–1777 . . . from the unique original in the collection of R.B. Adam, Esq.* (London: Humphrey Milford, 1925), xviii; see also, for example, *Corr: Life,* xxx–xxxvi; Frederick A. Pottle, "The *Life of Johnson*: Art and Authenticity," in *Twentieth Century Interpretations of the Life of Johnson,* 70–72; Irma S. Lustig, "Boswell at Work: The 'Animadversions' on Mrs. Piozzi," *Modern Language Review* 67 (1972): 11; *Later Years,* 289–91.

25. No age has been more critical of grammatical "errors" in published writings than the age of Johnson. For severe censorship of such faults as ambiguous pronoun reference and misplaced modifiers in major writings by Addison, Steele, Swift, Bolingbroke, and many others, see Kames, Campbell, and Blair as cited above, plus Robert Lowth, *A Short Introduction to English Grammar* [1762] (Menston: Scolar Press, 1967); see also McIntosh, *Common and Courtly Language,* chap. 1.

26. See Randolph Quirk, Sidney Greenbaum, Geoffrey Leech, and Jan Svartvik, *A Comprehensive Grammar of the English Language* (London: Longman, 1985), 1361–67.

27. I am assuming that Johnson deserved his reputation for speaking *Ramblers.* So many people testified to the formal precision of his ordinary conversation, to the deliberateness and care with which he chose his words, that I am reluctant to believe that the style of his talk was in all cases different from the style of *The Rambler.* But there isn't a single *Rambler*-style speech in the *Life.* Even if Johnson only spoke *Ramblers* occasionally, the fact that he never speaks *Ramblers* in the *Life* confirms my argument.

28. Brady, *Later Years,* 440–41; "simple, effective, and fluid": Passler, *Time, Form, and Style,* 112; "graceful" and "purposefully unobtrusive": Rader, "Literary Form," 20.

29. Donald Greene, "'Tis a Pretty Book, Mr. Boswell, But—," in *New Questions, New Answers,* 110–46 (earlier version in *Georgia Review* 32 [1978]); Harold Bloom, Introduction, *James Boswell's Life of Samuel Johnson* (New York: Chelsea House, 1986), 5.

"Casts a Kind of Glory Round it": Metaphor and the *Life of Johnson*

WILLIAM PAUL YARROW

> The greatest thing in style is to have a command of metaphor. This power cannot be acquired; it is a mark of genius, for to make good metaphors implies an eye for resemblances.
>
> Aristotle, *The Poetics*

The *Life of Johnson* is a great sprawling masterpiece of biographical information and observation, unexpectedly engaging and lifelike. Critics, almost unanimous in their assessment of the work's enduring value, have taken great pains to account for both its vividness and its longevity—the "life," the "liveliness," the "living quality" of the *Life of Johnson.* Boswell's dramatic presentation of Johnson has been particularly praised, but his framing of Johnson's conversation, his deliberate inclusion of competing levels of discourse, and his presentation of secondary characters, himself among them, have also elicited comment. What has received scant attention, however, is the role of figurative language in the book. Specifically, the way in which metaphor is used to intensify the presentation of Johnson has passed unremarked. I use metaphor here in its largest sense, the sense that Hugh Blair refers to in his *Lectures on Rhetoric and Belles Lettres*: "the word metaphor is sometimes used . . . for the application of a term in any figurative signification, whether the figure be founded on resemblance, or on some other relation, which two objects bear one another. . . . Aristotle, in his Poetics, uses metaphor in this extended sense, for any figurative meaning imposed upon a word."[1] Close attention to the use of tropes in the *Life of Johnson* reveals Boswell's unflagging effort to originate, incorporate, and encourage the use of metaphor in the book. One might go as far as to say that his design there was to *maximize* metaphor.

Boswell had been interested in metaphor since the time he was a young man. Metaphor was, for him, a function of wit. Like the green and silver suit he wore in Holland, it was a way to be "fine" (*Boswell in Holland* 131). Throughout his journals we find Boswell collecting metaphors he likes, preserving his successes, experimenting with language:

> How easily and cleverly do I write just now! I am really pleased with myself; words come skipping to me like lambs upon Moffat Hill; and I turn my periods smoothly and imperceptibly like a skilful wheelwright turning tops in a turning-loom. There's fancy! There's simile! (*London Journal* 187)

> Satire is like a nettle. If you touch it gently and timidly, it will sting you. But if you come boldly up and seize it firmly, it is crushed and becomes quite harmless. (*Defence* 79)

> It is wonderful how he will dwell on a trifle sometimes, like an ox in warm weather running after a fly—if that ever happens, which I am not quite sure. (*Ominous Years* 95)

> The gardens were like those of Babylon. The lady was like a Peruvian princess. I mean, all was like romance. (*Boswell in Extremes* 98)

More extensive quotation would reveal Boswell's almost consuming interest and pride in making metaphors. "My simile of the hares (my metaphor, rather)," he writes self-consciously in his *London Journal*, "is pretty well" (76). Throughout his journals, Boswell is often thinking about metaphors and, more often than not, thinking about using them in some way. Seizing on a good idea, he writes, "Upon some occasion when my imagination is warmer and my expression more fluent I may expand it. It is a bud which would have an excellent appearance if fully and beautifully blown" *Defence* 32). The telling word here is "appearance." For Boswell, the ornamental rather than the explanatory aspect of comparisons predominates.

Some of the felicitous metaphors in his journals are effectively recycled into his *Hypochondriack* essays. For example, this paragraph from his March 1783 essay, "On Diaries," concludes with three particularly successful ones.

> But it is a work of very great labour and difficulty to keep a journal of life, occupied in various pursuits, mingled with concomitant speculations and reflections, in so much, that I do not think it possible to do it unless one has a peculiar talent for abridging. I have tried it in that way, when it has been my good fortune to live in a multiplicity of instructive and entertaining scenes, and I have thought my notes like portable soup, of which a little bit by being dissolved in water will make a good large dish; for their substance by being expanded in words would fill a volume. Sometimes it occurred to me that a man should not live more than he can record, as a farmer should not have a larger crop than he can gather in. And I have regretted that there is no invention for getting an immediate and exact transcript of the mind, like that instrument by which a copy of a letter is at once taken off.[2]

Many of the metaphors in Boswell's journals never find their way into any other of his writings.[3] This absence is significant, for it shows a development in Boswell's attitude toward his work, a growing sense of appropriateness in the use or abandonment of metaphors from his journals. He comes to understand that not everything that is good is fitting. The following passage from *Boswell for the Defence*, dated 10 April 1772, is excluded from the *Life of Johnson*. It is as starkly eloquent and heartfelt as almost anything else in Boswell, an authentic poetry of honest feeling, but, as Boswell himself recognized, it belongs more properly in a biography of James Boswell than in the biography of Samuel Johnson.

> I dined at General Oglethorpe's. . . . Mr. Johnson and Dr. Goldsmith and nobody else were the company. I felt a completion of happiness. I just sat and hugged myself in my own mind. Here I am in London, at the house of General Oglethorpe, who introduced himself to me just because I had distinguished myself; and here is Mr. Johnson whose character is so vast; here is Dr. Goldsmith, so distinguished in literature. Words cannot describe our feelings. The finer parts are lost, as the down upon a plum; the radiance of light cannot be painted. (*Defence* 104)

A similar example can be seen in the transformation of the following entry from the journal for 29 May 1783 to its appearance eight years later in the *Life of Johnson*.

> I said he [Bennett Langton] was the reverse of the insect which is first snail and then butterfly, for he was first butterfly then snail. JOHNSON.

> 'Who said this of him?' BOSWELL. 'I say it now.' JOHNSON. 'It is very well said.' BOSWELL. 'I say very good things sometimes.' (*Applause* 151)

By the time this passage gets to the *Life of Johnson* Boswell clarifies the meaning of the metaphor and turns the focus away from himself and onto Johnson:

> 'He has reversed the Pythagorean discipline, by being first talkative, and then silent. He reverses the course of Nature too: he was first the gay butterfly, and then the creeping worm.' Johnson laughed loud and long at this expansion and illustration of *what he himself had told me* [my emphasis].(*Life* 3: 261)[4]

A comparison of metaphoric passages in the *Life of Johnson* with those in *The Journal of a Tour to the Hebrides* (1785) and in Boswell's private journals reveals this subordination of Boswell and his increased attentiveness to the presentation of Johnson. The following two instances of Boswell devising metaphors to describe his rough treatment by social companions clearly illustrate the point:

> I shall make no remark on her grace's speech. I indeed felt it as rather too severe; but when I recollected that my punishment was inflicted by so dignified a beauty, I had the kind of consolation which a man would feel who is strangled by a *silken cord.* (5: 359)

> BOSWELL. 'I said to-day to Sir Joshua, when he observed that you tossed me sometimes—I don't care how often, or how high he tosses me, when only friends are present, for then I fall upon soft ground; but I do not like falling on stones, which is the case when enemies are present.—I think this is a pretty good image, Sir.' JOHNSON. 'Sir, it is one of the happiest I have ever heard.' (3: 338)

In the second example, Boswell uses himself to illustrate qualities in Johnson. Johnson's comment underscores his capacity for kindness after severity, the point of the larger passage. In the first instance, there is no illumination of Johnson. The "silken cord" metaphor merely demonstrates Boswell's cleverness.

A similar development from *The Journal of a Tour to the Hebrides* to the *Life of Johnson* can be seen in the following passages which, as canine metaphors, are strikingly similar, but from one to the other show a significant change in tone and intention.

> A ludicrous, yet just image presented itself to my mind, which I expressed to the company. I compared myself to a dog who has got hold of a large piece of meat, and runs away with it to a corner, where he may devour it in peace, without any fear of others taking it away from him. 'In London, Reynolds, Beauclerk, and all of them, are contending who shall enjoy Dr. Johnson's conversation. We are feasting upon it, undisturbed, at Dunvegan.' (5: 215)

> He kept it [his book] wrapt up in the tablecloth in his lap during the time of dinner, from an avidity to have one entertainment in readiness when he should have finished another; resembling (if I may use so coarse a simile) a dog who holds a bone in his paws in reserve, while he eats something else which has been thrown to him. (3: 285)

The "ludicrous, yet just image," evident in and perhaps even characteristic of *The Journal of a Tour to the Hebrides,* disappears or is transformed in the *Life of Johnson.* In the passage from the *Life of Johnson,* Boswell's dog image is inspired by Mrs. Knowles's immediately preceding comment that Johnson "gets at the substance of a book directly; he tears out the heart of it" (3: 284–85). Boswell, it should be noted, acknowledges the danger inherent in such a comparison in his appeal to the readers' indulgence: "if I may use so coarse a simile." The focus of attention in the first passage is on Boswell, the maker of the metaphor; in the second, it is on the tenor of the metaphor, Johnson.

One can see further examples of the transformation of the "ludicrous, yet just image" to the "just and fitting image" if one focuses on the metaphors for Johnson himself that Boswell presents in these two works. The following examples are not exhaustive lists by any means, but they are sufficient to suggest the strategy Boswell employs. To make Johnson live in the reader's mind, Boswell attempts to locate Johnson's virtues and idiosyncrasies in specific pictoral images, objective correlatives, if you will, through the use of metaphor. Two vivid instances are Percy's metaphor for Johnson's conversation, which he compares to a statue from antiquity "where every vein and muscle is distinct and bold" (3: 317), and Tom Tyers's description of Johnson himself as a ghost that will not speak unless first spoken to (3: 307; 5: 73). As these examples illustrate, not all the metaphors for Johnson in the *Life of Johnson* are Boswell's, but Boswell's incorporation of metaphors by others is part of his strategy to present a textured, metaphoric picture of Johnson.

We learn in the *Life of Johnson* that Johnson blows out his breath "like a Whale"[5] (1: 486), laughs "like a rhinoceros" (Tom Davies, 2: 378), tosses and gores people like a bull (2: 66), is like an ox (2: 79), seems a bear (Baretti, 2: 66; Mrs. Boswell, 2: 269 n. 1; Lord Auchinleck, 2: 347–48; 5: 384), and has qualities of a lion (Cuthbert Shaw, 2: 32; William Strahan, 2: 107; 2: 138; 4: 107). We are told that his judgment is "like a mighty gladiator" combating "those apprehensions that, like the wild beasts of the Arena, were all around in cells, ready to be let out upon him" (2: 106), and that the force of his wit was such that, like a sharp sword, he was "through your body in an instant" (2: 365).

To particularize Johnson's temperament and intellect, natural phenomena are invoked. Boswell tells us that Johnson is a tempest (3: 273; 3: 275; 3: 290; 3: 385), the wind (1: 486), a cloud (2: 324, 3: 315), the ocean (Orme, 2: 300), a tree (3: 260; 4: 1), a garden (3: 183), a fountain (2: 144; 3: 268), a fire (3: 190), and a star (3: 221). Boswell even suggests that Johnson is one of "two great continents" (2: 80).

The last class of metaphors for Johnson in the *Life of Johnson* may be termed "literary" in that they are either allusions or refer to Johnson's contribution to belles lettres. Johnson is called "the infant Hercules of toryism (1: 38),[6] Ajax (4: 109), Goliath (2: 63), Gargantua (3: 255–56), even Socrates (5: 21).[7] Johnson is "the English Juvenal" (1: 118), the "Colossus of Literature" (4: 158), the great CHAM of literature" (Tobias Smollett, 1: 348, 1: 349 n. 5), "the Caliban of literature" (Gilbert Cowper [*sic*][8], 2: 129), and finally the "MONARCH OF LITERATURE" (3: 82).

These metaphors suggest the immense stature and the intense presence of Johnson. Goldsmith calls him "the big man" (2: 14); the Reverend Dr. Blair calls him "The Giant" (1: 396). Johnson is gigantic, larger than life, one of the elemental forces in the world. How could he not be, not seem so, associated by Boswell as he is with heroes, the great beasts, nature itself?

We also see this association (albeit less full) with nature, great beasts, heroes, and so forth, in *The Journal of a Tour to the Hebrides*, yet there it is a cruder, less subtle, less assured use of metaphor.

> Let it however be observed, that the sayings themselves are generally great; that, though he might be an ordinary composer at times, he was for the most part a Handel. (5: 18)

> There was a stratum of common clay under the rock of marble. (5: 20)

> He stalked like a giant among the luxuriant thistles and nettles. (5: 55)

> Besides, so great a mind as his cannot be moved by inferior objects: an elephant does not run or skip like lesser animals. (5: 111)

> Dr. Johnson sat high on the stern like a magnificent Triton. (5: 162)

Boswell runs afoul of some of the faults of metaphor Hugh Blair enumerates in chapter 15 of his *Lectures on Rhetoric and Belles Lettres.* Reversing Boswell's own formulation, one might say that the images are "just, yet ludicrous." Imagining the sixty-four-year-old Johnson sitting in a small boat as a Triton (with the head and trunk of a man and the tail of a fish) is ludicrous enough; "magnificent" Triton makes the case too strongly. An elephant has the size but lacks the dignity of the great beast; furthermore, the image of an elephant skipping imparts a certain hilarity to what is presented as a serious idea. It should be noted, moreover, that the metaphor does not clearly illuminate the idea. The association of giant and thistles (not to mention common clay and marble) works against the intended awe of the image; "luxuriant" thistles is perhaps intentionally humorous, but the humor is misconceived here. The fault of the first metaphor is better illustrated in the context of the whole passage, which praises Johnson but simultaneously qualifies that praise.

> The *Messiah,* played upon the *Canterbury organ,* is more sublime than when played upon an inferior instrument: but very slight musick will seem grand, when conveyed to the ear through that majestick medium. *While therefore Dr. Johnson's sayings are read, let his manner be taken along with them.* Let it however be observed, that the sayings themselves are generally great; that, though he might be an ordinary composer at times, he was for the most part a Handel. (5: 18)

By the time Boswell writes the *Life of Johnson,* his interest has shifted properly from metaphor (the display of wit) and the metaphor-maker (himself) to Johnson, the biographical subject. It was difficult for the naturally ebullient James Boswell to suppress himself completely, to disappear into his text, but in the *Life of Johnson* he attempts to foreground his subject and subordinate himself in the interests of presenting Johnson's *character*.[9] Boswell's investment is not in using metaphors for their own sake, much less his own sake, but in making *Johnson* metaphoric. Boswell realizes that it is only through particulars, and metaphors supply those particulars, that Johnson can truly be seen[10]: "Only by the minutest detail, by endless particularities which bear vividly all the character of the whole, and, as they spring up from a wonderful depth, give some feeling of that depth—only in such a manner would it have been in some degree possible to give a representation of this remarkable personality; for the spring can be apprehended only while it is flowing."[11]

One might guess that Boswell was the author of the foregoing quotation, but it comes from Goethe, a writer not normally linked to Boswell. The philosophies of representation through particulars in the *Life of Johnson* and *Dichtung und Wahrheit* are surprisingly similar. But for the actualization of pictoral presentation through small detail, one must turn to a writer like William Blake. Blake's aphorism on prudence ("Prudence is a rich ugly old maid courted by Incapacity")[12] is a particularly striking example of just the kind of vivid particularization Boswell is after. "Johnson" is a similar abstract concept which needs to be made vivid through detail: his ill-fitting wig, his ravenous appetite, his orange peels, Hodge his cat. All particularize the portrait, color in the abstract outline, finalize "the Flemish picture" (3: 191).

To make Johnson live, Boswell must think metaphorically and present Johnson imagistically, enshroud him in a metaphoric nimbus. Otherwise he, too, would slip away into abstraction, the way Nekayah and Pekuah, Rasselas and Imlac, do. *Rasselas*, a work Boswell loved, represents the danger of relying wholly on largely abstract speech to present character. The characters in *Rasselas* are often indistinguishable.[13] Boswell fights against this propensity in the *Life of Johnson*. The weapon he uses is the visual detail. "The minute diversities in every thing," he exclaims, "are wonderful" (3: 163).

Boswell, Goethe, and Blake all understand that metaphor is a primary mode of transmitting those "minute particulars." Johnson's metaphors— "a woman's preaching is like a dog's walking on its hinder legs" (1: 463); "a great city is, to be sure, the school for studying life" (3: 253); "a vow is a horrible thing, it is a snare for sin" (3: 357)—crystallize Johnson's *thought*; Boswell's metaphors crystallize *Johnson*: "I compared him at this time to a warm West-Indian climate, where you have a bright sun, quick vegetation, luxuriant foliage, luscious fruits; but where the same heat sometimes produces thunder, lightning, and earthquakes, in a terrible degree" (3: 299–300). This distinction between metaphor that crystallizes the abstract (and thus particularizes the author of the thought) and metaphor that crystallizes the concrete object or person is crucial. Both, Boswell realizes, are necessary for the presentation and full realization of Johnson in the *Life of Johnson*. Hence Boswell's insistence on the display of Johnson's conversational imagery (Johnson's metaphors) as well as his insistence on a metaphoric description of Johnson himself (Boswell's and others' metaphors).

Johnson needed to be crystallized metaphorically because the picture of Johnson for most readers, Boswell recognized, was an abstract one. Johnson, associated with the process of clear thought, personified Man Thinking. His thoughts, as presented in his literary works, defined him. He was the poet of "London," the author of *Rasselas*, the authoritative critic of the English poets. His contemporaries, James Clifford tells us, termed him "Dictionary Johnson."[14] This association of Johnson with his productions is most strongly seen, perhaps, in the public's identification of Johnson with "The Rambler," the eponymous author of his most famous essays. In *The Journal of a Tour to the Hebrides* Boswell frequently refers to Johnson as "The Rambler."

> Not finding a letter here that I expected, I felt a momentary impatience to be at home. Transient clouds darkened my imagination, and in those clouds I saw events from which I shrunk; but a sentence or two of the *Rambler's* conversation gave me firmness, and I considered that I was upon an expedition for which I had wished for years, and the recollection of which would be a treasure to me for life. (5: 128)

> Our bad accommodation here made me uneasy, and almost fretful. Dr. Johnson was calm. I said, he was so from vanity.—*Johnson*. 'No, sir, it is from philosophy.'—It pleased me to see that the *Rambler* could practice so well his own lessons. (5: 146)

> I awaked at noon, with a severe head-ach [*sic*]. I was much vexed that I should have been guilty of such a riot, and afraid of a reproof from Dr. Johnson. I thought it very inconsistent with that conduct which I ought to maintain, while the companion of the *Rambler*. (5: 258)

It is significant that Boswell's practice of substituting the epithet "The Rambler" for Johnson's name largely stops by the time he writes the *Life of Johnson.* The change represents Boswell's clearer, more particularized, vision of Johnson and results in an improved strategy for presenting him. Boswell has come to understand that to call Johnson "Dictionary" or the "Rambler" is to think of him only in terms of scholarship and knowledge, rationality and wisdom. Consequently, through physical descriptions, particularizing touches, pictorial adverbs appended to conversation, but above all with metaphor, he presents Johnson-the-man as opposed to Johnson-the-mind.

The tendency of the *Life of Johnson* to be abstract, through its preponderance of abstract discussion, is continually challenged by Boswell's insistence that the work be concrete. Bombarding the reader with continual specific visual metaphors for Johnson, exhibiting Johnson's metaphoric abilities in his conversation and writings, prodding, encouraging, and challenging Johnson to be himself metaphoric, and embedding metaphors in the text through the use of interpolated poems, letters, and diary extracts, thwart the possibility of viewing Johnson abstractly. When the conversation in the *Life of Johnson* is on the verge of being unrelievedly abstract, Boswell will "enliven"[15] the text with metaphor, or, as in the following instance, relieves the reader's tedium with a characteristically Johnsonian device, revealing the metaphor hidden in the cliché, and producing a characteristically Boswellian response, calling forth metaphor in others, in this case Edward Gibbon: "BOSWELL. 'Well now, let us take the common phrase, Placehunters. I thought they had hunted without regard to anything, just as their huntsmen, the Minister, leads, looking only to the prey.' J. [Gibbon]. 'But taking your metaphor, you know that in hunting there are few so desperately keen as to follow without reserve. Some do not choose to leap ditches and hedges and risk their necks, or gallop over steeps, or even to dirty themselves in bog and mire'" (3: 234–35).

When we think back on the *Life of Johnson,* the image that remains is of the physical Johnson speaking. So vivid is that picture that we remember not just his wit, wisdom, and good sense but often the context of his words. One line ("I refute it *thus*") can summon up a whole scene: "After we came out of the church, we stood talking for some time together of Bishop Berkeley's ingenious sophistry to prove the non-existence of matter, and that every thing in the universe is merely ideal. I observed, that though we are satisfied his doctrine is not true, it is impossible to refute it. I never shall forget the alacrity with which Johnson answered, striking his foot with mighty force against a large stone, till he rebounded from it, 'I refute it *thus*'" (1: 471). Johnson's passion for empirical truth is here linked to the indelible visual image of his agitated and repeated assault on the small boulder, "till he rebounded from it." This might be termed the dramatic presentation of Johnson through metaphor, in which Johnson himself takes on metaphorical qualities. As William Siebenschuh writes, "Boswell's dramatic images of Johnson are almost always metaphors that automatically link personal qualities and visual images in our minds" (389).

Johnson, on the other hand, is not particularly interested in details and is not naturally metaphoric. A typical and characteristic expression of his position may be found in his "Life of Cowley": "Great thoughts are always general, and consist in positions not limited by exceptions, and in descriptions not descending to minuteness."[16] He tells Boswell, "he always laboured when he said a good thing" (3: 260, 5: 77), by which he sometimes means a striking idea, a comment of luminous clarity which breaks a verbal deadlock, as in the following exchanges:

> 'I think (said Hicky,) gentility and morality are inseparable.' Boswell. 'By no means, Sir. The genteelest characters are often the most immoral. Does not Lord Chesterfield give precepts for uniting wickedness and the graces? A man, indeed, is not genteel when he gets drunk; but most vices may be committed very genteelly: a man may debauch his friend's wife genteelly: he may cheat at cards genteelly.' Hicky. 'I do not think *that* is genteel.' Boswell. 'Sir, it may not be like a gentleman, but it may be genteel. Johnson. 'You are meaning two different things. One means exteriour grace, the other honour. It is certain that a man may be very immoral with exteriour grace.' (2: 340–41)

> Miss Seward. 'There is one mode of the fear of death, which is certainly absurd; and that is the dread of annihilation, which is only a pleasing sleep without a dream.' Johnson. . . . 'The lady confounds

> annihilation, which is nothing, with the apprehension of it, which is dreadful. It is in the apprehension of it that the horrour of annihilation consists.' (3: 295–96)

More often, however, a "good thing" means to Johnson a striking phrase, an image, a metaphor, often a function of conversational wit, but never at the expense of the idea: Johnson's definition of patriotism as "the last refuge of a scoundrel" (2: 348), his characterization of Wilkes as "the phoenix of convivial felicity" (3: 183), or his comment on the characters in *Evelina*: "Such a fine varnish of low politeness!"[17]

Johnson thinks grandly and abstractly. He thinks in ideas. "There is no position," he suggests, "however false in its universality, which is not true of some particular man" (3: 42). A poet like Blake, on the other hand, presents a model of a different kind of mind, a mind that seems to think in images. One might posit two poles, one extreme inhabited by highly imagistic works—*The Book of Revelation*, Traherne's *Centuries of Meditations*, Smart's "Jubilate Agno," Rimbaud's prose poems "A Season in Hell" and "The Illuminations," Woolf's *The Waves*, Marinetti's Futurist manifestoes, Cela's *Mrs. Caldwell Speaks to Her Son*, or the lady Lord Kames knew "who talked for two hours at a time and not a word plain but all figure" (*Applause* 38)—and at the other end works which embody Johnson's sense of the word "notion," an abstract concept, an image of which cannot be formed in the mind, the "exceeding dry and hard" (3: 173) style of Lord Monboddo, certain works of philosophy. The two poles define a continuum along which writers might be placed according to their inclination toward literal or figurative language, marking their "notional" or metaphoric habits of mind, thinking in ideas or thinking in images. Comparing a few aphorisms from Johnson's conversation in the *Life of Johnson* and from the "Proverbs of Hell" section of Blake's "The Marriage of Heaven and Hell" illustrates the difference:

> JOHNSON: The happiness of society depends on virtue. (3: 293)
> BLAKE: The road of excess leads to the palace of wisdom. (35)
>
> JOHNSON: A man would never undertake great things, could he be amused with small. (3: 242)
> BLAKE: The eagle never lost so much time. as when he submitted to learn of the crow. (36)

> JOHNSON: All severity that does not tend to increase good, or prevent evil, is idle. (2: 435)
> BLAKE: The cut worm forgives the plow. (35)

For Blake, the ideas are embodied in the image. For Johnson the idea is all. Metaphors are literally an afterthought:

> 'Mudge's Sermons' are good, but not practical. He grasps more than he can hold; he takes more corn than he can make into meal. (4: 98)

> Sir, that is the blundering œconomy of narrow understanding. It is stopping one hole in a sieve. (3: 300)

> They have no object for hope. Their condition cannot be better. It is rowing without a port. (3: 255)

For Johnson, metaphors don't exist independently of their explanations. But whether the metaphor is affixed to an idea as a postscript, as in the examples above, or precedes the conceptual exposition, as in the examples below, it is always clearly in the service of the idea which called it into being:

> Their learning is like bread in a besieged town: every man gets a little but no man gets a full meal. (2: 363)

> Greek, Sir, is like lace; every man gets as much of it as he can. (4: 23)

> Sorrow is a kind of rust of the soul, which every new idea contributes in its passage to scour away.[18]

These a posteriori explanations also serve to limit and define the terms of the metaphoric comparisons which begin surprisingly, provocatively, even shockingly, but then decline into common sense. Johnson in his use of them is being "striking," though the distance of two hundred years renders them more unusual to our ears than they would have been to his audience. Blake, on the other hand, was not adverse to shocking his readers, not averse to leaving uncircumscribed the terms of his metaphors. The Blakean version of a Johnsonian idea might have been something like this: "Sorrow is the rust of the Soul."[19]

For Blake, the explanatory tags would have been irrelevant; for Johnson, they are the metaphors' raison d'etre. Metaphor is subordinated to the idea which it exemplifies. The idea, conveying the meaning, is of primary importance. In this, Johnson was typical of his century. As I.A. Richards pointed out, the eighteenth century believed that "figures are a mere embellishment or added beauty and that the plain meaning, the tenor, is what alone really matters."[20] Scott George elaborates this idea: "The metaphorical principle was supposed to be, not one of the constitutive modes of language, but something adventitious and ornamental. According to this view, metaphor is simply an added 'trick' of language, the kind of thing one does when he wants to leave the path of ordinary linguistic usage, for some reason or another. It is a device the writer can take or leave alone. No matter which he does, the real idea he is trying to impart remains the same. Metaphor only dresses it up a bit."[21] Yet within this sense of metaphor as ornament, there are two distinct uses—explanation and embellishment—which Hugh Blair makes clear. "All comparisons whatever may be reduced under two heads, *explaining* and *embellishing*. For when a writer likens the object of which he treats to any other thing, it always is or at least always should be, with a view to either make us understand that object more distinctly, or to dress it up and adorn it" (182).

Though both Boswell and Johnson relish metaphors, they approach them in a different way. Boswell sees metaphors primarily as "embellishing"; Johnson primarily as "explaining." Both take delight in being metaphoric, but Boswell's delight is often the exercise of a sensuous imagination whereas Johnson's is more typically a virtuoso athleticism of the mind. Exploiting the potential of metaphors to awaken striking connections in the mind is what Johnson means when he asks that metaphors be used with "propriety." Used in that way, "metaphorical expression . . . is a great excellence in style" (*Life* 3: 174). He criticizes Swift because "The rogue never hazards a metaphor."[22] As Johnson reads his own words in the journals Boswell shows him, he is delighted when he sees "that his conversation teemed with point and imagery" (3: 260). He takes Lord Loughborough[23] to task for being conversationally dull. "I never heard any thing from him in company that was at all striking" (4: 179). One must be "striking" in company. After all, Johnson reminds us, it is in conversation that we discover what our "real abilities are" (4: 179). Yet constant conversational striving is wearying. Goldsmith, he says, "was not an agreeable companion for he talked always for fame" (3: 247). Burke "is not so agreeable as the variety of his knowledge would otherwise make him, because he talks partly from ostentation" (3: 247). Johnson comments to Boswell that one speaks "Either to instruct and entertain, which is a benevolent motive; or for distinction, which is a selfish motive" (4: 223).

Understanding this caution, Johnson still wants to be "striking," and we see this desire for preeminence throughout the *Life of Johnson*, which is, among other things, testimony to his success in this regard. That he is within its pages a "striking" figure is unarguable, whether one thinks of Johnson's separation of the two fighting dogs by "striking" their heads together (5: 329, 2: 299) or his winning over his antagonists in argument by "striking" them down intellectually or rhetorically. After all, "He could, when he chose it, be the greatest sophist that ever wielded a weapon in the schools of declamation; but he indulged this only in conversation; for he owned he sometimes talked for victory" (5: 17). Johnson employs metaphor often to create an impression, to be intellectually striking. Using metaphor is an aggressive demonstration of his powers; it is part of his conversational arsenal. As he tells Boswell, "A man cannot strike till he has his weapons" (3: 316).

Despite Johnson's theoretical and practical interest in metaphors (clearly illustrated not just by the ample evidence in the *Life of Johnson* but by the *Lives of the Poets* and *Rasselas* as well),[24] Johnson's writing has been criticized precisely for a deficiency in this regard. A characteristic example, echoed by many earlier writers, is W.K. Wimsatt's criticism of Johnson as an "exceptionally general and abstract" writer. This characterization has been challenged by a number of writers in the twentieth century who set out to correct the impression "that neoclassical prose and poetry, especially Johnson's, are devoid of imagery in their pursuit of general truths." Cecil Emden's "Dr. Johnson and Imagery," Donald Greene's essay "'Pictures to the Mind': Johnson and Imagery," and O.F. Christie's study *Johnson the Essayist* are notable examples,[25] but we even have the contemporary, albeit idiosyncratic, opinion of Lord Monboddo, who disapproved of "the richness of Johnson's language, and of his frequent use of metaphorical expressions" (3: 174). The case for Johnson as an imagistic prose writer, persuasively argued by Emden, Greene, and Christie, is well summed up in Christie's words: "It is in 'imagery' that Johnson excels, in picturesqueness of phrase, in apt and concentrated and vivid expressions. This is Johnson's predominant quality, in which, as a prose writer, he has never since been surpassed" (57). Even Wimsatt in *Philosophic Words* admits to this quality in Johnson: "Johnson's assimilation of scientific images to the prevailing abstraction of his style is so thorough, or to put it an opposite way, his realization of the imagery latent in even the most abstract philosophic word is so keen, that a very accurate degree of metaphoric interaction between abstract and ordinarily almost imageless words often occurs in his writing."[26]

Comprehensive analyses of Johnson's conversation, as separate from his prose and poetry, are rare, however. In addition, Johnson's comment that he "laboured when he *said* a good thing" (3: 260) has not been taken sufficiently into account. About Johnson's conversation, William Vesterman suggests that "Johnson tends to move the terms of argument from the abstract to the simple, the commonplace, and the concrete, while his literary manner moves from a proposition expressed abstractly to the ramifications and complexities of it without leaving the level of the abstract."[27] While it is true that a significant portion of Johnson's conversation is grounded in "the commonplace and the concrete" and is often picturesquely imagistic, a larger portion is not particularly metaphoric at all. The second group of the following quotations is no less memorable or quotable than the first group, but the charm of the quotations does not depend upon metaphor.

> Truth, Sir, is a cow which will yield such people no more milk, and so they are gone to milk the bull.[28] (1: 444)
>
> Sometimes things may be made darker by definition. (3: 245)
>
> Were it not for imagination, Sir, . . . a man would be as happy in the arms of a chambermaid as of a Duchess. (3: 341)
>
> Taking away her Greek, she was as ignorant as a butterfly. (*Johnson & Burney*, 62 n. 2)
>
> No, no, always fly at the eagle! down with Mrs. Montagu herself! (Ibid. 71)
>
> In conversation you never get a system. (2: 361)
>
> No man is a hypocrite in his pleasures. (4: 316)
>
> All theory is against the freedom of the will; all experience for it. (3: 291)
>
> Questioning is not the mode of conversation among gentlemen. (2: 472)

> Madam, you are here, not for the love of virtue, but the fear of vice. (2: 435)

> Depend upon it, Sir, when a man knows he is to be hanged in a fortnight, it concentrates his mind wonderfully. (3: 167)

Johnson is, however, characteristically metaphoric in his conversation when he is describing a man or his work:

> Garrick's conversation is gay and grotesque. It is a dish of all sorts, but all good things. There is no solid meat in it: there is a want of sentiment in it. (2: 464)

> One species of wit he [Foote] has in an eminent degree, that of escape. You drive him into a corner with both hands; but he's gone, Sir, when you think you have got him—like an animal that jumps over your head. (3: 69)

"Goldsmith was a plant that flowered late" (3: 167); "Huggins has ball without powder, and Warton powder without ball" (4: 7); Gray's *Odes* are "forced plants raised in a hot-bed" (4: 13). Burke's "stream of mind is perpetual" (2: 450). When asked whether Derrick or Smart is the better poet, Johnson responds, "Sir, there is no settling the point of precedency between a louse and a flea" (4: 192–93). And of Boswell himself, Johnson, inspired by events before him, brands his companion indelibly:

> I teized him with fanciful apprehensions of unhappiness. A moth having fluttered round a candle, and burnt itself, he laid hold of this little incident to admonish me; saying, with a sly look, and in a solemn but quiet tone, "That creature was its own tormentor, and I believe its name was BOSWELL.' (1: 470)

> When we had landed, Dr. Johnson said, 'Boswell is now all alive. He is like Antaeus; he gets new vigour whenever he touches the ground.' (5: 309)

The other exceptional instance of "metaphorical exuberance in Johnson's discourse"[29] can be found in Mrs. Thrale's diary, *Thraliana*, where a radically different picture of Johnson is presented from the one we get in the *Life of Johnson*, and even from what we get in her *Anecdotes*, five-ninths of which is made of "227 separate fragments, taken from the matrix of the *Thraliana*, recombined, altered, and mixed with new matter."[30] The Johnson presented in *Thraliana* is a man of indefatigable conversational exuberance, of invigorating metaphoric ebullition. In the course of just the opening pages of her second volume Johnson calls money "Poyson" because "a small Quantity would often produce fatal Effects" (168); terms expense "a kind of Game wherein the Skilful Player catches and keeps what the unskilful suffers to slip out of his Hands" (168); suggests Murphy "displays more knowledge than he really has; like Gamesters who can play for more Money than they are worth" (169); says of Lady Cotton: "one no more thanks her for being sweet than one thanks a Honeycomb; it is her Nature and she cannot help it" (169); characterizes Lady Catherine Wynne "as like sower small beer" (169); compares Lady Macdonald to a dead nettle, for "were she alive She would sting" (169); and likens Mrs. Thrale to a rattlesnake, "for many have felt your Venom, few have escap'd your Attractions, and all the World knows you have the Rattle" (169). Of Peter King's mind he comments, "It is a Mind in which nothing has grown up of itself & where whatever has been transplanted—has degenerated" (169). Of Ralph Plumbe he quips, "Such people are like Cork'd Bottles you may put them into Water, if you will, & under Water, but they get no fuller" (170). A whimpering wife is like a "creaking door" (170). "Life is a Pill which cannot be swallowed without gilding" (180). "Ignorance to a rich man is like fat to a sick Sheep, it only serves to call the Rooks about him" (171). These examples are among many others.

Like Boswell, Mrs. Thrale was enamored of *ana*, and *Thraliana* began as a collection of *ana*—a miscellany of anecdotes, bons mots, witticisms, puns—whatever struck her fancy and memory. "It is many years since Doctor Samuel Johnson advised me to get a little Book and write in it all the little Anecdotes which might come to my Knowledge, all the Observations I might make or hear, all the Verses never likely to be published, and in fine ev'ry thing which struck me at the Time" (1). Thus, in Mrs. Thrale's section on Johnson, we have Johnson concentrated, condensed. Yet what accounts for the tour de force of his metaphors in *Thraliana*? One possible explanation is that Johnson plays to his audience, that he is metaphoric in mixed company and abstract in the company of men. The evidence in *Thraliana* above is substantiated in the *Life of Johnson*, where, as the conversations are predominately more male, they are proportionately less metaphoric.

Well aware of this, Boswell makes every effort in the *Life of Johnson* to compensate for that part of Johnson's conversation that is unembellished, unadorned by metaphor, as in the following examples. In the first quotation, Boswell revivifies and expands the dead metaphor in Johnson's criticism of Lord Bute. In the second, he picks up a buried metaphor ("calls forth all my powers") in Johnson's comment about Burke and presents its implications, makes it explicit:

> 'Lord Bute . . . took down too fast, without building up something new.' BOSWELL. 'Because, Sir, he found a rotten building. The political coach was drawn by a set of bad horses: it was necessary to change them.' JOHNSON. "But he should have changed them one by one." (2: 356)
>
> And once, when Johnson was ill, and unable to exert himself as much as usual without fatigue, Mr. Burke having been mentioned, he said, 'That fellow calls forth all my powers. Were I to see Burke now, it would kill me.' So much was he accustomed to consider conversation as a contest, and such was his notion of Burke as an opponent. (2: 450)

When Johnson is abstract, Boswell forces him into metaphor.

> JOHNSON. 'Sir, as a man advances in life, he gets what is better than admiration—judgement, to estimate things at their true value.' I still insisted that admiration was more pleasing than judgement, as love is more pleasing than friendship. The feeling of friendship is like that of being comfortably filled with roast beef; love, like being enlivened with champagne.
> JOHNSON. 'No, Sir; admiration and love are like being intoxicated with champagne; judgement and friendship like being enlivened." (2: 360)

At those times when Johnson is explicitly metaphoric, Boswell is more metaphoric.

> A gentleman attacked Garrick for being vain. JOHNSON. 'No wonder, Sir, that he is vain; a man who is perpetually flattered in every mode that can be conceived. So many bellows have blown the fire, that one wonders he is not by this time become a cinder.' BOSWELL. 'And such bellows too. Lord Mansfield with his cheeks like to burst: Lord Chatham like an Aeolus. I have read such notes from them to him, as

> were enough to turn his head.' JOHNSON. 'True. When he who every body else flatters, flatters me, I then am truly happy' (2: 227)

In the following instance Boswell expands Johnson's commonplace ("the tide of life"), not in the actual dialogue but in the text itself:

> When I expressed a wish to know more about Mr. Ballow, Johnson said, 'Sir, I have seen him but once these twenty years. The tide of life has driven us different ways.' I was sorry at the time to hear this; but whoever quits the creeks of private connections, and fairly gets into the great ocean of London, will, by imperceptible degrees, unavoidably experience such cessations of acquaintance. (3: 22)

One has the sense that in these rhythmic phrases Boswell's design is not just to make the text metaphoric, but to make himself Johnsonian. Almost from the time he first met Johnson he had been advising himself to "Be Johnson." The progress and extent to which Boswell makes himself "Johnson" in the *Life of Johnson* is of great thematic importance in coming to terms with the literary structure of the text. The preceding passage thus presents a wonderful dovetailing of Boswell's two motives in the *Life of Johnson*: through specific metaphor to make Johnson live and through imitation to take on the qualities of his subject and idol.

Boswell is so aware of the need for metaphor in the *Life of Johnson* that, as even a cursory reading reveals, he fills it with examples from letters, poems, and selections from works by Johnson himself. He amasses instances of metaphors for Johnson by other persons, of others playing his role by setting up a conceit for Johnson to develop, and of still others who take part in expanding Johnson's images. Mrs. Thrale, Reynolds, Scott, Paoli, and, in this final example, Mr. John Spottiswoode the younger, are among those who aggressively or unwittingly goad Johnson into metaphor:

> JOHNSON. 'Wine gives a man nothing. It neither gives him knowledge nor wit; it only animates a man, and enables him to bring out what a dread of company has repressed. It only puts in motion what has been locked up in frost. But this may be good, or it may be bad.' SPOTTISWOODE. 'So, Sir, wine is a key which opens a box; but this box may be either full or empty.' JOHNSON. 'Nay, Sir, conversation is the

> key: wine is a pick lock, which forces open the box and injures it.' (3: 327)

All the examples above suggest a dialectic at work, the mutual creation of metaphor. Part of the delight in reading the *Life of Johnson* is watching the formation of these collaborative tropes, the synthesis of antithetical minds. A particularly pure example of this can be seen in *The Journal of a Tour to the Hebrides*:

> *Johnson.* 'No, Sir; I never heard Burke make a good joke in my life.'—*Boswell.* 'But, sir, you will allow he is a hawk.'—Dr. Johnson, thinking that I meant this of his joking, said, 'No, sir, he is not the hawk there. He is the beetle in the mire.'—I still adhered to my metaphor,—'But he *soars* as the hawk.'—*Johnson.* 'Yes, sir, but he catches nothing.' (5: 213)

It is as if we are watching two comics indulging in a kind of intellectual vaudeville. Rhythmically the interchanges of Boswell and Johnson are indistinguishable from the rhythm of the classic comedy routine. The straight man's exasperation with his comic sidekick is familiar to devotees of Laurel and Hardy, Abbott and Costello, Gleason and Carney, Rowand and Martin, or, as Gordon Turnbull has suggested to me, Don Quixote and Sancho Panza.

> I will not be baited with *what* and *why*; what is this, what is that? why is a cow's tail long? why is a fox's tail bushy? . . .
>
> Why, Sir, you are so good, that I venture to trouble you.
> Sir, my being so *good* is no reason why you should be so *ill.* (3: 268)

The exchanges of Boswell and Johnson often culminate in these exasperated Johnsonian "punchlines." The "Yes, sir," "No, sir," "Why, sir" formulations punctuate the dialogue in exactly the same way as the parenthetical "Mr. Bones" interjection does in the vaudeville skit. It is no coincidence that the author of *Waiting for Godot* left unfinished at his death a play about Samuel Johnson. Samuel Beckett recognized the comic dialectic at the heart of the *Life of Johnson.*

This comic dialectic is also the grandest in the book, the one that pits Boswell, the champion of Fielding, passion, and wine, against Johnson, the defender of Richardson, reason, and tea.

Though this antithesis is provocative, it is ultimately superficial. Boswell is Johnson's antithesis in only a comic sense. In a more profound sense they are part and parcel of each other. Boswell is not being sentimental when he says that in the presence of Johnson he felt "elevated as if brought into another state of being" (2: 427). And Johnson is not being hyperbolic when he says, "Sir, if I were to lose Boswell, it would be a limb amputated" (4: 82 n. 3).

There are other dialectics at work in the *Life of Johnson.* William Dowling in *Language and Logos in Boswell's Life of Johnson* has discussed the competing worlds of the book, its levels of language, text, letters, prayers, talk . . . and its versions of Johnson, "the idealized and disembodied Johnson whom his readers imagine as a force behind the moral writings and the rough and uncouth Johnson whom they encounter in the actual surroundings of drawing room and tavern." In Dowling's words: "[the] principle of structure that guides my interpretation . . . is the principle of antithesis, or antithetical relations among the plurality of worlds contained in the *Life.* For it is not simply that the *Life* is a work radically discontinuous in its structure, or that its very discontinuities point unwaveringly to a plurality of worlds rather than a single world identical with its narrator's consciousness, but that these worlds exist in subversive or antagonistic relation to one another.[31]

Yet a dialectical relationship is as potentially synthetic as it is antithetical. In some sense the dialectical structures small and large throughout the *Life of Johnson* can be seen as the tenors and vehicles of a larger metaphoric relationship. The small specific metaphors throughout the text all point to the large metaphor which is the text. One might say, echoing Max Black, that Boswell and Johnson are the two terms in an "interaction metaphor."[32] Boswell "filters and transforms" (289) our view of Johnson just as the presence of Johnson filters and transforms our view of Boswell. The dialectical tension between Johnson and Boswell, between the tendency of the book to be abstract and its insistence on being concrete, is ultimately resolved in the happy synthesis of parts that is the work itself.

The *Life of Johnson* presents, simultaneously, two great truths, two ways of seeing the world—the world through concrete image and the world through abstract idea. We see Johnson through the lens of Boswell and we see Boswell behind the screen image of

Johnson, not alternately but simultaneously. This curious double vision is in part owing to the texture of metaphor in the book, Johnson's metaphors and Boswell's. But more important, it is due to the oxymoron of language itself, its spirit of abstraction and the will to metaphor.

If one stands back from the *Life of Johnson*, far enough away to be unable to discern the specific metaphors so carefully sewn into the fabric of the text, one half-glimpses the central metaphor of the work, Boswell's undying insight. What the *Life of Johnson* ultimately teaches us is that life *is* conversation, that the real vitality of living is not in action or production, but in communication, the social impulse as embodied in the meetings of the Literary Club or the late night chats with Johnson in Bolt Court; that as much as life is conversation, solitude and silence are death. Boswell's innate sense that required him to keep journals, to preserve conversation, to "embalm" himself for posterity, was the life force surging through him. The *Life of Johnson* asks that we oppose insulation, isolation, the ineffable loneliness of absolute silence with social discourse, intimate talk, the sheer implacability of speech itself.

Addison said, "A noble Metaphor, when it is placed to an Advantage, casts a kind of Glory round it, and darts a Lustre through a whole Sentence."[33] The *Life of Johnson* is such a noble metaphor and, as such, endures as a work of great art.

Notes

1. Hugh Blair, *Lectures on Rhetoric and Belles Lettres* (1783; New York, 1826), 158–59.

2. *The Hypochondriack: Being the Seventy Essays by the celebrated biographer, James Boswell, appearing in the London Magazine, from November, 1777, to August, 1783, and here first Reprinted*, ed. Margery Bailey, 2 vols. (Stanford: Stanford University Press, 1928), 2: 259.

3. See, for example, *Ominous Years* 133, 135; *Boswell in Extremes* 87, 158; *Applause* 108, 152, 229, 230; *Great Biographer* 86.

4. Because quotations in this essay are primarily from the *Life of Johnson*, citations to it will be made hereafter without title and by volume and page only, unless clarity demands otherwise. Volume 5 alludes to Boswell's published *Journal of a Tour to the Hebrides*, printed together with the Hill-Powell *Life* (see Cue Titles).

5. "The sentences that follow, about blowing out his breath like a

whale, as if he had made the argument of his opponents fly like chaff before the wind, first appear in the third edition." R.W. Chapman, "Boswell's Revises of the *Life of Johnson,*" in *Johnson & Boswell Revised by Themselves and Others: Three Essays by David Nichol Smith, R.W. Chapman and L.F. Powell* (Oxford: Clarendon Press, 1928), 35.

6. For Johnson as Hercules see also *Life* 1: 224, 3: 242, 5: 19.

7. Garrick calls him Diogenes (*Defence* 118).

8. John Gilbert Cooper, miscellaneous author.

9. See Ralph W. Rader's "Literary Form in Factual Narrative: The Example of Boswell's *Johnson,*" in *Essays in Eighteenth Century Biography,* ed. Philip B. Daghlian (Bloomington and London: Indiana University Press, 1968), 3–42.

10. William Siebenschuh, "Boswell makes his version of Johnson accessible to our imagination visually by hundreds of brilliant dramatic and descriptive touches; verbally, in the great conversational records; and dramatically, in the famous 'set pieces.'" "Dr. Johnson and Hodge the Cat: Small Moments and Great Pleasures in the *Life,*" in *Fresh Reflections on Samuel Johnson: Essays in Criticism,* ed. Prem Nath (Troy, N.Y.: Whitston Publishing, 1987), 388.

11. *The Autobiography of Johann Wolfgang von Goethe [Aus meinem Leben: Dichtung und Wahrheit],* trans. John Oxenford, 2 vols. (Chicago and London: The University of Chicago Press, Phoenix Books, 1974), 1: 244.

12. "Proverbs of Hell," in "The Marriage of Heaven and Hell," *The Poetry and Prose of William Blake,* ed. David V. Erdman (Garden City, N.Y.: Doubleday & Company, Inc., 1970), 35.

13. *Rasselas* "is a story that hangs motionless, suspended in debate by characters whose voices are virtually indistinguishable, and who sometimes forget which side of an argument they have taken." Steven Lynn, "Sexual Difference and Johnson's Brain," in Nath, 125.

14. James L. Clifford, *Dictionary Johnson: Samuel Johnson's Middle Years* (New York: McGraw-Hill Book Company, 1979), vii.

15. See Shenstone's letter of 9 February 1760 to Graves, quoted by Boswell. "I have lately been reading one or two volumes of *The Rambler*; who, excepting against some few hardnesses in his manner, and the want of more examples to enliven, is one of the most nervous, most perspicuous, most concise, most harmonious prose writers I know" (*Life* 2: 452–53).

16. *Lives of the English Poets,* ed. George Birkbeck Hill, 3 vols. (Oxford: Clarendon Press, 1905), 1: 21.

17. *Dr. Johnson & Fanny Burney: Being the Johnsonian Passages From the Works of Mme. D'Arblay,* introduction and notes by Chauncey Brewster Tinker (London: Andrew Melrose, 1912), 32.

18. *The Rambler,* ed. W.J. Bate and Albrecht B. Strauss, *The Yale Edition*

of the Works of Samuel Johnson, vols. 3–5 (New Haven and London: Yale University Press, 1969), 3: 258.

19. For this form in Blake compare "Exuberance is Beauty," "Opposition is true Friendship," "Energy is Eternal Delight" (*Poetry and Prose of William Blake* 37, 41, 34).

20. *The Philosophy of Rhetoric* (1936; New York: Oxford University Press, 1950), 100.

21. *The Eighteenth Century Philosophy of Metaphor* (Nashville: Joint University Libraries, 1945), 6.

22. Note the use of the word *hazard* here. The use of metaphor implies a risk, yet hints at reward. Herbert Read, *English Prose Style* (New York: Pantheon Books, 1952), 24.

23. Alexander Wedderburn. The Hill-Powell edition of the *Life of Johnson* cites Mrs. Piozzi's identification of him in her annotated 1816 edition (4: 179). Boswell identifies him only as "another law-Lord" (4: 178).

24. See W. Jackson Bate's *Samuel Johnson* (New York and London: Harcourt, Brace, Jovanovich, 1977). "Johnson's ordinary speech teemed with images, apt, pithy, and surprising. In his critical writings he repeatedly regrets the relative lack of original and forceful imagery in the poetry of his own time, and he uses the term 'image' more frequently and favorably than any other critic before the twentieth century" (285).

25. W.K. Wimsatt, *The Prose Style of Samuel Johnson* (New Haven: Yale University Press, 1941), 96; David Passler, *Time, Form and Style in Boswell's Life of Johnson* (New Haven: Yale University Press, 1971), 135 n.; Cecil S. Emden, "Dr. Johnson and Imagery," *Review of English Studies,* n. s., 1(1950): 23–38; Donald J. Greene, "'Pictures to the Mind': Johnson and Imagery," in *Johnson, Boswell and Their Circle: Essays Presented to Lawrence Fitzroy Powell in Honour of His Eighty-Fourth Birthday* (Oxford: Clarendon Press, 1965), 137–58; O.F. Christie, *Johnson the Essayist: His Opinions, Morals, and Manners: A Study* (1924; New York: Haskell House, 1966).

26. *Philosophic Words: A Study of Style and Meaning in the Rambler and the Dictionary of Samuel Johnson* (New Haven: Yale University Press, 1948), 66.

27. *The Stylistic Life of Samuel Johnson* (New Brunswick: Rutgers University Press, 1977), 14.

28. If one accepts Paul Korshin's recent argument ("Johnson's Conversation in Boswell's *Life of Johnson,*" in *New Light on Boswell,* 174–93) that this is a well-known and well-worn metaphor, a "proverbial statement" (176), we see a characteristic example of the way in which Johnson revivifies old metaphors. Johnson takes the cliché "to milk the bull" and expands its implications, makes it explicit, and reclaims the phrase for poetry. "Truth, Sir, is a cow which will yield such people no more milk."

That's Johnsonian in the best sense. See Donald Greene's comment, "Johnson often 'freshens' a cliché . . . by continuing the metaphor" ("'Pictures to the Mind': Johnson and Imagery," 144). William Wimsatt's comment about Johnson's imagery is also apropros here. "Perhaps this is the thing most characteristic of Johnson's 'imagery,' a tendency to reverse dead metaphors, to force them back to their etymological meaning so that they assume a new metaphorical life" (in this case the verb "to milk"; Wimsatt, *Prose Style,* 66). See also Bate's comment about the imagery in "The Vanity of Human Wishes." "What is typical of Johnson is that his imagination follows up and completes the rather conventional metaphor (torrent of fate) so that now man is pictured as actually rolling down it" (285).

29. Raman Selden, "Deconstructing the *Ramblers,*" in Nath, 279.

30. *Thraliana: The Diary of Mrs. Hester Lynch Thrale (later Mrs. Piozzi) 1776–1809,* ed. Katherine C. Balderston, 2 vols. (Oxford: Clarendon Press, 1942), 1: xxiii.

31. (Princeton: Princeton University Press, 1981), 149, xv–xvi.

32. Max Black, "Metaphor," *Proceedings of the Aristotelian Society* n. s., 55 (1955): 285. See also Black's extended discussion of the "interaction metaphor" as distinct from the "substitution view of metaphor" (the idea that "a metaphorical expression is used in place of some equivalent *literal* expression" [279]), or the "comparison view of metaphor" (the idea that "metaphor consists in the *presentation* of the underlying analogy of similarity" [283]), and his comment that "substitution-metaphors and comparison-metaphors can be replaced by literal translations . . . —by sacrificing some of the charm, vivacity, or wit of the original, but with no loss of *cognitive* content. But interaction-metaphors are not expendable" (292).

33. *The Spectator,* 3 July 1712, in *Addison and Steele: Selections from the Tatler and the Spectator,* 2d ed. (New York: Holt, Rinehart and Winston, Inc., 1957), 415.

"Over Him We Hang Vibrating": Uncertainty in the *Life of Johnson*

ISOBEL GRUNDY

Large in bulk, weighty in mass, definite in outline, such is by general assent Boswell's Johnson. Nothing could be more different from the shimmering, evanescent glimpses proffered in place of the old biographical certainties by Virginia Woolf and other modernist challengers of the givens of life-writing. Yet it appears that Woolf picked up from Boswell her favorite image of the biographer as ceaselessly in motion, ceaselessly expectant before the ceaselessly elusive truth. Boswell, after judiciously weighing the case for and against Savage, concludes "that the world must vibrate in a state of uncertainty as to what was the truth." Woolf, in a paragraph in *Jacob's Room* on that same state of uncertainty, elaborates: "something is always impelling one to hum vibrating, like the hawk moth, at the mouth of the cavern of mystery, endowing Jacob Flanders with all sorts of qualities he had not at all. . . . What remains is mostly a matter of guess work. Yet over him we hang vibrating."[1]

Boswell was constructing a permanent monument to a human landmark of literature; Woolf was midway in the first of her several works of fiction designed in part to suggest the impossibility of the biographer's project. The first observer of Jacob once he is out of childhood says, "Nobody sees any one as he is. . . . They see a whole—they see all sorts of things—they see themselves" (28–29). Yet the possibility that Woolf borrowed Boswell's "vibrate" invites some questions. Does Boswell the biographer hang vibrating? Does he express uncertainty over Johnson as he does over Savage, or find in Johnson the mystery which tantalizes, disturbs, and sometimes delights him in himself?[2] Does he confront, as Woolf so persistently does, the intrusions of guesswork, the tendency of the biographer to endow the subject with imaginary qualities, the problematics of identity? Does he perhaps not, after all, wholeheartedly seek (as most critics assume he does) to "explain" Johnson?

Let us first look at the evidence against these propositions. Woolf herself (true to her generation, which had not yet thought of Johnson as Boswell's hero or Boswell's fictional character) admired Boswell for his scrupulous observation of "truth of fact," his "astonishing power over us . . . based largely upon his obstinate veracity." By means of facts, she believed, Boswell's "genius" had "set free" Johnson's personality, and in this context (five years after writing *Jacob's Room*) she seemed not to question the wholeness and solidity of that personality. It is still the general consensus of scholars that Boswell ascribes to Johnson a "monumental stability of character."[3]

As a diarist, indeed, Woolf might have noted Boswell doing sometimes what she does regularly and piercingly herself: noting factual details of which the meanings or implications remain hauntingly unclear, observing the fluctuations of self. Her perceptions of an "incessant shower," a "myriad impressions" impinging on the mind, and of a single person's having "a great variety of selves," six or seven or as many thousand,[4] are foreshadowed in Boswell's diarizing, though they are perceived with reluctance: "I am vexed at such a distempered suggestion's being inserted in my journal, which I wished to contain a consistent picture. . . . It presents a strange and curious view of the unaccountable nature of the human mind. I am now well and gay. . . . I am now again set a-going (*London Journal* 205–6). Johnson's comments on diary-keeping expect such unaccountability: the "great thing to be recorded . . . is the state of your own mind . . . for it will not be the same a week afterwards" (*Life* 2: 217).

But such perceptions are nowhere suggested in Johnson's comments on life-writing. When he mentions the "volatile and evanescent" nature of "the incidents which give excellence to biography" he means nothing more than their tendency to disappear from the record. Woolf, indeed, sounds more like a descendant of Hume, who maintained that he was unable to discern any interior self apart from the perception of the moment, and that others too were "nothing but a bundle or collection of different perceptions . . . in a perpetual flux and movement," who found no answer to the question "Where am I, or what?" And the power of Hume's perceptions to disturb and upset Boswell is well known.[5]

So even the proponent of vibration finds certainty in Boswell. Boswell would have loved Woolf's phrase "obstinate veracity." His claims to this quality form a *leitmotif* in the *Life*, often sounded in unison with that of the inaccuracy of others (especially Sir John Hawkins and Hester Piozzi). Boswell claims not only to produce the truth ("a true and fair delineation"; "he will be seen as he really was"); he even claims to possess reliable methods of infallibly producing it.[6] These are attention to "minute particulars," a "nice perception which was necessary to mark the finer and less obvious parts of Johnson's character," generous infusions of the words of Johnson himself, and supplementing his own testimony with that of other Johnsonian intimates (1: 27–34; cf. 3: 209, 229–30). Some of these methods are precisely those queried by the narrator in *Jacob's Room*, who notes that the intimate friend's report reflects himself as much as his subject, and that of conversation, half "was too dull to repeat; much unintelligible (about unknown people and Parliament); what remains is mostly a matter of guess work" (72).

Boswell too is sensitive to the provisional nature of reports and guesses. But his sensitivity is generally that of a lawyer, ready to explode a dubious testimony only in order to substitute a more reliable one. He navigates delicately among differing degrees of authority, in a manner perhaps most noticeable when he treads the unstable ground of Johnson's early childhood. For instance, he clearly offers the toddling Sam Johnson's precocious "zeal for Sacheverel" as a construct first made by the proud father (whose interpretation of the child's behavior is introduced with "he believed," as if even he declined to be on oath) and then filtered through two intermediaries, Mary Adye's grandfather and Mary Adye herself (1: 38–39). Lucy Porter's authority for the duck story (derived, she said, from Johnson's mother) is made to bow to the authority of the adult Johnson, in the same way that, at a later period, suspect witnesses like Hawkins and Piozzi are made to bow to Boswell's "own knowledge" or to an "unquestionable authority" like Sir Joshua Reynolds (1: 40, 481).

In the matter of tracing chains of evidence Boswell is not infallible: he gives an imprimatur to another early anecdote, that of little Sam on his hands and knees reconnoitering the kennel, as coming from Johnson "himself, upon the authority of his mother," forgetting that she was not present but relied on the testimony of the schoolmistress. It is therefore necessary that three witnesses should each be reliable, in order for this story to escape the condition of volatility and evanescence (1: 39). Boswell was, nevertheless, a persevering questioner of witnesses, if not such a habitual questioner of the rules of evidence, or of the relation between truth and "the weight of common testimony," as Johnson himself (e.g., 1: 428; 2: 79).

Boswell takes Johnson's own authority for belief that a great mind does not fluctuate or waver, but makes consistent "progress" (1: 38). He credits Johnson with "inflexible dignity of character," with being incapable of a particular inconsistency (1: 131, 231). He sometimes ascribes motives, professing himself a reliable guide to the subjectivity of Johnson. He tells us, for instance, why Johnson founded the Ivy Lane Club while at work on the *Dictionary*: "His enlarged and lively mind could not be satisfied without more diversity of employment." He tells us what Johnson felt at the prospect of meeting Wilkes: he was positively abashed, though he "resolutely set himself" to go through with the meeting as a result of Boswell's skillful manipulation (1: 190; 3: 68).

Johnson's motives are again transparent on the occasion when he rephrases "a bottom of good sense" into "fundamentally sensible": "His pride could not bear that any expression of his should excite ridicule, when he did not intend it; he therefore resolved to assume and exercise despotick power."[7] Boswell finds no difficulty in reconciling Johnson's fear of death with his carelessness of danger: "his fear was from reflection; his courage natural." With similar confidence he interprets opinion: Johnson's prejudice against Scotland was without ill will, "of the head, and not of the heart"; his talk of the pleasure of cursing the House of Hanover was "most certainly, an affectation of more Jacobitism than he really had" (2: 298, 301; 1: 429).

Often, too, Boswell assumes a broad human universality which will give his readers as well as himself access to understanding Johnson. "We may easily conceive with what feeling a great mind like his" would utter the line "SLOW RISES WORTH. . . ." Any "man of clear judgement" will reject the idea that Johnson sought to damage Milton's reputation (1: 130, 231). Such explanations, like Pope's "clue," the ruling passion, are held to "unravel" difficulties of interpreting another's mind:[8] Johnson's "account of his reading, given by himself in plain words," at once "reconciles any seeming inconsistency [about his application or idleness] in his way of talking upon it at different times" (1: 446). Like Pope in a different context, it seems, Boswell professes to hold the clue to the maze.

Yet Boswell's very certainties imply uncertainties. These appeals to the universal and to the reconciliation of inconsistency occur in contexts of some doubt or dispute. When he asserts our understanding of the feelings expressed in "London," Boswell is confronting the discrepancy between Johnson's patriotic flag-waving of 1738 and his later, better-known attitudes, and seems to be hesitating over whether actually to allege that the neglect of which Johnson complains in the poem was something he had brought on himself by opposition or by apathy. When he preempts our judgment of Johnson's intentions over Milton, he is using Johnson's known, practical benevolence to the poet's granddaughter to prevent any suspicion that Johnson might have felt a Rochefoucauldian satisfaction in diminishing his great predecessor's reputation.

An even more marked uncertainty hangs over the issue of Johnson's alleged constitutional idleness. When Boswell asserts that Johnson's inconsistency on this topic is only "seeming," not real, he is covering over a resounding silence. He discusses Johnson's far-from-idle youth, his early, assiduous reading. He quotes the old gentleman at Oxford asserting that energy for study diminishes with age. In omitting to say anything about Johnson's self-castigations for *later* idleness, Boswell implies that the old gentleman is refuted by mention of the vivacity of Johnson's later works. But this is no refutation: according to Johnson's own comments on the use of time, he might well have been generally idle, yet produced lively writings. We may suspect the biographer, who has given hostages to fortune undreamed of by the novelist, of being ready to claim a factitious certainty of interpretation, so that any unsolved mysteries or dilemmas of understanding are to be resolved not by his text but by his exclusions, his silences.

In each of these cases ("Slow rises worth," Lauder's allegations against Milton, Johnson's assiduity or otherwise in studying) there exists an option of reading Johnson's behavior as having an irrational, a self-damaging, or a culpable aspect. In each case Boswell, by implication, closes off this option. Writing of the year 1763, he seems unwilling to reveal the "idleness" of the elderly Johnson which, when he comes to his narrative of Johnson's later years, he will in due course acknowledge. Boswell's "any man of clear judgement" makes an appeal to us, the jury in the Milton case, to find Johnson "distinguished for ardent curiosity and love of truth" as well as for magnanimity in this particular case; when he quotes Johnson's own words on the subject he treats them as those of a star witness: "Is this the language of one who wished to blast the laurels of Milton?" (1: 231).

It seems therefore that Boswell sometimes asserts the consistency and stability of his subject as part of a process of defence against not only the accusation of, but the perceived possibility of, inconsistency or confusion. At other times such possibilities apparently find him more nearly "capable of being in uncertainties, Mysteries, doubts, without any irritable reaching after fact & reason."[9] In several instances where Johnson's behavior is hard to read, he refrains from over-determination. When, in a *reprise* of the idleness discussion, he expresses his wonder that Johnson does not find "more pleasure in writing than in not writing," this draws down on him the repressive "Sir, you *may* wonder" (2: 15). Boswell neither glosses, mitigates, nor attempts to soften this, but leaves his reader, in turn, wondering or vibrating.

Permitted areas of uncertainty begin, then, to appear in the *Life*. About some aspects of his friend Boswell is content to report, to hazard a guess, without fully explaining. On Johnson's physical eccentricities he leaves the field wide open for more recent speculation. The same is true of the sources of Johnson's mental unhappiness and the way it fluctuates from day to day or year to year, if only because Boswell's linking of it with sexual irregularity is withheld until a stage when it appears as it is—a construct appealing to would-be explainers. Johnson's extreme unpredictability in social relations causes ripples of discomfort on the surface of the *Life*, but the more closely Boswell is involved in such incidents the more likely he is to resist the impulse of irritable reaching for fact and reason. Rather than explanation, his preferred technique is to delimit the unsettling effects of such moments by labelling them slight or trivial.

It is a commonplace that Boswell depicts Johnson, as he knew him, only in middle and old age. It has been less recognized that the last quarter or third of the *Life* reads like nothing less than a study of old age, of a massive intellect and formidable personality undergoing irregular but inexorable dilapidation. Boswell's Johnson is far from static, but exists and changes inside a context of time. It is not just because Boswell is so often cited in bite-sized pieces that gradual process is not immediately obvious, but because his method, like Woolf's, proceeds by small accretions. Nevertheless, the last few years of the *Life* trace a gradual decline in which any existing certainties are eroded. Johnson is more frequently unaccountable than before. The instances of his rudeness or savagery in conversational debate become steadily more outrageous, suggesting an increasing problem with self-control, a spread or seepage of the area of Johnson's behavior governed not by reason but by chance associations and displaced rages. It is inconceivable that Boswell the respectful acolyte could have offered the kind of explanation for Johnson's vagaries that Johnson offered for those of Polonius; yet he leaves this interpretation open to his readers.

In weaving into the *Life* a thread of close attention to his own relation with Johnson, Boswell reverted to a topic—himself—on which he was accustomed to interrogate detail, to doubt identity, to hold contradictions in close juxtaposition. His probing of his own behavior in interaction with Johnson is the source of much that is tentative, suggestive rather than stated, in his biographical portrait—paradoxically, since his own need is clearly implicated in the degree to which he makes Johnson monolithic or ever-fixed. His book charts an ongoing, shifting relation of biographer to subject, as well as a now-completed relation of younger man to mentor. The sifting of testimony, an appropriate and necessary technique for Johnson's past and hidden years, involves faith that testimony can deliver truth, and that anecdotes are meaningful. As the mimetic treatment of talk and human contacts gradually takes over from the sifting of testimony, we are asked to believe that talk encapsulates character. As representations of Johnson through his talk begin to be joined by emblematic moments (Johnson in a coach, Johnson at a waterfall), we are increasingly asked to contemplate images of Johnson in poses we cannot read.

No more than Johnson's other friends did Boswell ever venture "to ask an explanation" of the weird "particularity" of apparently obsessive ritual movements and countings or mutterings. In a first attempt at reporting these peculiarities, in his *Journal of a Tour to the Hebrides*, he lumped them together with habits of dress and fondness for fresh air, hazarded the half-explanation of "mere habits, contracted by chance," and appealed to the non-threatening commonplace that studious persons habitually talk to themselves (5: 306). In writing up the *Life* for the year 1764 he expands the report of eccentricity: "It appeared to me some superstitious habit, which he had contracted early, and from which he had never called upon his reason to disentangle him" (1: 484). He marks each of these accounts with his own uncertainty: "I suppose," "I conjecture." The second time around in the *Life*, he comes closer to admitting authorial unease by dropping the ideas of chance and of mere scholarly absentmindedness, adding the ideas of superstition and of involuntary entanglement, or evoking the grim force of Johnson's depiction of habit in, for instance, "The Vision of Theodore."[10]

Admitting unease cannot be equated with admitting mystery, but the two are related. The publication of Johnson's *Prayers and Meditations* by George Strahan in 1785 meant that to the first readers of the *Life* his inner unhappiness was already "certainly known." Speculation suggests that Boswell may have been saved from some fabulation or fabrication by Johnson's truth-telling in these private pages; as it was, he attempted to guide reader response to their revelations (and to minimize the suggestion of inconsistency) by insisting that "every generous and grateful heart . . . must respect that dignity of character which prevented him from complaining" (2: 66–67). It becomes Boswell's task, in another adaptation from Pope,[11] to demonstrate that discord is harmony misunderstood, and partial evil is universal good. He attempts to enforce these beliefs both by establishing a relation between Johnson's legible surface and his murky depths, and by his own steady disposition toward generous respect.

When, for instance, Johnson admits turning his thoughts "with a very useless earnestness upon past incidents," the biographer notes the "philosophick heroism" of assuming an appearance of "manly fortitude to the world, while he was inwardly so distressed" (2: 190). Strength is discovered in weakness. Since, however, Boswell does not speculate as to the past incidents that induced such guilt and pain, mystery tacitly remains. A similar, perhaps unconscious use of openness for purposes of concealment occurs when

Boswell, agonizing in public as to how much he should reveal about Johnson's sexual irregularities, writes that his reason for mentioning them at all is that they account for Johnson's fear to die (4: 396–98). That is, he declines to ask either of two potentially destabilizing questions: whether such irregularities (of a highly conventional kind) indeed took place, or whether they would adequately explain such fear of death.

Boswell is not innocent of over-simplification about other people, particularly those divided from him by obvious markers like class, race, or gender. He routinely uses the tag "Francis Barber, his faithful negro servant" (2: 62); he boils down Hester Thrale's motives for years of assiduous attention to Johnson to the simplistic summary, "her vanity" (4: 157). (*She* related that her feelings for Johnson ran the gamut from "Veneration . . . reverence . . . delight" to "habitual endurance of a yoke.")[12] But Boswell spares Johnson such reach-me-down summations.

Sometimes his explanatory urge, focusing on others, seems by that very means to leave Johnson himself unexplained. For instance, in a conversation of 7 May 1773, Boswell unhesitatingly professes to read Goldsmith's wish to shine, his disappointment, and his resulting envy and spleen. He reads, too, Goldsmith's misreading: his taking Johnson's inattention as contempt. But in relating the quarrel that followed on Goldsmith's transparent behaviors (and in relating its aftermath) he offers no reading whatever of Johnson's feelings or motives (2: 253–56). When he writes (apropos bringing Johnson and Wilkes together) of "that intellectual chymistry, which can separate good qualities from evil in the same person" (3: 65), he presumably locates such compounds in Wilkes exclusively: Johnson must not become a mixed character to this event.

Yet even interpretations of motive may be proffered with some hesitancy. Boswell cannot explain Johnson's hatred of having his birthday noticed, "unless it were" as a reminder of approaching death (3: 157). He often gives several alternative possible explanations: for Johnson's "unaccountable caprice" in rejecting his offer to produce Lord Marchmont as a source of information about Pope; for his refusal to be ruffled at a report that he was taking dancing lessons; for a hyperbolic statement of his own internal contradictions: "Alas! it [his liveliness and brilliance] is all outside; I may be cracking my joke, and cursing the sun. *Sun, how I hate thy beams*!" Faced with Johnson's self-identification with Milton's Satan cursing the sun, Boswell admits "I knew not well what to think of this declaration," before hazarding some guesses. In the cases of Lord Marchmont and of the dancing lessons, some of the guess-work motives are to Johnson's credit and some are not; over the dancing as well as over the parallel with Satan, jesting complicates the issue.[13] Especially in Johnson's closing years, his religious pronouncements, in talk or in his journal, often "seem to imply" readings which Boswell nevertheless chooses to leave open (4: 122, 139, 272). On one occasion he alludes to the temerity inseparable from speaking for another when he pronounces himself "as certain as I can be of any man's real sentiments" how Johnson felt (4: 55).[14]

Sometimes, indeed, Boswell confesses himself baffled as freely as does Woolf, or Woolf's narrator. One famous example is the occasion on which Robert Chambers's drawing up a will for Bennet Langton provoked from Johnson an outburst of fantastical jokes, culminating in the excess of paroxysmic midnight laughter in the open street by Temple Bar (2: 260–63). Boswell explicitly traces the source of the fun to Johnson's zeal for male succession, in opposition to Langton's "devising his estate to his three sisters, in preference to a remote heir male." But even this is far from certain: within three years Johnson was to send Boswell a letter which on balance supports inheritance by females (2: 416–18). The *Life* recognizes the disproportion of the laughter to any assignable cause. It seems quite probable (since Johnson was "very ill" at the time, and grumpy about receiving medical advice) that he was painfully amused at Langton's and Chamber's shortsighted enjoyment of the death-related activity of will-making; but this too is speculation. Boswell persists in classing the incident as among "the slightest occasional characteristicks" of Johnson, but he makes his perturbation open and clear.[15]

Boswell offers few guideposts as to how far Johnson's psychic or emotional state varied from time to time; such guideposts do not seem to be part of his plan. At Ashbourne for a visit, Johnson is "more uniformly social, cheerful, and alert, than I had almost ever seen him" (3: 189); but does this reflect fondness for John Taylor? for the country? for being looked after? or some other cause? This visit included another emotional reaction as unreadable as that at Temple Bar: it was odd that Johnson should take delight in clearing an artificial cascade of unsavory rubbish, odder still when the rubbish contained a large dead cat (Boswell had experienced, and suffered from, Johnson's love of cats). As with the laughter at Temple Bar, Boswell takes refuge in presenting the inexplicable as the "trifling," which nevertheless will be pleasing to "true, candid warm admirers of Johnson" (3: 190–91).

Similarly, he relates without either linking or contrasting them those occasions (only a week apart) when Johnson denies that anyone can be happy in the present moment without being drunk, and then experiences "such good spirits, that every thing seemed to please him as we drove along." A conversation nearly a year later suggests that the possible connection had not escaped Boswell (2: 350–51, 361, 3: 5). He makes no comment on another puzzling sequence involving use of, and attitudes towards, alcohol. Over a couple of days during a period of abstention from alcohol (28–29 April 1778), Johnson gave his reasons for drinking as "To get rid of myself, to send myself away." He then repeatedly harangues others against drink, sometimes with personal accusations of drunkenness (3: 329, 335). When, three years later (28 March 1781), we meet Johnson as a drinker once more, Boswell refrains from using this as a possible clue to change in his emotional state. In his portrait, Boswell comments at this point on Johnson's doing things by extremes, never with moderation (4: 72); in private, he was "delighted" to see Johnson more cheerful. But he does not speculate about implications for reading Johnson's emotional vagaries.[16]

Comparative reticence about Johnson's inner life does not extend to Boswell's own. His claims to objectivity in principle are matched by candid revelations of his actual subjectivity.[17] Early in his acquaintance with Johnson his own response becomes a topic in the *Life*: not only the qualities of Johnson's talk, but also the "orthodox high-church sound of the MITRE,—the figure and manner of the celebrated SAMUEL JOHNSON . . . and the pride arising from finding myself admitted as his companion," contributed to producing "a variety of sensations, and a pleasing elevation of mind beyond what I had ever before experienced." His record of that evening, he says, is hopelessly inadequate to the reality (1: 401); indeed, the imperfection of his record of Johnson is directly attributable in part to his being "wrapt in admiration of his extraordinary colloquial talents" (1: 421). Years later, a day in May 1781 remembered as "placid," and another (20 April 1781) described as "one of the happiest days that I remember to have enjoyed in the whole course of my life," whose "general effect . . . dwells upon my mind in fond remembrance," are equally unproductive of verbal record (4: 110, 96).

To this extent Boswell, like Woolf, constructs a fallible observer. Paradoxically, his candor about his own unsteadiness opens for his readers an opportunity to question the steadiness he attributes to Johnson. "I complained of a wretched changefulness," he writes of the Ashbourne visit. "It was most comfortable to me to experience, in Dr. Johnson's company, a relief from this uneasiness. His steady vigorous mind held firm before me those objects which my own feeble and tremulous imagination" presented waveringly (3: 193). But this apparent use of Johnson's solidity to "anchor and stabilize his own flickering sense of reality"[18] is recorded under the same date (22 Sept. 1777) as an unusual confession from the steady and mentally vigorous Johnson: of his hypochondria, his being not "the same one day as another" (3: 192). Again, if Boswell does not reveal puzzlement, he reveals grounds for puzzlement. On the following evening he relates a series of wild fluctuations in his feelings about Johnson, from intense and sentimentally devoted reverence and protectiveness (under the influence of music), through enjoyment of philosophic calm, through the urge to contradict him (though "with all deference"),[19] through a quarrel which is violently agitating to Johnson as well as Boswell, to eventual reconciliation (3: 198–207).

From this it appears not only that Boswell's construction of Johnson as stable and venerable is connected with his construction of himself as wretchedly changeable and unworthy of respect; but also that his awe and veneration are liable to slippage into revolt (as would be only normal according to Johnson's views on human reluctance to admit inferiority),[20] or into attack on Johnson's stability which can only be expressed by contradiction of his statements. The motives Boswell exposes in himself *are* volatile and evanescent: intense feeling has a natural tendency to reverse into its opposite.

He recognizes the principle of resistance, reaction, or cussedness as shaping his own behavior, though he prefers not to identify it in Johnson's. When he attains a state of ease, relaxation, and equality with Johnson, as he does on 30 March 1778, he reacts against it. "I missed that aweful reverence with which I used to contemplate MR. SAMUEL JOHNSON, in the complex magnitude of his literary, moral, and religious character. I have a wonderful superstitious love of *mystery*; when, perhaps, the truth is, that it is owing to the cloudy darkness of my own mind" (3: 225). He condemns this inconsistency of his own as foolish and immature; but in the *Life*, though not in the original journal, he acknowledges it anyway.[21]

Johnson's behavior as Boswell describes it would often be susceptible to a similar reading. Indeed, Boswell brings himself to follow Joshua Reynolds's lead in amusement at one instance: when Johnson begs to be told his faults and then flies into a passion at the telling: "a penitent . . . belabour[ing] his confessor" (4: 281). But more characteristically he depicts Johnson's irrationalities without so calling them, leaving the reader to vibrate between awe and amusement, sympathy and condemnation. A terrifying and apparently inexplicable outburst of rage against Americans (15 April 1778) follows on Johnson's contradicting Mary Knowles (a highly articulate Quaker) about the equality of women, talking with her of death, then magisterially endorsing her views on John the beloved disciple (3: 286–90). It is plausible that Johnson's former stance of antagonism, repressed out of politeness or gallantry, returned under stormier guise; indeed, mildness and violence continued to alternate during the whole evening, a dozen pages of the *Life*. In the same manner, Johnson, having gone out of his way on 12 April 1778 to repair breaches and maintain appearances in the presence of a potential patron of his friend Thomas Percy, falls into "intemperate vehemence of abuse" against Americans on the reappearance six days later of the patron figure. On Boswell, who attempts to restrain him, he executes a delayed revenge which seems to Boswell bewilderingly unprovoked (3: 275, 315–16). It is tempting to suppose that the Americans have twice served as scapegoats: that the astonishing rage might be accounted for, but could not be made to appear rational; that we are left vibrating to prevent our opinion fixing itself in condemnation of Johnson.

The emotional involvement which makes Boswell willing to tolerate such behavior when directed against himself makes him also willing to expose it, to delineate it scrupulously as part of their ongoing relationship. This he is increasingly willing to do in Johnson's last few years. But rather than calling Johnson irrational, unstable, or unpredictable (though he comes close to it once or twice), he prefers to use an aggrandizing imagery of thunder and tropical storms (e.g., 3: 345, 315). In recounting another falling-out with his mentor, on 2 May 1778, he names his own anger, vexation, and hurt pride, but does not identify Johnson's conflicted feelings, though he assigns a feeble enough motive: desire for more attention than he was getting. It is as if he averts his eyes while exposing the patriarch's nakedness (3: 337). A Johnson who cannot be wholly approved cannot be investigated, though when Boswell judges himself culpable (he was drunk and pressing Johnson to discuss sexual fantasies), Johnson's feelings "may easily be conceived" (4: 109).

The later stages of the *Life* make increasing though usually muted reference to inconsistencies and mysteries of Johnson's. He shows "the heterogeneous composition of human nature" in admitting (for all his acclaimed liberality to those in distress) that he too is "occasionally troubled with a fit of *narrowness*" (4: 191). When Boswell praises Johnson's old college friend Edwards for readiness to talk, he notes that Johnson lacks this quality (3: 307). He sees himself as having regularly "ventured to dissipate the cloud, to unveil the mystery" of Johnson, though he attaches this boast to Johnson's trivial concealment of daily details, not to his more suggestive (and then recent) remark that no one can "be sure he is wise, or that he has any other excellence" (3:323–25). He places under Johnson's last year the story from an earlier date of his indignantly rejecting the notion that his fellow Club members are familiar with his mind: "Sir, you have not travelled over *my* mind, I promise you" (4: 183).

Also noticeable during the final years of the *Life* are instances of a novelistic technique: the vignette or visual image, in which appearance replaces utterance. In these glimpses the unreadable exterior stands in for the subjectivity of the other, but in doing so emphasizes the significance of that identity which must be assumed because, though it can be loved, it cannot be known. Johnson is seen as opaque and other, as he was at Temple Bar. The technique is central in Woolf's art, mimicking an operation of the mind that Johnson had memorably described in "Yet still he fills affection's eye."[22]

Of this kind is the scene Boswell observes on returning to a room left untenanted except for Johnson talking with John Wilkes "literally *tete-a-tete*; for they were reclined upon their chairs, with their heads leaning almost close to each other, and talking earnestly, in a kind of confidential whisper" (4: 107). The topic they have reached in conversation is then mentioned; but, by first making his reader share the sense of exclusion that comes to an intruder on a *tête-à-tête*, Boswell offers a reminder how much remains unshared. What insights may we and he have just missed!

Johnson is similarly, tantalizingly, present and not present in his own astonishing fantasy of himself fallen on hard times: "I should like to come and have a cottage in your park, toddle about, live mostly on milk, and be taken care of by Mrs. Boswell" (4: 226). This idea pictures a region of Johnson's mind seldom or never travelled. Boswell gives it its elusive, haunting shape by a sleight of hand suggestive of the novelist rather than the biographer. His journal shows that for this intense imaginative rendering of Johnson as older than he was ever in fact to become, the biographer fused two separate ideas which Johnson floated in conversation: of himself turning to Boswell for accommodation, and of himself decrepit and dependent (*Applause* 152). The sharply unified image is a joint creation of Johnson and his friend.

It is matched by a vignette which bears the superadded coloring of finality: Johnson "without looking back, sprung away with a kind of pathetick briskness, if I may use that expression, which seemed to indicate a struggle to conceal uneasiness, and impressed me with a foreboding of our long, long separation" (4: 339). Here Johnson moves beyond the ken of the biography, which catches itself in the very act of fabricating interiority for him, since communication is denied by his movement into solitude. Boswell could find only banal words ("venerably pious") for the solitary Johnson he never saw, writing in the summer house at Streatham (4: 135). Into such domestic privacy the biographer cannot, as *Rambler* 60 had suggested, follow his subject. When Johnson moves beyond his vision on this last occasion, he chooses to reflect a sense of his own limitation which brings him very close to the novelist of *Jacob's Room*, recording her "sudden vision that the young man in the chair is of all things in the world the most real, the most solid, the best known to us—why indeed?—For the moment after we know nothing about him" (70–71).

The *Life* as a whole moves steadily—consistently?—toward its peroration, Boswell's "character" of Johnson (4: 426–30). This, when it comes, squarely confesses Johnson's inconsistency: "At different times, he seemed a different man." Then it backpedals ("in some respects; not, however, in any great or essential article") and tries to limit the inconsistency to matters not of behavior but only of opinion and mood. The whole "character" is positioned under the umbrella of service to a universal truth: it opens, "Man is, in general, made up of contradictory qualities." About what is implied by these contradictions, Boswell himself enters immediately into contradiction. They may be suppressed, if not eradicated, "by long habits of philosophical discipline" (such as one might expect Johnson to have built up); but they are more prominent when combined with "native vigour of the mind" (4: 426). Johnson's inconsistency, then, seems to be a victory for nature over nurture.

Johnson's enduring, reliable qualities as the "character" presents them are exactly those which the body of the *Life* has returned to again and again in particular instances. He is sceptical yet prejudiced, "hard to please, and easily offended . . . but of a most humane and benevolent heart"; he is melancholy, yet fond of flattery, usually grave, yet given to frequent merriment, cantankerous in talk yet pious in his writings, uniting "a most logical head with a most fertile imagination." Even without reading the *Life*, a reader of the "character" alone might anticipate the kinds of baffling contrarieties which Johnson exhibits in the biography. In his conclusion Boswell continues consistently to hold a delicate balance between the constant and the contradictory.[23]

As a man of the Enlightenment, he would be shocked at the modern novelist's profession of inability to know, her embrace of the fleeting. If Johnson is contradictory, a Johnsonian adage is trustworthy; if Johnson cannot be relied on not to change, permanent truth can subsume the impressions of particular moments. Still, Boswell's obstinate veracity has allowed contradiction to prevail: he has brought himself to follow Shakespeare in converting his hero into a changeable, timeworn man.

Notes

1. *Life* 1: 174; Woolf, *Jacob's Room* (London: Hogarth, 1922, repr. 1980), 72. Boswell later remarks that Johnson exemplifies "that vibration between pious resolutions and indolence, which many of us have too often experienced" (3: 401). William R. Siebenschuh makes Boswell and

Woolf *almost* meet (*Fictional Techniques and Factual Works* [Athens: University of Georgia Press, 1983], 4); Catherine N. Parke brings Woolf together both with Boswell and with Johnson as biographer ("'The Hero Being Dead': Evasive Explanation in Biography [The Case of Boswell]," *Philological Quarterly* 68 [1989]: 346; *Samuel Johnson and Biographical Thinking* [Columbia and London: University of Missouri Press, 1991], 132–34).

2. E.g., "Was I then the very Boswell whose history you know?" (Boswell to Temple, 23 July 1764, *Grand Tour I* 36). "There is no accounting for our feelings, but certain it is that what strikes us strongly at one time will have little influence at another" (31 Dec. 1775, *Ominous Years* 207–8). William C. Dowling discusses Boswell's "need for mystery" in *The Boswellian Hero* (Athens: University of Georgia Press, 1979), 118, 121; and Felicity A. Nussbaum provides a useful analysis of Boswell's struggle to contain the flux of "serial identity" in *The Autobiographical Subject: Gender and Ideology in Eighteenth-Century England* (Baltimore and London: Johns Hopkins University Press, 1989), 107ff.

3. Woolf, "The New Biography," *New York Herald Tribune* (30 Oct. 1927), repr. in *Granite and Rainbow* (London: Hogarth, 1958), 150–52, 154–55; "The Art of Biography," *Atlantic Monthly* (April 1939), repr. in *The Death of the Moth* (London: Hogarth, 1942), 187–97. Cf. Liisa Saariluoma, "The Biographical Mode in the Novels of Virginia Woolf," *Orbis Litterarum* 45 (1990): 169–88; Gordon Turnbull, "Boswell and Sympathy: The Trial and Execution of John Reid," in *New Light on Boswell*, 105.

4. Woolf, "Modern Fiction" (revised from a *TLS* article of 1919), in *The Common Reader, First Series*, 1925, ed. Andrew McNeillie (London: Hogarth, 1984), 150; *Orlando, A Biography* (London: Hogarth, 1928, repr. 1978), 278.

5. *Rambler* 60, ed. W.J. Bate and Albrecht B. Strauss (New Haven and London: Yale University Press, 1969), 1: 323; David Hume, *A Treatise of Human Nature*, 1739–40, ed. Ernest C. Mossner (Penguin: Harmondsworth, 1969), 300, 316; e.g. Susan Manning, "'This Philosophical Melancholy': Style and Self in Boswell and Hume," in *New Light on Boswell*, 126–40.

6. Cf. Greg Clingham, "Truth and Artifice in Boswell's *Life of Johnson*, in *New Light on Boswell*, 207–29.

7. *Life* 4: 99. In his journal Boswell was less certain: "Then, I believe, choosing a still more ludicrous word, and looking awful to show his power of restraint over us" (*Laird* 328–29).

8. "Epistle to Lord Cobham, Of the Knowledge and Characters of Men," 1733, 1: 178.

9. John Keats to George and Thomas Keats, 21 Dec. 1817, *Letters*, ed. Hyder Edward Rollins, 2 vols. (Cambridge, Mass.: Harvard University

Press, 1958), 1: 193. Boswell critics have shown an understandable interest in explaining Boswell, establishing fact and reason. Most read Boswell as defensive of Johnson: e.g., George Mallory, *Boswell the Biographer* (London: Smith, Elder, 1912), 234–35; Siebenschuh, *Form and Purpose in Boswell's Biographical Works* (Berkeley, Los Angeles, London: University of California Press, 1972), 51–77, and Ralph W. Rader sees his defences as enforcing his own unifying, internalized idea of Johnson ("Literary Form in Factual Narrative," in *New Questions, New Answers*), 30, 33–34. Marshall Waingrow noted his "pattern of suppression" regarding Johnson's various weaknesses, and that the suppression is always incomplete (*Corr: Life* xxxvi). Maaja A. Stewart sees Boswell as "controlling and formulating the facts of his subject's life to match his own desires. . . . Boswell has appropriated Johnson" ("Nabokov's *Pale Fire* and Boswell's Johnson," *Texas Studies in Literature and Language* 30 [1988], 231). Nussbaum reads him as "display[ing] the contradictions of identity within a vision of a coherent and fully comprehensible character" (117). Unusually, Philip Davis sees him as "asking: Who, what was Johnson" (*In Mind of Johnson, A Study of Johnson the Rambler* [Athens: University of Georgia Press, 1989], 43).

10. *Rasselas and Other Tales,* ed. Gwin J. Kolb (New Haven and London: Yale University Press, 1990), 206–12.

11. *An Essay on Man* (1733), 1: 291–92.

12. Hester Lynch Piozzi, *Anecdotes of Samuel Johnson,* ed. Arthur Sherbo (London: Oxford University Press, 1974), 156.

13. *Life* 3: 344–45, 4: 79–80, 304. The subtext to the first occasion may be Johnson's suspicion of what Boswell apparently concealed: Marchmont's initial anti-Johnsonian stance (*Boswell in Extremes* 335–36).

14. A contemporary critic calls refusal to speak for another "implicit acknowledgment of the dangers of assuming an essential human . . . psyche and of divorcing the psyche's construction from its historical moment" (Jo-Ann Wallace, review of Lorelei Cederstrom, *Fine-Tuning the Feminine Psyche, English Studies in Canada* 17 (1991): 240.

15. Noted by Siebenschuh (*Fictional Techniques* 94–96) and others.

16. *Laird* 297.

17. Parke maintains that Boswell makes a place for himself in relation to his subject "by moving that subject slightly to one side" ("The Hero Being Dead," 345).

18. Stewart, "Nabokov's *Pale Fire* and Boswell's Johnson," 236.

19. In editorial asides in the *Life* Boswell freely and frequently contradicts a Johnson who is no longer able to overpower him: e.g., on Frederick the Great (1: 435), on the proper management of servants (1: 436), on Rousseau (2: 12), on Richardson and Fielding (2: 49, 175), on learning in women (2: 76), on moral standards in clergymen (2: 172), on Robertson's history ("it is not easy to suppose, that he should so widely

differ from the rest of the literary world," 2: 238), and on Hamilton of Bangor's poems ("I comforted myself with thinking that the beauties were too delicate for his robust perceptions," 3: 151). He remains "confident that I was in the right" in an argument over the feasibility of a cheerful old age, in which he has unwittingly paraphrased both Gulliver's rhapsody on first hearing about, but not *all* about, the Struldbrugs, and the mistaken interlocutor of Johnson's great tragic poem (*Life* 3: 337; Swift, *Gulliver's Travels* [1726], III. x; "The Vanity of Human Wishes," *Poems,* ed. E.L. McAdam with George Milne (New Haven and London: Yale University Press, 1964), 105.

20. See Isobel Grundy, *Samuel Johnson and the Scale of Greatness* (Athens: Georgia University Press, 1986), 184–85.

21. The journal has him wholly satisfied, contradicting Pope's "Man never is, but always to be blest" (*Boswell in Extremes* 229–31).

22. "On the Death of Dr. Robert Levet," line 9, *Poems,* ed. McAdam with Milne.

23. I owe this point to Professor Gwin J. Kolb.

Pilgrimage and Autonomy: The Visit to Ashbourne

JOHN B. RADNER

Between 14 September and 24 September in 1777, after months of advance planning in letters, James Boswell visited Samuel Johnson at John Taylor's house in Ashbourne. Johnson wrote briefly about the visit in the nine letters he sent Mrs. Thrale between 8 and 29 September and in a few journal entries that collectively fill about one page. Boswell described his time with Johnson in the relatively full journal he wrote partly at Ashbourne but mostly the next month in Edinburgh and Auchinleck, and he also included some material on the visit in the separate notebook he began using in 1776 for data concerning Johnson's early life.[1] Later Boswell transformed the carefully written Ashbourne journal into a significant section of the *Life of Johnson*, making numerous small cuts and additions, changing individual words or phrases, and also adding substantially from his notebook, from other sources, from memory, and from his feelings as he reviewed all his material. Most of the changes, along with Boswell's careful placing of this visit within his larger narrative, help prepare for the significant shift in his relationship with Johnson from reverential awe to poised judgment that Boswell described in his journal entry for 20 March 1778. On that date, the first evening he spent with Johnson after the Ashbourne visit, he first notes that "We were quite easy, quite as companions tonight," and then regrets the absence of "that awful reverence with which I used to contemplate MR. SAMUEL JOHNSON, in the complex magnitude of his literary, moral, and religious character" (*Boswell in Extremes* 225).

When Boswell told Johnson on 20 September 1777 "that I was not now afraid of him, but I had an awe of him which made me happier in his company," or two weeks later when he wrote the entry for 20 September and noted that "I felt this [awe] at the time" (169), Boswell did not know that his awe would soon disappear, that on 20 March 1778 he would "view Dr. Johnson with a steadier and clearer eye" (225). Later Boswell saw this as an important event in his personal life and in his preparation to be Johnson's biographer, and after an initial hesitation decided to include in the *Life* part of the journal entry for 20 March that described the change.[2] Though Boswell characteristically did not explain directly how this change occurred, his revision of the Ashbourne journal suggests that he thought it derived from his willingness to challenge Johnson's published views on America when they were alone on their last night together. But the original Ashbourne journal, if examined as Boswell's dramatic response to the visit, and especially to Johnson's "quite violent" reaction to Boswell's challenge, suggests an important addition to the explanation in the *Life*: that Boswell's distress at Johnson's scary anger prompted him to find a less confrontational, less threatening way to assert his grownup status to a man who angered him deeply by denying him full respect, a new kind of intellectual collaboration with Johnson that would prove Boswell's autonomy without risking Johnson's rage.

In order to assess the story Boswell tells in the *Life*, therefore, and his revisions, it is necessary carefully to examine the Ashbourne journal. And to appreciate this journal fully, it is essential first to infer from all the available documents just what the visit was like for each man. This is a tricky task, however, since the major source for any account of the Ashbourne visit is Boswell's journal, most of which was written while Boswell was still surprised at having defied Johnson on their last evening together, and still worried about Johnson's final reaction. More important, a truly complete account of this visit, and of the key changes that occurred between September 1777 and March 1778, is impossible without a more thorough examination than I have space for here of Boswell's entire relationship with Johnson, especially as this relationship changed once Boswell made clear his intention to write the *Life*.

Though distinctive in offering Johnson and Boswell "much time to ourselves" with few outside distractions, as Johnson promised Boswell on 22 July (*Letters SJ* 3: 40), the time together at Ashbourne in many respects was typical of the Johnson-Boswell relationship after Johnson had read Boswell's Hebrides journal and saw what sort of materials Boswell was gathering for the *Life*, and especially after Johnson thwarted Boswell's wish to publish a companion to Johnson's *Journey to the Western Islands* (1775) based on the Hebrides journal.[3] Each man came to this carefully arranged visit with certain expressed wants and expectations, and certain needs of which he might not have been fully aware. Each was mostly satisfied, but in important ways disappointed. To some extent disappointment was inevitable, since some of Johnson's wishes conflicted with some of Boswell's, and especially since certain wishes of each man conflicted with some of his other wishes.

Boswell wanted to view Johnson as the proper object of "a pilgrimage" (*Extremes* 143) partly because he needed Johnson's advice and stabilizing influence, partly because, as with his father, he found the experience of awe reassuring (34). But he also wanted Johnson to regard him as an autonomous grownup, someone able to appreciate and assess Johnson's arguments and to judge his conduct, and also as his "intimate friend" (173). Johnson saw Boswell's "kindness [as] one of the pleasures of my life, which I should be very sorry to lose" (*Letters SJ* 2: 9), had been delighted with the Hebrides journal, and mostly assisted Boswell's preparations for the *Life*. But he resisted Boswell's efforts to manage his life, was troubled that all the preparations for the *Life* pointed to his death, and was uncomfortable at his biographer's power to judge him, especially since he knew that in the Hebrides journal Boswell had "found my faults, and laid them up to reproach me" (Johnson to Mrs. Thrale, 19 June 1775, *Letters SJ* 3: 228). Johnson tried to maintain control by supplying the authority Boswell needed, while withholding some of the respect he knew Boswell wanted. Boswell responded both to what Johnson gave him, and to what he was denied. The Ashbourne visit, like Boswell's visits to London in 1775 and 1776, was a mixed experience for each man.

Johnson's letters make clear that Boswell's "good humour" and "his usual vivacity" (*Letters SJ* 3: 74, 68) provided cheering diversion from the eternal sameness of Ashbourne, relief especially welcome because of Johnson's recent encounters with sickness (Anna Williams and Elizabeth Aston) and death (Catherine Turton and Harry Jackson) (3: 51, 57–58, 64–65). Johnson could show Boswell the local attractions, and Boswell was an audience when Johnson challenged Taylor about monarchs or bulldogs. Boswell also introduced topics ranging from Hamilton's poetry to Hume's death, giving Johnson a chance to exercise his mind and hold forth authoritatively. Having enjoyed reading Boswell's Hebrides journal as it was being written, Johnson had the mostly pleasing consciousness that "nothing that [he said] for this Week at least will be lost to Posterity" (as Mrs Thrale wrote on 18 September 1777).[4] But Johnson regretted not getting to see the Ashbourne journal (*Letters SJ* 3: 79). He was also deeply disappointed that he and Boswell failed to arrange "some other little adventure" like the trip to Sweden and Russia they had discussed on Skye, a journey that "can fill the hunger of ignorance, or quench the thirst of curiosity" (*Letters SJ* 3: 57, 65–66, 74). He grew remarkably angry when Boswell told others that 18 September would be Johnson's birthday, as he had also done in 1773 (*Letters SJ* 2: 75; *Hebrides* 183), reminding an aging Johnson that it was time to account for one more year of his allotted lifetime. (Boswell's steadily collecting information, and recording what Johnson did and said, for a work that would only be written after Johnson had died, inevitably called to Johnson's mind God's final, definitive assessment of his life.) Finally, at the end of their last day together at Ashbourne, after Johnson had dictated the legal brief Boswell requested and offered to "sit up *all night*," Boswell angered Johnson by opposing the position on America that Johnson had argued two-and-a-half years earlier in *Taxation No Tyranny* (*Extremes* 183).

Boswell's experience at Ashbourne was also mixed. Throughout the visit Johnson was remarkably helpful with the biographical project, bringing Boswell everything he had written for William Dodd, and answering all Boswell's questions without the testy complaints of 1776 (*Ominous Years* 295). (Johnson postponed dictating his letter to Lord Chesterfield, however, despite Boswell's repeated requests [*Extremes* 183], perhaps to make clear that his death was not imminent.) Boswell also heard decisive and original reflections about his most pressing concerns. At both ends of this visit, in striking contrast to some earlier moments in their relationship, Johnson was even willing to talk at length with Boswell about death and personal immortality. On 16 September he responded with assuring arguments to Boswell's distress that Hume, while believing in annihilation, had died cheerfully; and on 23 September, one day after Boswell recorded (and declared "too gloomy") Johnson's comment on 16 September that even the best people must fear death, since no one "can be sure that he is in a state of acceptance with God" (155), Boswell received an unexpected bonus when Johnson seemed to agree that despite the "strong" Biblical words about damnation, it is not unreasonable to hope there will be no eternal punishment.[5]

Boswell also got encouragement and practical advice about moving to London once he became laird of Auchinleck (169–71); and Johnson's "old feudal enthusiasm"—his insistence that "were he in my father's place, he would be against my going to live in London in a settled way, as Auchinleck would be deserted"—added force to his economic argument that Boswell "might indulge [his] love of London without a violation or neglect of any duty" (*Extremes* 169–70; cf. *Ominous Years* 99–100). Throughout the visit, Johnson's conversation had "an immediate cordial effect" on Boswell's melancholy (165, 173, 178, 181; cf. *Ominous Years* 256); and Boswell was clearly delighted when he recorded that Johnson's analysis of melancholy and madness "philosophically" explained what Boswell had "often and often experienced" (168–69). He was less pleased, however, when Johnson urged his standard remedies for melancholy, like reading ("You talk to me . . . as if I had keen desires for reading, but unluckily that is not the case" [181]) or when he tried to stop Boswell from drinking by saying that General Paoli was concerned that "my drinking . . . would make me go mad, for madness was in my family" (165).

In addition, Johnson was vexingly inexplicit in his approval. Boswell wanted the sort of endorsement Johnson enthusiastically had given him in 1763 and 1766 for his grounding assumption that he was truly exceptional (*London Journal* 326; *Grand Tour II* 282). He wanted considered praise for himself as "a settled advocate with a wife and children" (*Extremes* 144). He also wanted assurance that Johnson acknowledged him as someone who could help write the *Life of Thomson* (*Life* 3: 116–17, 122), who could offer Johnson himself Johnsonian consolation (3: 123), and who was fully qualified to produce Johnson's biography. Johnson appreciated Boswell's need for respect, and on their last afternoon together, when Boswell said, "We must meet every year if you do not quarrel . . . with me," Johnson first dismissed Boswell's talk of a quarrel, then declared that "My regard for you is greater than I can (almost) find words to express" (*Note Book* 23), a remarkable statement given Johnson's mastery of words. But during this visit Johnson's praise of Boswell was quite general, especially compared with what Boswell recorded Johnson saying about his Hebrides journal (*Hebrides* 188, 193, 226, 241–42, 245, 293), or with what Johnson published about Boswell in the *Journey to the Western Islands.*[6] Boswell's entry for 21 September expressed frustration that Johnson cleverly brushed aside what Boswell knew were good Johnsonian arguments for the value of tragic actors, and did so despite Boswell's clear request that Johnson take his arguments seriously ("My dear Sir! you may turn anything into ridicule. . . . But. . . ." [*Extremes* 175–76].) And the entry for the day he left Ashbourne indicates Boswell's disappointment that he got "little food for my vanity as a *celebrated man* upon this jaunt," since nobody mentioned "my *Account of Corsica*," and only "the Fellow of the College at Manchester" alluded to "my being an author" (184; cf. 161–62). (During this visit, however, Boswell did not show Johnson his current journal; and he does not report mentioning having just begun his *Hypochondriack* essays.)

More important, though Boswell had hoped that "Dr. Johnson should not say a single harsh thing to me or of me" during this Ashbourne visit (158), he wrote these words on 30 September just before describing the most biting insult he ever recorded. Alluding to Boswell's having announced Johnson's birthday, Johnson told Taylor in Boswell's presence that he "had a mind to have forbid him to mention it, but was in hopes he would have forgot it; and I thought he would do better from not knowing what was wrong than if he had been told to avoid it," a comment "representing [Boswell] as a being of little judgment or conduct" (*Extremes* 158). (Ironically this angry birthday insult is a striking example of the kind of "fault" I think most distressed Johnson in the Hebrides journal.) In addition, on their final evening together, 23 September, Boswell attacked Johnson's published argument about America, producing a "quite violent" response. The brief account in Boswell's journal suggests that this was a major breakthrough, their first sustained and heated argument, as Boswell confronted Johnson in private on a subject that mattered significantly to both men. Boswell used his defense of the colonists to express some of his own anger at Johnson's recent behavior; and Johnson's anger seems essentially respectful, since he kept arguing with Boswell "till three in the morning," when, "weary" (Johnson) and "jaded"

(Boswell), they decided to sleep (184).[7] But for reasons suggested when he mentioned his stand on America in earlier journals and letters, Boswell seems apprehensive about this assertion of intellectual independence.[8] He describes the confrontation as more or less accidental ("I got, I know not how, upon the American controversy"), denies having any wish to press the issue ("I would gladly have been off it again as soon as possible. For he was quite violent"), and presents himself as entirely calm yet fearful in the face of Johnson's rage ("I dreaded offending him. . . . I suggested. . . ."). He does not describe the argument as fully or as clearly as he does Johnson's quarrel with Taylor about the Stuarts (156–57), or his own debate with Johnson about actors (175–76). In fact, he seems reluctant even to write the entry for 23 September. He started it first on 10 October, when he wrote half a sentence (and at night got "mortal [drunk]" for the first time since Ashbourne and was "horrible to wife" [188]). He returned to it on 21 October, when he completed the first sentence but wrote just two in addition. He only finished this entry on 22 October, twelve days after he had begun writing it; and on this same day, either just before or just after he finally described what had happened on 23 September, Boswell balanced this account of his first angry debate with Johnson by writing his entry for 5 May 1777, an entry that describes "one of the best interviews that [Boswell had] had with [his father] of late years," a conversation in which Lord Auchinleck "was much softened, and my heart warmed to him" (120).

All Boswell's satisfaction and disappointment at the visit were on his mind when he wrote to Johnson two days after he returned to Edinburgh, the day before he resumed the Ashbourne journal. He begins by saying that "our late interview . . . appears to me to have answered expectations better than almost any scheme of happiness that I ever put in execution"; states a bit misleadingly that "My journal is stored with wisdom and wit" (since he had described only a third of the visit); and adds that "my memory is filled with the recollection of lively and affectionate feelings, which now, I think, yield me more satisfaction than at the time when they were first excited" (*Life* 3: 209). He then indicates his resentment at Johnson's not taking him sufficiently seriously by the way he asks Johnson to explain why "pleasure should be more vivid at a distance than when near," a question he had asked Johnson at least once before without getting an answer (*Hebrides* 329):

"I wish you may find yourself in the humour to do me this favour, but I flatter myself with no strong hope of it; for I have observed that unless upon very serious occasions, your letters to me are not *answers* to those I write" (*Life* 3: 209). The next day, when Boswell began writing the major portion of the Ashbourne journal, starting almost immediately with Johnson's birthday insult, he had strong and varied feelings about the visit.

On his first days of journal-writing at Ashbourne (16–18 September), after describing the trip as "a pilgrimage to some sacred place, . . . that I should have my soul elevated towards a better world and my understanding improved for this world" (*Extremes* 143). Boswell momentarily set aside the task of recording Johnson's "wisdom and wit" to tell what he himself did, saw and thought between Edinburgh to Ashbourne. In fact, on the day of the birthday insult, Boswell described fondling chambermaids, and somewhat defiantly suggested that his "keen sensations of desire for women" might not be "irreligious" or "immoral," despite Johnson's "opinion" (149). In the entry for 16 September (written on 22 September), he declared "too gloomy" Johnson's claim that no one can be sure of God's favor (155). And throughout the journal, especially the portion written in Edinburgh, Boswell assessed and judged Johnson's opinions (163, 174), authoritatively compared Johnson's current statements with those uttered earlier (165, 180–81), criticized his lack of "minute active benevolence" (161; cf. *Defence* 126), and described him as liable to "burst out" angrily with violent, volcanic eruptions (177, 181). He most persistently defied Johnson in the part of the entry for 22 September written on 10 October. First he firmly rejects Johnson's judgment that Lord Auchinleck "must have something of the family disease of mind to have a failure of memory at seventy," shrewdly accusing Johnson of seeking the explanation for his father's mental decline that threatened him least (180). Then, having stated that Johnson is wrong about Prior, some of whose poems "are rather too wanton for *modest women*, according to the established opinion," Boswell adds: "I have my own private notions as to modesty, of which I would only value the *appearance*: for unless a woman has amorous heat she is a dull companion, and to have amorous heat in elegant perfection, the *fancy* should be warmed with lively ideas" (180). He concludes the entry by rationalizing having surreptitiously copied Johnson's birthday prayer "and some short notes of a journal" (181–82).

On 30 September, however, when Boswell first resumed writing the journal in Edinburgh, he approached the birthday insult by finishing his account of Johnson's "violent" political argument with Taylor, noting at the end how Johnson's "old Oxford eloquence" awakened Boswell's "venerable mysterious notions of the sacredness of monarchy and my gallant affectionate feelings of loyalty" (156–57). Then, immediately after he recorded the insult, Boswell tried to assure himself that Johnson had not been in earnest by writing that "When he found that I was somewhat disconcerted, he retracted, or at least expressed himself in terms that showed he had been in jest" (158).[9]

The following day (1 October), Boswell discovered a new, non-defiant way to establish his independence. He produced collaborative reflections. Instead of endorsing Johnson's opinions while perhaps adding an example or an illustration, or rejecting Johnson's claims with arguments to support his opposition, Boswell incorporated but substantially augmented Johnson's positions. This sort of collaboration is anticipated in earlier journals,[10] but it is nowhere so fully developed, nor so dense, as here. As Charles McC. Weis and Frederick A. Pottle suggest (*Extremes* 155 n. 1), the frequency of such reflections in this portion of the Ashbourne journal might arise from Boswell's having just begun writing the *Hypochondriack* essays. (In fact he read page proofs for the first essay on the day he wrote the first "collaboration," on the fear of death, which closely resembles the fifth paragraph of the essay he began to write twelve days later.) But it seems more accurate to say that in these first Ashbourne entries written in Edinburgh, and also in his monthly essays, Boswell was trying to establish his autonomy on large moral issues without defying Johnson, as he had done on America and on sexual morality.

The first example occurs right after Boswell tells that the ladies who heard about the birthday the night before "plague [Johnson] unknowingly by wishing him joy." Having noted that Johnson's "dread of death has sometimes shocked me," Boswell contrasts Johnson's constant fear of death with his own ability "at times" to view death with "no great horror." He puts this contrast in conventional terms ("Perhaps such minds as his may be assailed with more violent terrors than feebler and more confined ones, as oaks are torn by blasts which shrubs escape by their lowliness"), but adds that he "was now led to have a new state of reflection as to death." Then drawing on Juvenal and Pope, using Paoli's idea about fear of death, which Johnson endorsed on 16 September, and also assuming what Johnson says about life after death on 16 September and 23 September, Boswell uses almost three hundred words to outline a thoughtful, balanced stance toward death that differs both from Johnson's position and from his own before this reflection (*Extremes* 158–59).

In the entry for 19 September, there is an even longer collaboration (written on 3 October), beginning with Boswell's report that he has "learnt from Dr. Johnson during this interview not to think with a dejected indifference of the works of art and the pleasures of life, because it is uncertain and short, but to consider such indifference as a failure of reason, a morbidness of mind" (163). Boswell then explains this Johnsonian perspective, drawing throughout on Johnson's example of "contemplating a large mass of human existence," but citing and quoting Young and Berkeley, Gray and Pope rather than Johnson. Addressing morbid ideas he had expressed and tried to resolve earlier in 1777 (80, 91, 102), he now produces something at once Johnsonian and Boswellian, original but not defiant, and in the process he proves himself to be an autonomous Johnsonian. In between these reflections on death and on happiness Boswell produced a slightly different sort of collaboration (also written on 3 October). He links his remarks about his pleasure walking through unfamiliar towns to Johnson's comments about how variously men shave themselves, using a generalization that might have come from either man ("The minute diversities in everything are wonderful"). Then he endorses Johnson's claim "that of a thousand, two do not shave so much alike as not to be distinguished," a claim Boswell initially rejected, by finding his own apt analogy: "when one considers what variety of sounds can be uttered by the windpipe, in the compass of a very small aperture, we may be convinced how many degrees of perpendicularity there may be in the application of a razor" [163].[11]

Creative collaborations like these affirmed Boswell's intellectual maturity without defying Johnson, hence without risking his anger as more defiant gestures might, though I think Boswell produced them here precisely because he had already expressed some of his anger by openly challenging Johnson. They were not shown to Johnson as the Hebrides journal had been, so they could not earn Johnson's praise. But after 1775, when Johnson frustrated Boswell's wish to publish some version of his Hebrides journal, Boswell could produce such collaborations only because Johnson was *not* nearby, and would *not* become a reader. (The same might be said of the *Hypochondriack* essays, which Boswell only shared with Johnson in 1784 [*Applause* 261].) Though they were not shown to Johnson, these collaborations helped produce significant changes in Boswell's attitude and behavior the following year, beginning with the triumphant letter he wrote Johnson on 28 February 1778.

This letter makes clear that the ministry's shift away from Johnson's position on America was one reason Boswell became "quite easy" with Johnson on 20 March. Having first posed a question about Parnell, Boswell then asks Johnson, "What do you say to *Taxation No Tyranny*, now, after Lord North's declaration, or confession, or whatever else his conciliatory speech should be called?" (*Life* 3: 221). He confirms that like Johnson he is "a steady and a warm Tory," but confidently asserts that he was correct in opposing Johnson's errors on "the Middlesex Election, and the Taxation of the Americans by the British *Houses of Representatives*" (cf. *Life* 4: 259). Though he closes the letter by writing, "But, enough of this subject; for your angry voice at Ashbourne upon it, still sounds aweful 'in my mind's *ears*'" (3: 221), Boswell clearly no longer fears Johnson's anger about America, as he still did while completing the Ashbourne journal. Lord North's shift left him the victor.

The circumstances surrounding the letter of 28 February 1778 suggest that the collaborative writing Boswell had begun early in October 1777 also enabled him to triumph over Johnson in this letter, and contributed to the loss of "awful reverence." Boswell rejoiced at Lord North's conciliatory speech in letters he wrote on 24 February to Sir John Pringle (L1082), and on 26 February to the Earl of Pembroke (L1038); but he said nothing about this speech in the long letter he wrote to Johnson on 26 February (*Life* 3: 219–20). Then on 28 February Boswell wrote Johnson again, chiefly to gloat about North's reversal. It is, of course, impossible to say for sure why Boswell was silent concerning North in his first letter, or why he then wrote a second, triumphant letter. But it seems significant that in his brief journal entries for 26–27 February Boswell reports that on these days he "wrote well" and "wonderfully" *Hypochondriack* 6 (*Extremes* 209), a poised reflection on melancholy in which Boswell incorporates many ideas he had heard from Johnson starting in 1763 (and especially in 1776–77), while giving them an original, Boswellian stamp.[12] After finishing this collaborative essay and then crowing over Lord North's concessions, Boswell experienced the surge of energy or confidence that is evident as his journal entries move from an average of three (printed) lines per day for the last fifteen days of February, to fourteen lines per day for the first six days of March, to almost twenty-six lines per day for March 7–12 (208–16), when Boswell left Edinburgh for London.

Having already noted on 20 September 1777 that he "was not now afraid of [Johnson], but . . . had an awe of him which made me happier in his company" (169), and then having weathered Johnson's anger about America and been vindicated, Boswell was not so wary of Johnson's angry disapproval as he once had been.[13] Having judged and defied Johnson in his journal, he was not so reverential as in the past; and having found a way to establish himself as an independent Johnsonian, he was not so needy. (Also just before he started out for London in 1778, Boswell had heard three men he respected but did not revere—Lord Monboddo, Lord Kames and Sir William Forbes—all speak of dying with none of Johnson's gloomy fear [210, 231, 215].) So Boswell was ready to discover that he no longer regarded Johnson with "awful reverence."

In the *Life*, Boswell confirmed that his having challenged Johnson on America and Middlesex contributed to the loss of awe on 20 March by tellingly expanding his account of their dispute on 23 September 1777, by including his letter of 28 February, and by inserting into the account of 20 March 1778 something Wilkes told him the following day: "*Liberty* is as ridiculous in [Johnson's] mouth as *Religion* in *mine*" (3: 224). In addition, he minimized the change he recorded in his journal for 20 March, and hence the need to explain it, by revising the Ashbourne journal to emphasize his independence and intellectual poise throughout the visit. Boswell used in the *Life* all the major episodes and almost every conversation from the Ashbourne journal, many virtually unchanged but some substantially modified.[14] He also made some key additions, like their conversation on 23 September about earthly unhappiness and what lies beyond death.[15] His overall account of what he and Johnson did and said during the visit is therefore roughly the same in the *Life* as in the journal, though there are a few telling differences. But Boswell created images of Boswell, of Johnson, and of their interaction during the visit that are strikingly different from those in his original journal.

In part because reviews of the *Journal of a Tour to the Hebrides* made Boswell wary of too much self-exposure, but chiefly to confirm what he later saw as a key shift in his relationship with Johnson, he presents himself in the *Life* as stronger, more independent, and more in control than in the journal. Boswell understandably drops his reflections about why at Ashbourne he had "no incitements to amorous desires" (*Extremes* 173) and his "private notions" about female modesty (180); and he eliminates his scheming "to enjoy the satisfaction of drinking wine" (165) and his surreptitiously copying Johnson's birthday prayer (181–82). He also cuts most indications of his radical neediness. We hear nothing, for instance, about how Johnson's presence rescues Boswell from melancholy (165, 178); he also drops his statement that he "had an awe of [Johnson] which made me happier in his company," keeping away "indolence, folly, nay, melancholy" (169). He avoids mentioning his personal distress when he describes their talking about a father who lacks tenderness (173–74; *Life* 3: 182) and about the possibility of being snubbed by a duke (179; *Life* 3: 189). He still reports telling Johnson that "David Hume's persisting in his infidelity, when he was dying, shocked me much," but he significantly reduces his remarks on how his mind was "much firmer than formerly" during this discussion (154–55; *Life* 3: 153–54);[16] and he cuts his enthusiastic response to Johnson's "old Oxford eloquence" (*Extremes* 157) the next day, and his reflection in the entry for 21 September that "while I sat in an *English Church*, and saw *Dr. Samuel Johnson* in the seat with me, and had my imagination filled with all the circumstances of learning, genius, worth, and literary distinction which that name conveys, and considered that he was my *intimate friend*, I was as serenely and steadily happy as I suppose man can be" (173).

A few cuts from Johnson's conversation also confirm this image of a stronger, more independent Boswell (though a few misleading additions to what Boswell originally reported Johnson saying show readers of the notebook and journal Boswell's enduring neediness).[17] The demeaning birthday insult is gone, for instance, though not Johnson's displeasure that Boswell mentioned the birthday; and though Johnson still worries about Boswell's drinking, he simply says that drinking water will keep Boswell sober (*Life* 2: 169), not that drinking wine "would make me go mad" (*Extremes* 165).[18] Boswell still complains to Johnson "of a wretched changefulness, so that I could not preserve, for any long continuance, the same view of any thing"; and he still notes that Johnson's "steady vigorous mind held firm before me those objects which my own feeble and tremulous imagination frequently presented, in such a wavering state, that my reason could not judge well of them" (*Extremes* 181; *Life* 3: 193). But whatever he experienced when he reflected on this passage, knowing that Johnson was dead, Boswell presents himself here and throughout the *Life* as someone who has achieved the steadiness of vision illustrated by his reflection on happiness, a man of enlightened sensibility who plays a significant role in their talks about this life and eternity.

Boswell also prepared for his self-assertion concerning America, and the loss of "awful reverence," by stressing more than usual his assiduity and confidence as biographer. By introducing into the *Life* most of his correspondence with Johnson from 4 April 1777 onwards, he makes clear how he produced this visit, because of which we have so much of Johnson's wisdom and wit. He glosses Johnson's brief comment about the *Lives of the English Poets* in his letter of May 3 by inserting, out of chronological order, a letter Edward Dilly wrote Boswell on 26 September, which shows Boswell's diligence in gathering detailed information, lets us know in advance that he and Johnson eventually have an "interview" in 1777, and alludes to the Ashbourne visit as a time when Boswell's "stock" of information will be "much increased" (3: 110). Later Boswell justifies the expense of the trip by noting the "many [biographical] particulars" Johnson communicated to him (3: 196; cf. *Extremes* 176). And when he finishes describing the Ashbourne visit in the *Life*, and before he quotes from the letter he wrote to Johnson on 29 September 1777, he first notes that "From this meeting at Ashbourne I derived a considerable accession to my Johnsonian store," then glosses this claim (which his text has already amply illustrated) by inserting what Sir William Forbes wrote in December about the Ashbourne journal, including Sir William's notion that "there is not a man in the world to whom he [Johnson] discloses his sentiments so freely as to yourself" (3: 208). In his account of 22 September, he pauses to call attention to his biographical method ("the Flemish picture which I give of my friend . . . in which . . . I mark the most minute particulars"), and to "bid defiance" to his critics (3: 190–91). At both ends of his account of this visit he also demonstrates how carefully he gathers information and weighs evidence by including biographical "particulars" that might fit better elsewhere: the complete story of Johnson's involvement with Dodd the previous May–June (3: 139–48), and the true story of what happened between Johnson and the Honorable Henry Hervey years earlier (3: 194–96). Both examples also affirm Johnson's confidence in Boswell as biographer.[19]

Boswell modified the "Johnson" of the Ashbourne journal in part to fit with his sustained image of Johnson,[20] but chiefly to anticipate the change in their relationship. Several small changes prepare for Boswell's new point that "During this interview at Ashbourne, Johnson seemed to be more uniformly social, cheerful, and alert, than I had almost ever seen him" (*Life* 3: 189).[21] Boswell also drops his complaint that "Dr. Johnson is deficient in minute active benevolence" (*Extremes* 161), though he adds the uncharitable suggestion that "Johnson paid great attention to Taylor" because "he had been told by Taylor he was to be his heir" (*Life* 3: 181; cf. 3: 207).[22] Johnson still gets angry at the thought of being pitted against Mrs. Macaulay; but as in the journal, his anger is expressed clearly and directly, then mitigated as he seeks "to be more gentle," then redirected at Bennet Langton after Boswell apologizes (3: 185–86; *Extremes* 176–77). And in his account of their final evening together, Boswell inserts this remarkable exchange based on his notebook:

> I said to him, 'My dear sir, we must meet every year, if you don't quarrel with me.' JOHNSON. 'Nay, Sir, you are more likely to quarrel with me, than I with you. My regard for you is greater almost than I have words to express; but I do not choose to be always repeating it; write it down in the first leaf of your pocket-book, and never doubt of it again.' (*Life* 3: 198)

But Boswell also prepares readers for the quarrel about America, which in the first edition of the *Life* begins less than two pages after this affirmation of regard, by adding references to the stunning loudness of Johnson's "voice and manner" (3: 139), his ability to "roar . . . down" opponents (3: 150), and his tendency to start arguments from a "spirit of contradiction" and then grow "outrageous" (3: 155). By changing "I said" (*Extremes* 155; *Note Book* 22) to "I ventured to tell him . . ." (*Life* 3: 153) and "I ventured to ask . . ." (3: 155), while twice repeating "I ventured" from the journal (3: 170, 188), Boswell emphasizes that despite Johnson's remarkable cordiality, it is still dangerous not only to criticize or contradict him, but even to ask him about certain subjects.

In several ways Boswell enhanced the portrait in the Ashbourne journal of Johnson's massive intellect, which was "foiled by futurity" (*Extremes* 155; *Life* 3: 154) but by little else. Instead of praising Hugh Blair as "a very great man," which Boswell considered "too high an epithet" and "heedlessly uttered" (*Extremes* 165), Johnson in the *Life* praises Blair's sermons with judicious understanding of "fashionable fame" (3: 167). And Boswell modified the passage suggesting that Johnson is "not . . . quite clear" (165) about the effects of drinking on health so that it emphasizes Johnson's "usual intelligence and accuracy of enquiry" (*Life* 3: 170). At the same time, the revised account of the Ashbourne visit recalls and confirms a contrast Boswell has been developing throughout the *Life* between Johnson's violent narrowmindedness and Boswell's enlightened poise, the contrast Boswell summed up at the end of his biography by adding to the "character" of Johnson in the *Tour of the Hebrides* (1785) that he "had, perhaps, at an early period, narrowed his mind somewhat too much, both as to religion and politicks" (*Life* 4: 426; cf. 5: 17).

Johnson remains the authority on a variety of issues. But Boswell emphasizes his own significant contributions (e.g., 3: 188, 199–200); and he includes most of his own collaborative reflections as if they were part of the original, shared experience. In addition, Boswell continues to present himself as a firm and rational opponent of Johnson's "almost heretical" opinion about tragic actors (3: 185) and his imperceptive scorn of the power of music (3: 197). And before quoting Johnson's statements about melancholy and madness, all of which Boswell enthusiastically corroborated in the journal from his own experience (*Extremes* 168–69), Boswell writes that he "always thought" Johnson was "erroneously inclined to confound" these two conditions, and then explains why "there is, in my opinion, a distinct separation between them" (*Life* 3: 175; cf. 1: 36, 65–66). (Boswell begins his account of 1777 by sympathetically noting that throughout this year Johnson suffered from what Johnson himself described as "disturbances of the mind, very near to madness" [3: 98–99].)

Throughout the *Life*, Boswell also prepares for the debate on 23 September by criticizing Johnson's views on America, often linking America to the Middlesex election (Wilkes). On both issues Boswell aligns himself with reason and justice, and with what later events clearly show was the correct policy, against Johnson's prejudice and violence (1: 134; 2: 112, 286; 3: 312); and he claims he avoided talking with Johnson about *Taxation No Tyranny* in 1775 because its "extreme violence" was "unsuitable to the mildness of a Christian philosopher" (2: 312; cf. 3: 316). Immediately before describing their only full-scale dispute about America, Boswell mentions both *Taxation No Tyranny* and Wilkes (along with "the brave Corsicans") in elaborating on his claim that Johnson "had always been very zealous against slavery in every form, in which I, with all deference, thought that he discovered 'a zeal without knowledge'" (3: 200–1).[23]

Then Boswell presents an expanded version of their quarrel about America as a battle in which a reasonable Boswell holds his ground against a violently prejudiced Johnson, and so deserves respect for courage as well as for astuteness. Instead of describing this confrontation as more or less accidental, as in the journal, Boswell accepts responsibility: "Had I been as attentive not to displease him as I ought to have been, I know not but this vigil might have been fulfilled; but I unluckily entered upon the controversy concerning the right of Great-Britain to tax America, and attempted to argue in favour of our fellow-subjects on the other side of the Atlantick" (3: 205). Boswell does not speculate about why, after years of avoiding America as a topic, he "unluckily" challenged a remarkably cordial Johnson on their final evening together. (In the manuscript of the *Life*, Boswell started to write "unfortun[ately]," replaced it with "very improperly," then shifted to the less apologetic "unluckily" [M144:555].) But he makes clear that he stated his case forcefully by replacing "I suggested that by allowing them a parliament like Ireland . . ." (*Extremes* 183) with "I insisted that America might be very well governed . . ." (*Life* 3: 205). ("I insisted that" is also more direct and energetic than the first two phrases Boswell wrote in the manuscript at this point: "I declared my sent[iments]" and "I wondered at the . . ." [M144: 555].) Boswell ascribes the tone of the argument to Johnson, who "could not bear my thus opposing his avowed opinion, which he had exerted himself with an extreme degree of heat to enforce; and the violent agitation into which he was thrown while answering, or rather reprimanding me, alarmed me so, that I heartily repented of my having unthinkingly introduced the subject"(*Life* 3: 205). But here, instead of simply repenting as in the journal, where Boswell describes himself as afraid of "offending him by even the gentlest doubts in favour of our fellow subjects on the other side of the Atlantic" (*Extremes* 183), Boswell admits what is implicit in the journal: in response to Johnson's violence, he too, "grew warm" (3: 205) in defending the colonists against thoughtless and brutal authority. He believed in this cause and was willing to take the consequences. Boswell also comes much closer than in the original entry to claiming this quarrel as a triumph. Despite being alarmed by Johnson's "violent agitation," he maintained his position and presumably continued reasoning in the face of Johnson's harsh scolding. Then, when Boswell shifted the focus to the corruption of the British Parliament, contrasting it with the Roman Senate, Johnson opposed him with reasoned assertions, as if in the course of an evolving debate that lasted for "an hour or two" Johnson recognized Boswell's right to be treated with serious arguments rather than abuse (cf. *Extremes* 183). When he describes going to Johnson's bedside the following morning, Boswell adds to the journal that "the storm of the preceding night was quite laid . . . and he talked with as much readiness and good-humour as ever" (*Life* 3: 206; cf. *Extremes* 184).

The revised Ashbourne journal, culminating in the quarrel about America, shows a strong and resolute Boswell, a biographer-to-be in full control of his material. He is poised, as in the journal, even when Johnson ignores his plea to be serious and fallaciously dismisses his strong arguments in favor of tragic actors. And unlike the Boswell of the journal, he is so resilient when faced by Johnson's violent anger that Johnson treats him with respect. The reader of this section of the *Life* will not be surprised by the defiance of Boswell's letter of 28 February 1778 ("What do you say to *Taxation no Tyranny*, now?" [3:221]), or by Boswell's somewhat sad realization on 20 March 1778 that his "aweful reverence" for Johnson was gone ("I felt a sort of regret that I was so easy" [3: 225]). The revised Ashbourne journal also prepares readers for Boswell's rebuking Johnson in public on 18 April 1778 by saying that he was "always sorry" when Johnson abused the Americans (3: 315; *Extremes* 300); for his firmly but politely rejecting Johnson's claim on 15 April 1778 that "one would rather exist even in pain, than not exist" (3: 295–96; not in *Extremes* 291); and for his directly telling Johnson on 8 May 1778 how very angry he had become when Johnson rudely attacked him six days earlier "before people who neither love you nor me" (3: 338). No longer the pilgrim he imagined himself when he started writing the Ashbourne journal on 16 September 1777 (*Extremes* 143), confident of his ability to distinguish mere prejudice from sound reasoning and to note how Johnson's "supposed orthodoxy" sometimes "cramped the vigorous powers of his understanding" (*Life* 2: 104), Boswell can determine that Johnson's attack on slavery reveals "a zeal without knowledge" without destroying Johnson's ability to dissolve Boswell's skepticism about Christianity or to marshal principled arguments in favor of subordination.

By removing Johnson's "harsh" insult and by crediting Boswell as thinker and writer, the revised Ashbourne journal made up for the deficiencies in the original visit and at the same time easily accounted for the letter of 28 February and the change reported in the journal entry of 20 March 1778. But in the process it misrepresented the visit. The revised Boswell is less needy and defiant than he appears in the original Ashbourne journal, or in other documents from the time. He does not tell Johnson on 20 September 1777 that "I had an awe of him which made me happier in his company" (*Extremes* 169), nor does he say to Johnson, on 7 April 1778, "I love to be under some restraint, some awe" (250). He criticizes Johnson's ideas about madness and melancholy, and his views on slavery, in ways that were far from Boswell's mind during this period, just as earlier in the *Life* we hear nothing of Boswell's initial strong delight with *Taxation No Tyranny* (*Ominous Years* 80).

These misrepresentations are worth remarking because the *Life* highlights the Boswell-Johnson relationship in the period between April 1777 and March 1778. As anticipated, the Ashbourne visit threw Johnson and Boswell together with few supporting characters. Boswell quotes from only one of twenty-five published letters Johnson wrote to Hester Thrale in July-October 1777, in a note, while for the period from February 1777 to February 1778 he quotes from fourteen of his fifteen letters to Johnson and all thirteen of Johnson's letters to Boswell.[24] (In contrast, Boswell quotes from only four of his thirteen letters to Johnson in 1776, and only one of his four letters to Johnson in the last half of 1778.) Except for Johnson's poised and sympathetic letter to Saunders Welch, which was added in the second edition (1793), only letters between Boswell and Johnson carry us from their quarrel about America to the time they next meet. In fact, after 1793, when Boswell corrected a mistake in the first edition by moving from the start of 1778 to the start of 1779 the paragraph announcing that "this year came out the first four volumes of his *Prefaces, biographical and critical, to the most eminent of the English Poets*" (3: 370), the year 1778 was left with no standard introduction about what Johnson had written and the enduring vigor of his mind. Instead we move directly from the letter Johnson wrote Boswell on 27 December 1777 to Boswell's response on 8 January 1778. Because his relationship with Johnson was such a significant feature in Boswell's account of this period when he found himself to have fully matured as Johnson's biographer, it is important to notice that Boswell failed to provide a completely accurate, richly nuanced explanation of one of the most significant changes in this relationship. It seems especially ironic that while rightly claiming credit for his extraordinary efforts in producing the *Life*, he overlooked how his confidence for this task, his assured independence, was fostered by his writing collaborative journal entries and essays.

A fitting emblem for this whole portion of the *Life* is an episode Boswell added, apparently from memory, to his account of 22 September 1777, the penultimate day of the Ashbourne visit.[25] On a sunny morning, Boswell and Johnson pass some time viewing "with placid indolence" the artificial waterfall Taylor had made in the river near his garden. Then Johnson takes a pole to push over the stone dike some of the branches and "other rubbish" that obstructed the flow, and when he finds "a large dead cat so heavy that he could not move it after several efforts," he asks Boswell to help, "which I accordingly did, and being a fresh man, soon made the cat tumble over the cascade" (3: 190–91). A whimsical Johnson, set in motion "partly from that inclination to activity which will animate, at times, the most inert and sluggish mortal," and comically incapable of completing his mock-heroic task, is carefully observed by an amused Boswell, who "stood quietly by, wondering to behold the sage thus curiously employed, and smiling with an humorous satisfaction each time when he carried his point." The episode demonstrates the richness of Boswell's memory (see also 3: 207), and his narrative skill in economically bringing the scene to life. It illustrates one sort of cooperation Boswell sees as central to the production of the *Life*: Johnson speaks and acts, at times behaving quite oddly, while Boswell notices, assesses, remembers, and later tells the story. The episode also expresses Boswell's wish that his relationship with Johnson had always been as mutually respectful, as free of conflict and anger and frustrated desires, as was their calm, philosophical talk about earthly happiness and immortality on their last day at Ashbourne. By the time he included this episode in the *Life*, however, Boswell knew that this wish had been as vain in 1777 as was Johnson's wish for another "adventure" with Boswell, a journey that might fulfill expectations as richly as Johnson then felt the trip to the Hebrides had done. The Ashbourne visit made clear that neither of these wishes would be satisfied, largely because Boswell's plan to write Johnson's biography pleased Johnson but also disturbed him, producing a resistance that in turn deeply troubled Boswell, helped produce bouts of deep melancholy in 1775 and 1776, and led him to devise new strategies for achieving the control and independence he both wanted and feared.

Notes

I am grateful to Amy Fulton-Stout for shrewd comments on the first version of this paper and to Irma Lustig for challenging and supportive criticism from start to finish.

1. On 16 September Boswell wrote the entries for 10–11 September, on 17 September the entry for 12 September, on 18 September the entries for 13–15 September, and on 22 September those for 16–17 September, a total of fourteen pages in the McGraw-Hill edition, six describing his trip to Ashbourne. Then on 30 September, in Edinburgh, Boswell resumed the journal "from notes" (*Boswell in Extremes* 157). Except for 6 October, he wrote every day through 10 October, filling twenty-five pages on ten different days, carrying the journal to the start of the entry for 23 September. He wrote entries for 23–27 September (five pages) in Auchinleck on 21–25 October, though on 21 October and 24

October he wrote only a few words. His account of this eighteen-day trip is two-thirds as long as his journal for the previous 252 days of 1777. Because in this essay I quote primarily from the Ashbourne journal, I have cited *Boswell in Extremes* by page number only except where clarity requires the use of the short title, as after an intervening title.

2. Sometime after he wrote the paragraph that begins "In my interview" (*Life* 3: 225), which incorporates the end of his entry for 20 March (*Extremes* 225) Boswell crossed it out, using several diagonal lines for the part on page 623 of the manuscript (M144) and one line for the rest. He also wrote to the left of his paragraph, "try some good man with this passage"; and later he wrote "stet." Material from the manuscript of the *Life* is printed with permission of Yale University and Edinburgh University Press.

3. See Mary Lascelles, "Johnson and Boswell on their Travels," *Facts and Notions:. Collected Criticism and Research* (Oxford: Clarendon Press, 1972), 155–69.

4. *The Letters of Samuel Johnson, with Mrs. Thrale's Genuine Letters to Him,* ed. R.W. Chapman, 3 vols. (Oxford: Clarendon Press, 1952), 2: 209.

5. *Boswell's Note Book 1776–1777,* ed. R.B. Adam (London: Humphrey Milford, 1925), 22–23.

6. Johnson praised Boswell's "gaiety of conversation and civility of manners," his "acuteness of observation," his "inquisitiveness . . . seconded by great activity," and his ability "sagely" to reproach Johnson's "sluggishness and softness" (*Journey* 3, 11, 117, 144, 71). He did not praise Boswell's writing, however, or acknowledge Boswell's journal as the fullest record of their trip.

7. In his letter of 26 April 1768, Boswell's lyrical defiance of Johnson's request than he "empty [his] head of Corsica" similarly expressed his frustration that during three evenings of talk in late March Johnson had teasingly withheld all comment on Boswell's book (*Letters JB* 1: 155). My conjecture about Johnson's respect is supported by comparing his parting advice the next day, urging Boswell to plant trees on his estate (*Extremes* 184), with his parting advice in 1776: "Don't drink. . . . Don't talk of yourself or of me" (*Ominous Years* 352).

8. In the year after Johnson blocked the publication of the Hebrides journal, Boswell nervously moved toward a clash with Johnson on America. He developed pro-American views "notwithstanding Dr. Johnson's eloquence" (summer 1775, *Ominous Years* 160). He warmly defended the Americans on 28 October 1775 (171–72) and then guiltily worried in December that Johnson has heard what Boswell had said and was angry (201–2). He told a group in London on 17 March 1776 that America "was the only great point upon which I had got from under Dr. Johnson," and then immediately regretted this "imprudence" (270).

9. Similarly in 1773, before describing Johnson's joke about Boswell the "eunuch" (*Hebrides* 177), Boswell reconfirmed that his "political notions" coincided with Johnson's (162–63). In 1773 Boswell then showed this passage to Johnson, along with the narrative that virtually asked Johnson to say that his "extraordinary raillery" was not "serious" (177), and expressed his frustration at Johnson's failure to respond when he recorded Johnson's next joking insult (294). In 1777, in part because Johnson had discouraged Boswell from publishing the Hebrides journal, the audience was not Johnson, and Boswell had to assure himself that the insult was "in jest."

10. See the first paragraph for 16 July 1763 (*London Journal* 304), for instance, or the eighth paragraph for 22 August 1773 (*Hebrides* 63–64), or the fifth and eleventh paragraphs for 22 March 1776 (*Ominous Years* 287–88, 290).

11. The paragraph about "the difficulty of rising in the morning" (*Extremes* 166) is a different kind of collaboration: Johnson describes an unsatisfactory method and Boswell speculates at length about alternatives. Boswell's accounts of their discussions of melancholy and madness (168–69) and of his own moving to London (169–71) ar also collaborative. Johnson does most of the talking Boswell records, but in the journal Boswell comments extensively.

12. While accepting Margery Bailey's claim that many of Boswell's essays were derivative (*The Hypochondriack* [Stanford: Stanford University Press, 1928]: 33–36), I would highlight their originality in tone and emphasis, something especially clear in *Hypochondriack* 6. (Note, for instance, how the final paragraph criticizes Johnson's responses to Boswell's melancholy.)

13. See *In Search of a Wife* 333–34; *Hebrides* 110–12, 263; *Ominous Years* 63–64, 322–23; and *Extremes* 25; and compare these reactions to unexpected, judgmental anger with Boswell's reaction to an expected "broadside" (*Defence* 122). In his entry for 17 March 1776, Boswell describes "the habitual awe which comes upon me in my father's presence when he disapproves of my conduct" (*Ominous Years* 270).

14. As usual, he protectively masked the identities of those discussed; and he moved some material, like Taylor's account of comforting Johnson when Tetty died (*Extremes* 159), to more appropriate points in the *Life* (1: 238).

15. Probably because it seemed important enough to be fully recorded as soon as possible, Boswell described this conversation at the end of the notebook he chiefly used for stories about Johnson's early life. Then, for some reason—perhaps because he had already recorded it, perhaps because he did not have his notebook with him in Auchinleck when he wrote this part of the Ashbourne journal, or perhaps because

their discussion of which man was "more likely" to "quarrel (or some such word)" with the other (*Note Book* 23) ironically anticipated the violent dispute about America that still troubled Boswell as he described it—Boswell did not include this rich conversation in his narrative journal for 23 September.

16. Boswell also distances himself from Hume by changing "he told me he was quite easy at the thought of annihilation" (*Extremes* 155) to "I had reason to believe that the thought of annihilation gave Hume no pain" (*Life* 3: 153).

17. In two cases Boswell has Johnson openly declare what Boswell originally only inferred: Boswell's "he seemed inclined to mitigate" (*Note Book* 23) becomes Johnson's "they may admit of a mitigated interpretation" (*Life* 3: 200); and "he has old feudal enthusiasm, for he said that . . ." (*Extremes* 169) becomes Johnson's "for I have the old feudal notions, and . . ." (*Life* 3: 177). Boswell also transforms some of his journal musings about Auchinleck and London (*Extremes* 170–71) into a list of ideas he told Johnson at the time, at the end of which he writes, "He listened to all this, and kindly 'hoped it might be as I now supposed'" (*Life* 3: 178). Though we can sensibly debate the accuracy of what Boswell's journal and notebook report Johnson actually saying, these texts are almost surely accurate when they report Johnson *not* saying something Boswell would have liked him to have said.

18. Similarly, Johnson's telling Boswell that he "must have my father's employment, or one as busy, to preserve me from melancholy" (*Extremes* 169) is transformed in the *Life* into a general statement about employment (3: 180).

19. A bit later Boswell records Johnson's approval of his scrupulous accuracy, in contrast to Mrs. Thrale's casualness (*Life* 3: 226–28, 243–45). In his account of 22 September 1777, Boswell even began to tell how his quest for information led him to copy from Johnson's diary (see *Extremes* 181–82); but the manuscript of the *Life* reveals that he stopped writing after he reported seeing Johnson's "Diary lying on the table," then crossed out the whole passage (M 144: 541).

20. For example, the Johnson of the *Life* does not say "may belch or f--t" (*Extremes* 154); and when he is told that the dying Hume was not troubled by the thought of annihilation, instead of "He lied" (155) says "It was not so, Sir" (3: 153; cf. 2: 106).

21. Boswell inserts "cordially" in the first sentence describing the visit (*Life* 3: 135), adds "obligingly" to the statement that "Dr. Johnson obligingly proposed to carry me to see Islam" (3: 187), and highlights his statement about Johnson's "remarkably cordial" behavior on the last day of the visit by moving it to the start of that day's entry (3: 196; cf. *Extremes* 182).

22. Unlike John J. Burke Jr., in "But Boswell's Johnson Is Not Boswell's Johnson" (*New Questions, New Answers,* 190), I think Boswell added this idea because he now suspected that Johnson's cordiality at Ashbourne, like his praise of Boswell in 1776 (e.g., *Ominous Years* 298) and especially in 1778 (e.g., *Extremes* 250, 290), was largely designed to coax Boswell into taking another trip. Note how just before introducing Johnson's letter of 11 September 1777, where Johnson writes "that I set a very high value upon your friendship, and count your kindness as one of the chief felicities of my life" (*Life* 3: 135), Boswell in a note quotes from the letter Johnson sent Hester Thrale two days later, including Johnson's lament that Boswell "has not a *better bottom*" for travel (3: 134 n. 1).

23. Similarly, Boswell contrasts Johnson's "old feudal notions" (*Life* 3: 177) with his own "old feudal principles" (3: 178; cf. 2: 316). At the start of the 1793 edition of the *Life* (1: ix [should be xiv]–xvi), Boswell added the brief Johnson dictated on 23 September to support a Negro claiming his liberty in Scotland, which in the 1791 edition Boswell noted he could not locate (2: 174 n. 1). Then he offered some of the arguments from his 1791 poem *No Abolition of Slavery,* as Frederick A. Pottle points out (*The Literary Career of James Boswell, Esq.* [Oxford: Clarendon Press, 1929], 147), to establish himself as someone who has "read, conversed, and thought much upon the subject" (*Life* 3: 203–4), in contrast to Johnson's prejudice and ignorant zeal. In the 1795 edition this three-page passage was somewhat distractingly placed between their "calm" discussion of happiness and the quarrel about America.

24. Boswell also reminds readers of the whole sweep of their relationship by including, in a footnote to Johnson's letter of 28 June 1777, two letters he wrote to Johnson in 1764 and 1775 but only sent in June 1777 (*Life* 3: 122 n. 2).

25. In writing the Ashbourne journal, Boswell initially used both sides of each sheet; but after the entry for 16 September, he began writing on only one side. Sometime later, perhaps when he showed this journal to a friend or perhaps only when he began to revise it for the *Life,* Boswell wrote a version of this touching story on the first blank page, his first words indicating he was not sure on which day this happened ("one morning after breakfast"). Later he moved it to a day when it almost surely did not occur, probably because it nicely balances Johnson's controlled anger at breakfast that morning, and then is held in readers' minds as we move through the poignant moments of 23 September to the heated quarrel that ends this final day.

"My Dear Enemy": Margaret Montgomerie Boswell in the *Life of Johnson*

IRMA S. LUSTIG

The world has known of Margaret Montgomerie Boswell's antipathy to Samuel Johnson since 1791, because for nine years Johnson insisted on it in letters to Boswell which he, in turn, published in the *Life of Johnson.* These letters, with a few responses from Mrs. Boswell and modest editorial links, constitute a forward-straining "sub-plot" not resolved until 1783. Johnson's genius makes the interplay of personalities vivid even in a chiefly one-sided correspondence. But, except for one frank and yet elliptical footnote to the text, Margaret Boswell's prolonged resistance to Johnson's offers of friendship is largely unexplained. Intuition will serve the reader well, but Boswell's journal, various letters, published and unpublished, and the knowledge we now have of the Boswells' relationship help us understand more fully the causes, course, and resolution of the estrangement.

Mrs. Boswell's hostility is commonly thought to have been triggered by Johnson's extended visit in Edinburgh before and after the tour of the Hebrides. Boswell reports that on the first night at their home in James Court she was charmed by Johnson's conversation into forgetting his external appearance (*Hebrides* 12). But he was their guest for thirteen nights and twelve days, from his arrival in Edinburgh on 14 August 1773 until he left with Boswell for St. Andrews on the 18th, and except for two nights at Lord Elibank's country seat, from the night of 9 November until he began his journey home, via Sir John Dalrymple's, on the 20th. Though they were "harassed by invitations," as Johnson said, on the mornings they breakfasted at home Mrs. Boswell had the "endless task" of pouring tea for a perpetual stream of visitors, from ten o'clock to one or two. There were also guests at dinner or supper on all three days of Johnson's first sojourn, and sometimes at both meals on the same day (*Hebrides* 12–32, and 377–91, passim). Margaret Boswell was a brisk and capable person, but she had very early shown symptoms of consumption (pulmonary tuberculosis). She sometimes pushed her strength to the extreme.

Her coolness to Johnson is first disclosed in the *Life of Johnson* on 27 November 1773, when Johnson announced his safe return to London the night before. "I know Mrs. Boswell wished me well to go," he wrote; "her wishes have not been disappointed" (*Life* 2: 268–69). Boswell, either obtuse or disingenuous, wonders, in a footnote, at Johnson's perspicacity, for Mrs. Boswell had paid him the "most assiduous and respectful attention." We who have seen, or been, grim but polite hostesses, like Johnson understand Mrs. Boswell; so also did her husband, for she was quick to speak her mind privately when overtaxed. Boswell went on in that important footnote to give three reasons for his wife's transparent impatience: Johnson's "irregular hours and uncouth habits" were disagreeable to her (the candle wax on the carpets is legendary); she did not admire Johnson as well as others did; and she thought he had too much influence over her husband. "'I have seen many a bear led by a man,'" she had once said, "with more point than justice," but "'I never before saw a man led by a bear'" (2: 269 n. 1). Though he qualified her statement, Boswell could not resist his pride in her tartness. But we do not know what answer, if any, he made to Johnson, for Boswell's next letter (2 December 1773) was edited for publication, as were almost all the others that followed Johnson's references to Margaret Boswell's dislike.

Early the next year after Johnson had visited Scotland, he himself acknowledged that he had been a burdensome guest. "Make my compliments to Mrs. Boswell," he wrote on 29 January 1774, "and tell her that I do not love her the less for wishing me away. I gave her trouble enough, and shall be glad, in recompense, to give her any pleasure" (2: 272). These sentiments recur systematically, and, in fact, like a formula, for several years: "Tell Mrs. Boswell that my good intentions towards her still continue. I should be glad to do any thing that would either benefit or please her" (7 February 1774, 2: 272); "I hope Mrs. Boswell and little Miss are well.—When shall I see them again? She is a sweet lady, only she was so glad to see me go, that I have almost a mind to come again, that she may again have the same pleasure" (5 March 1774, 2: 275).[1] In every letter thereafter Johnson makes his compliments to Mrs. Boswell, by 1775 with the recurring, sometimes playful, refrain, "though she does not love me" (27 May, 27 August, 16 November, 23 December, 10 January, and 3 February 1776). Occasionally he tries to tease Margaret Boswell out of her stiffness: "Pray teach Veronica to love me. Bid her not mind mamma" (2: 379). And in the same letter, "Make my compliments to Mrs. Boswell, though she does not love me. You see what perverse things ladies are, and how little fit to be trusted with feudal estates [a good-humored dig at Boswell's archaic principle of heirs male]. When she mends and loves me, there may be more hope of her daughters" (27 May 1775, 2: 380). The lady does not smile.

Obviously Johnson knew that Boswell would read at least these portions of his letters to Margaret. On 16 November 1775 he announced—disarmingly, one would have thought—what the Boswells (and we) have tacitly understood: "I know that she does not love me; but I intend to persist in wishing her well till I get the better of her" (2: 387).

Johnson might have thought that he had won her over in 1776. Boswell's conflict with his father over the entail to the estate had reached a frightening stage. Lord Auchinleck wished to entail Auchinleck on heirs general, male or female; Boswell stubbornly insisted on descent through males only, however remote. If he or his two sons should die (one has only to think of the Thrales to know that the threat was real), his daughters would be passed over. Moreover, Lord Auchinleck, mistrustful of his heir's competence, had named trustees to manage the estate when Boswell should succeed, thereby reducing his income. Still Boswell remained intransigent; but perplexed and uneasy, he wrote Johnson a "long, serious, and earnest" letter on 2 January 1776, setting the matter out fully and soliciting his opinion. With the postscript he added two days later, the letter ran to twelve pages measuring about nine by seven inches. Margaret, terrified that their children would be disinherited, also wrote to Johnson on 4 January, a "very sensible, clear letter," Boswell said, entreating his interest with her husband so that he might agree to Lord Auchinleck's settlement (*Ominous Years* 211, 214 and n. 2). Boswell printed nothing of either letter in the *Life of Johnson*, but the entail is the entire subject after Johnson's letter of 10 January 1776, from the bottom of page 412, volume 2 to the top of 423. An editorial interpolation of two pages sets out the history of the estate of Auchinleck and its transmission and, in a respectful but candid account, Boswell's differences with his father. He justifies his own arguments in a very long footnote (*Life* 2: 414 n. 2–415) and discloses that he had reason to apprehend "disagreeable consequences" from noncompliance with his father's wishes. There then follow five letters from Johnson related to the entail, 15 January and 3, 9, 15, and 24 February 1776.

Johnson replied only briefly to Boswell on 15 January, suggesting that he apply for guidance to Lord Hailes, "a Christian and a Lawyer." He was to tell Mrs. Boswell, however, that "I hope to be wanting in nothing that I can contribute to bring you all out of your troubles" (*Life* 2: 415–16). Believing for some time that Margaret's letter was written without Boswell's knowledge and required what he could not find, a "private conveyance," Johnson made no answer until 16 May 1776 (3: 85–86). But on 3 February 1776 he wrote to Boswell again, a long, cogent letter supporting heirs general (2: 416–18). Margaret wept in relief (*Ominous Years* 231). She did not express her gratitude to Johnson, however, probably because he had not responded to her letter.

Lord Hailes, as it turned out, was also firmly in opposition to Boswell's views. He sent Hailes's opinion to Johnson, who signified his agreement in a letter of 9 February, to which he added the postscript, "I hope I shall get some ground now with Mrs. Boswell" (*Life* 2: 420). A shorter exegesis on the entail on 15 February ends with a request to "Pray let me know if Mrs. Boswell is friends with me" (2: 422). Even so hasty and brief a letter as that of 12 March, announcing Johnson's departure from London, reads in the third and last line, "mention very particularly to Mrs. Boswell my hope that she is reconciled to, Sir, Your faithful servant, Sam. Johnson" (2: 424). In the letter he wrote directly to Margaret Boswell on 16 May he implored her, "Do not teach the young ones to dislike me, as you dislike me yourself" (3: 86). On 16 November he assumes that she is his "irreconcilable enemy," and desires her "not to transmit her malevolence to the young people" (3: 93). At the year's end, 21 December 1776, Johnson tells Boswell that if his wife "would but be friends with me, we might now shut the temple of Janus," an allusion to the Roman custom of keeping the doors to that temple open during times of war (3: 95; *Letters SJ* 2: 365 n. 7).

Within six months Johnson's description of Margaret's attitude has deteriorated from dislike to enmity, a term employed playfully, perhaps, but serious withal.

In the next year, however, she sent a peace offering, a jar of her own marmalade. No gift was so long a promise and so fulsomely acknowledged. Boswell announced that it was forthcoming in a letter of 24 February 1777, which also reported that his wife was "much honoured" by Johnson's professions of love on 18 February, though Johnson had also written that he did not suppose her yet reconciled to him (*Life* 3: 104–5). On 24 April Boswell again mentioned the marmalade; on 3 May Johnson replied whimsically that he will taste it cautiously at first. "Beware, says the Italian proverb, of a reconciled enemy." But when he finds that the marmalade does him no harm, he shall be thankful for it, "as a pledge of firm, and, I hope, of unalterable kindness" (3: 108–9). On 28 June 1777 Johnson could finally return "affectionate thanks" via Boswell (3: 120). On 22 July he wrote to Margaret directly. The sweetmeats gave him pleasure as a token of friendship. By having her kindness he has a "double security" for the continued kindness of her husband. He was always faithful to her interest and always endeavored to exalt her in Boswell's estimation. She must do the same for him. "We must all help one another" (3: 129).

The gift was so long in coming, even given the distance it had to travel, one suspects that Boswell had to manage it, perhaps from the first. Johnson's repeated and heartfelt acknowledgments suggest that he knew the gesture to have been difficult and feared that the reconciliation was tentative.

He was right. On 29 September 1777 he told Mrs. Thrale that the peace was "formal": he had learned from Boswell that his wife "does not love me quite well yet" (*Letters SJ* 3: 79). On 25 November 1777 she again appears in a letter in the *Life* as his "dear enemy" (3: 210). Still Johnson continued the campaign. On 24 January 1778 he offered, unsuccessfully, to give up his own apartments if Boswell would bring Mrs. Boswell to London to recover from the "severe cold" that had kept her housebound in Edinburgh for three months (3: 215–16). On 13 March 1779 Johnson promised her a set of both the *Lives* and the *Poets* in acknowledgment of her marmalade though she still harbored "ill-will" to him (3: 372). He did indeed send sixty volumes, and on 21 August 1780 notified Boswell that he would complete her collection. "I love your naughty lady, whom I never shall persuade to love me" (3: 436).

Johnson appears to have kept his promise: there were sixty-eight elegantly bound volumes in the Auchinleck library at the time of its dispersal (*Letters SJ* 3: 304 n. 8). Could they have induced the remorse that Johnson hoped for? On 17 October 1780 he wrote that he was pleased to learn he had been unjust in accusing Mrs. Boswell of ill will. He had love very ready for her if she thought it worthy of acceptance (*Life* 3: 442). But a genuine reconciliation was not affected for another two years.

Margaret was dangerously ill from consumption in the summer of 1782. On 30 August Lord Auchinleck died and Boswell succeeded to the estate. He had been devotedly attentive to his wife but was now restless for London. Though she was still spitting blood (always aggravated when he left her), Boswell persuaded himself late in September that Johnson's wisdom concerning his new role as laird was "highly requisite." He wrote to Johnson requesting permission to visit him, but set off for London without waiting for a reply. He was recalled to Auchinleck, however, from an inn two stages off because his wife's symptoms had become more violent. Three days later, on 27 September, Boswell received Johnson's reply (*Applause* 6).

Throughout the years Johnson had inquired about Margaret's health and counselled Boswell to protect her. He now wrote firmly against the proposed jaunt. When composing the *Life* Boswell thought one paragraph of the letter, "equally just and tender," proper for publication: "One expence, however, I would not have you to spare: let nothing be omitted that can preserve Mrs. Boswell, though it should be necessary to transplant her for a time into a softer climate. She is the prop and stay of your life. How much must your children suffer by losing her" (4: 155).

Without prompting, Margaret wrote to Johnson inviting him to Auchinleck. In the letter of his own (1 October 1782) in which her letter was enclosed, Boswell described it as the "spontaneous effusion of her heart." But he published only Johnson's reply on 7 December (incorrectly dated 7 September in the *Life*). The journey was too great for him to attempt at that late season, Johnson wrote, "but if my health were fully recovered, I would suffer no little heat and cold, nor a wet or a rough road to keep me from you." He implored her, for his sake, "among other greater reasons," to spare no expense in taking care of her health, to procure all the attendance necessary for her ease, keep her mind quiet, and give him an account of her recovery. Margaret, "made happy" by his letter, and flattered, as she also said, by his concern, reported on 20 December that she was better and hoped to convince him by her attention of "how much consequence I esteem your health to the world and to myself" (*Life* 4: 155–57, 501).

Subsequent events proved her sincere, but Johnson never took her friendship for granted. On 29 May 1783, his last meeting with Boswell that year, Johnson averred that there was no man to whom he would sooner turn if he were in distress. "I should like to come and have a cottage in your park, toddle about, live mostly on milk, and be taken care of by Mrs. Boswell.[2] She and I are good friends now, are we not?" The question appears to be rhetorical, yet it also seeks affirmation, as Boswell's journal makes plain: "I told him yes" (4: 226; *Applause* 152).

In March 1784 Margaret again invited Johnson to Auchinleck (*Life* 4: 264). To the end of his life he asked Boswell to pay his respects to "dear Mrs. Boswell" (and to "teach the young ones to love me," another tender and poignant refrain [4: 379]). In the last, painful letter before his death, inquiring on 3 November 1784 about Boswell's long silence ("Are you sick, or are you sullen?"), Johnson beseeched him for assurances that he was well, "and that nothing ill has befallen dear Mrs. Boswell, or any of your family" (4: 380).

Margaret Montgomerie respected Johnson as an author and quoted him approvingly even before she was Mrs. Boswell. "The Rambler has a very good paper on foolish passion [No. 11]. He has drawn a most natural picture of a domestic tyrant," she wrote to Boswell on 10 October 1769, shortly before their marriage (*In Search of a Wife* 335). In context, the citation is almost certainly a jab at Lord Auchinleck's prospective remarriage, which obsessed Boswell. She couldn't have pleased him more than to quote his mentor against his father. "I have read Mr. Johnson what you lately wrote to me in praise of your friend the Rambler," Boswell replied on 24 October. "He was much pleased, saying 'Very pretty Very pretty. Were I in Scotland I would give her away,'—you know that is the english form."[3]

But however wide Johnson's fame and astute or noble his sentiments, to Margaret Boswell he was only an author. She was conscious of station, though Lord Auchinleck scorned *her* as a poor relation (she was the daughter of his sister). The youngest of five orphaned children, Margaret Montgomerie brought to her marriage no connections and only the interest on an annuity of £1000. She had no hope of succeeding to the family estate of Lainshaw, which was encumbered by long incompetence and by 1777 in bankruptcy (*Later Years* 166). The Lainshaw Montgomeries were cadets, however, of the Earl of Eglinton (Margaret called him her "chief") and had a genuine but unsuccessful claim to the ancient peerage of Lyle (*Earlier Years* 402–3). Though she was "poor" and dependent, Margaret Boswell had the class prejudices of the landed gentry. She knew herself married, moreover, into a proud family of ancient lineage. Though she mocked them for their self-importance, her husband's obeisance to the son of a tradesman, a man of ungainly appearance and "uncouth habits," obviously rankled. She was angry, for example, at Johnson's scathing rebuke of Boswell for seeking permission to read publicly the Latin verses on Inchkenneth which Johnson had sent him.[4]

No matter in what respect Margaret Boswell came to hold Johnson, she was so socialized as to remain contemptuous of his birth and manners. Boswell regretted in a letter to Malone of 11 November 1785, after the publication of the *Tour to the Hebrides,* that any part of the censorship of Lord Macdonald identified him by name. "My Wife says that attacking his *cheer,* is adopting Dr. Johnson's *lowbred* notion of the importance of a *Good table*; and she thinks I had no right to *report* Dr. Johnson's saying that Sir A. was 'utterly unfit for his situation' which she thinks a severe reflection which will stick both to himself and his family" (*Corr: Garrick, Burke, Malone* 278).

The difference in Margaret Boswell's attitude toward General Paoli is instructive. In the letter to her of 24 October 1769 from which I have quoted above, Boswell wrote, "I have often shewn you Mr. Johnson's manner, which with his figure and the aweful idea we have of him would strike you with reverence and a kind of fear. And yet I doubt not but you would soon be able to converse with him, and would be very good company to him." Boswell then turned to her fear, needless, as it turned out, that Paoli would attend their wedding.[5] She would make a "very awkward figure," she had written the week before, on 17 October. "Consider me living at Lainshaw, unaccustomed to see the face of a creature except our own family, and you will not wonder at my being apprehensive of appearing greatly to the disadvantage before so great a man" (*In Search of a Wife* 336). Boswell understood her trepidation regarding the "illustrious General," but assured her that Paoli had the art of making people easy beyond anyone else he had ever known.

Margaret's esteem for a man "so great" because he was a dignified military and civic hero was enduring. She met Paoli in 1771, when he visited Scotland and impressed everyone with his stateliness. He spent his last night in Edinburgh at the Boswells' home; six months after his departure Paoli recalled that Mrs. Boswell had given him a "convoy" as far as Haddington (*Defence* 22, 59).[6] Paoli and Boswell became intimate friends, and from May 1775, after repeated invitations, Paoli's house became Boswell's headquarters in London until he moved his family to the city in 1786. When John Wilkes "very improperly" attacked Paoli at dinner at the Boswells' home on 30 May 1787 (Boswell does not give the reason), Mrs. Boswell, "with a just warmth, drank his health, declaring her high respect, and desired there might be no more of it" (*English Experiment* 138). The quick, outspoken, and firm command, as well as the loyalty, were characteristic of her.

Not only class but gender, nation, and religion also affected Margaret Boswell's attitude toward Johnson. She was retired and provincial, without her husband's opportunities or taste for a wider sphere. Before their marriage she had accompanied him to Ireland, as his cousin, but until he moved the entire family to London, she was in England only once, a jaunt with Boswell to Northumberland and Durham in August 1771. She enjoyed it thoroughly (*Later Years* 22). Yet Boswell explained that she did not much like to travel when on 26 February 1778 he declined Johnson's invitation to be their guest (*Life* 2: 219). Given the fragile state of her health, Edinburgh or Auchinleck was certainly more comfortable, and though she was often lonely, she did not like to leave home or five small children for long periods of time. On 9 August 1785, during the six months that Boswell was in London completing the *Tour to the Hebrides*, she confided to the Honorable Mrs. Margaret Stuart, another "privileged" and overburdened woman, that "In Ed.[r] I spent fourteen years of My life in retirement Without the Comfort of such a friend as you to Consult in any time of difficulty & Who is there Without them—& yet I was satisf'd."[7]

Margaret Boswell's domesticity reinforced her identity as a Scot and a Presbyterian. Having never been Anglicized, she was not ambivalent, dazzled by the south, like her husband. She became an experienced hostess, but the distinguished guests at her table were chiefly Scots friends and relations. Paoli was indeed a foreigner, but Johnson was English. She would have made the conventional upper-class accommodation to the Union ("You know I have often told you I am a coward, and in some measure a slave to public report," she wrote Boswell on 4 August 1769 [*In Search of a Wife* 247]). But Mrs. Boswell was surely as offended as her relations and friends by Johnson's criticisms of Scotland in *Journey to the Western Islands.* They discomfited Boswell, too.

Lord Auchinleck's heated argument with Johnson was probably unique in the family only in its intensity. Loving Boswell was "the only thing in which I have the honour to agree with you," Johnson wrote to Margaret on 16 May 1776 (*Life* 3: 86). What contentious topics had they discussed in Edinburgh almost three years earlier? Johnson could not long contain his opinions despite his best efforts at self-control; Margaret Boswell was also capable of vigorous discourse, and enjoyed it. She had been a "little nettled" when, shortly before their marriage, Boswell taxed her with "a too great degree of frankness to gentlemen," though she was aware, she conceded, that she was "on many occasions too free." Experience had taught her the necessity of a "prudent reserve" (*In Search of a Wife* 227). The retreat exemplifies the conflict between a natural assertiveness and learned submission which is evident throughout her relationship with Boswell.[8] Opposing Johnson intellectually and holding out against his protestations and cajoling was a declaration of rights.

It is not to be forgotten, moreover, that Johnson remained the outsider. Margaret's first impressions were indelible: she never saw him again after his visit in 1773. Her idea of him over the eleven years remaining to his death was from his letters, his books (he did not mention her in *A Journey to the Western Islands*),[9] and from report, primarily Boswell's.

Johnson was from the first a major cause of Margaret Boswell's deepest wound, a suspicion of her husband's attachment. Her confidence in it was undermined even before their marriage, when his love was ardent. The episode bears reviewing because it established a pattern different only in details. Boswell was suffering in the summer of 1769 from a venereal infection, the consequence, Pottle suggests, of a visit to a brothel in Ireland in June (*Earlier Years* 409; see also *In Search of a Wife* [14 July 1769] 230). Although Dr. John Gregory, Professor of Medicine at the University of Edinburgh, thought that the cure was progressing and could have been completed in Edinburgh, Boswell insisted that he must go to London for a course of Dr. Kennedy's "Lisbon Diet Drink." Margaret yearned for him not to leave her so close to the wedding. He had told her all his faults and much of his past. She worried about his roistering and hard drinking, particularly its effect upon his weakened health. She obviously had no control except by written entreaties when he was in London—to any devout Scot the center of sin. But in addition to procuring the miraculous potion, Boswell found it requisite, of course, to talk with Johnson "on the conduct of the married state" (*Life* 2: 76). Their conversations were part of the intellectual and social mission for which the "Diet Drink" was largely a pretext. Margaret protested feebly that if his health were not in question Boswell could see Johnson some other time.

Boswell went to London on 28 August 1769, made side trips to the Shakespeare Jubilee at Stratford and to Devonshire, and after eleven weeks returned to Edinburgh 13 November 1769, twelve days before their marriage at Lainshaw. It was not just for her to conclude, he had written on 5 September, that his affection was not so strong as hers because he could go such a distance from her so early. Even attending the Jubilee was recovering his health, acquiring an additional stock of ideas with which to entertain her, and "dissipating melancholy clouds." She was, however, his "constant object." He adored her (*In Search of a Wife* 249–53, 277).

Boswell was faithful to Margaret in the first years of their marriage, but in the autumn of 1772 he yielded to temptation after drinking too much port. She knew that he was uneasy about a genital problem and made him send for a surgeon, who after a few days declared him safe (*Later Years* 41). Thus her apprehensions about his fidelity were renewed before she met Johnson. There is no need to review over the subsequent years Boswell's many long jaunts to London, to which, as Frank Brady has written, Johnson was the "deep sustaining tie" (32). Readers of Boswell's journals (or his biography) are also acquainted, perhaps more than they should like to be, with his compulsive whoring at home and abroad and the drunken outbursts, sometimes violent, when Boswell chafed at confinement in Scotland. Johnson, too, knew about his licentiousness: broad hints in the *Life*, even in a letter there to Mrs. Boswell, explicit rebukes in Boswell's journals, and Johnson's letters to Mrs. Thrale furnish conclusive evidence. How could Johnson not have known that Boswell suffered from a venereal infection in London in the spring of 1776, for example? Johnson wrote with good cause to Mrs. Boswell that it was well she had her husband home. He had led a "wild life" during this visit. "Pray take care of him, and tame him" (16 May 1776, *Life* 3: 86).

Johnson may sometimes have enjoyed Boswell's uninhibited pleasures vicariously—he, too, would have visited Margaret Caroline Rudd were it not for the newspapers (3: 79). But he was made of sterner stuff (think only of the "Extraordinary Johnsoniana-*Tacenda*," printed in *The Applause of the Jury* 110–13), and he was repelled by the grossness of Boswell's sexual adventures. Although Johnson reprimanded Boswell sometimes, even contemptuously, he knew that he could not control him. He would not violate their friendship by specific revelations to Mrs. Boswell. Thus he sympathized helplessly with her in her trials.

Like many another spouse, Margaret probably found it less painful to blame his friends for her husband's defections than to acknowledge his deteriorating character. Ultimately she could not deceive herself, certainly not after Johnson's death and in the last years of her life, when Boswell, though tormented and still protesting his love, neglected her shamefully. Johnson's reiterated appeals to Boswell to protect "dear Mrs. Boswell," and in 1782 to stay at home when she was perilously ill, coincided with her disillusionment. Then she could accept that Johnson was not deliberately luring her husband from home and that his wish for her friendship was sincere.

Johnson had prepared her for that acceptance by addressing earlier the root cause of her skepticism, what Boswell identified as Johnson's too great influence on him. Although Margaret suffered immeasurably from Boswell's infidelities, they were transient, and no particular woman threatened her supremacy until Boswell conducted an affair with Margaret Caroline Rudd in 1785–86. Johnson's moral and intellectual authority, on the other hand, for many years undermined the primacy of the marital relationship. Johnson's wishes—or, more properly, Boswell's self-interested interpretation of his wishes—outweighed Margaret's. The need to consult Johnson or gain an accession of his wisdom was a frequent explanation for the journeys south. Boswell also made the long and hazardous Hebridean tour despite her objections.

There is vivid evidence in the journal that Margaret Boswell recognized Johnson's preeminence. She used him both to punish Boswell and to shock him out of a prolonged period of drunkenness. Let Boswell tell it:

> SUNDAY 10 JULY [1774]. . . . A circumstance occurred this morning which I hope will have a lasting impression upon me. There had come a letter to me from Mr. Samuel Johnson last night. My wife improved it well. She said she would not give me it, as I did not deserve it, since I had put myself into a state of incapacity to receive it when it came, and that it would not have been written to me had the writer of it known how I was to be. She would therefore send it back. She thus made me think how shocking it was that a letter from Mr. Samuel Johnson should find me drunk. She then delivered it, and it was a more than ordinary good one. It put me in the best frame, and I determined vigorously to resist temptation for the future. (*Defence* 224–25).

Even after Johnson's death Boswell's dedication to him prevailed over family life. While Boswell was in London editing the *Tour to the Hebrides* and seeing it through the press, Margaret lived at Auchinleck "quite a Lady Abbess—I attend My children from ten till twelve & from four to six & superintend all their little attempts to accomplish themselves by Musick & reading &c" (Margaret Boswell to Mrs. Margaret Stuart, 9 August 1785).[10] It was not only Boswell's desire to transfer to the English bar, moreover, that compelled him to uproot his family and undertake the disastrous migration to London in 1786. Malone encouraged the "experiment," because he, too, believed that only in London could Boswell finish the *Life of Johnson.* They were doubtless right, among other reasons because Malone was there. The physical and emotional consequences of the move were fatal to Margaret. Given Boswell's indulgence by the "Gang," his eminent friends in London, and the indifference of most of them to her welfare, she probably longed for Johnson even as she regretted his biography.

Johnson's attitude toward Margaret Boswell also evolved over time, from courtesy to genuine concern. On 3 November 1773, on a rainy day at Auchinleck in the final stages of his Scottish tour, he made an unvarnished appraisal of her in response to an inquiry from Hester Thrale. "Mrs. Boswel has the mien and manners of a Gentlewoman," he wrote, "and such a person and mind, as would not be in any place either admired or contemned. She is in a proper degree inferiour to her husband; she cannot rival him, nor can he ever be ashamed of her" (*Letters SJ* 2: 111). Johnson acknowledged Margaret Boswell's breeding in this letter but judged her otherwise unexceptional, and by the general standards of the day, which he here obviously upholds, an appropriate wife to Boswell. (Did Johnson also truly believe Hester Thrale inferior to Henry Thrale, his "Master"?)

If this early appraisal of Margaret Boswell represents Johnson's settled opinion, his subsequent behavior is the more impressive: it demonstrates that he valued her, as he did many other persons, not on intellectual grounds but because she was human. It should be pointed out, however, that Mrs. Boswell was not at Auchinleck during Johnson and Boswell's visit in 1773. As the result of an unexplained encounter in the autumn of 1770 with Lord and Lady Auchinleck (married the year before, on the same day that the Boswells were wed), Margaret did not re-enter the house until Boswell succeeded to the estate in 1782 (*Later Years* 19). Johnson's report to Mrs. Thrale was based, therefore, upon only the three days that Mrs. Boswell was his hostess after he arrived in Edinburgh late Saturday 14 August 1773. During this visit he was sightseeing with Boswell, or Mrs. Boswell poured tea while Johnson conversed with numerous other guests (with the exception of the Duchess of Douglas, all male). On his second sojourn with the Boswells, except for two nights, from 9 to 20 November 1773, Johnson was feted by all ranks at breakfast, dinner, and supper; still, he had in that period another and more extended opportunity to observe Margaret Boswell. Did he discover then the acuteness and strength of mind which she exhibited consistently over the years? Did admiration grow, perhaps, with sympathy?

Boswell assumed in marriage what he always needed, both freedom and security. Johnson learned that Margaret Boswell—sensible, straightforward, unfailingly loyal—was pivotal to Boswell's stability and to his happiness. Johnson had read Boswell's Hebrides journal in progress and was privy to his distress at the long separation from Margaret, the comfort her letters gave him, his anguish about *her* fate when they were endangered at sea, and his joy at returning home. Johnson also knew the strains that the Boswells' radical differences in temperament put upon the marriage. Margaret lacked his romantic imagination, Boswell lamented; he wished that she understood the "various workings" of his mind better (*Applause* 166–67). Her sexual desires were low-keyed, certainly compared to his. Boswell's reckless libertinism caused many quarrels and even temporary exile from their bed. But the whole course of Boswell's journals and the extant correspondence between him and Margaret reveal that they were close-knit despite their differences and his behavior. Ultimately she deferred to him, or was worn out by his entreaties, but as an example of her stature and the seriousness of their exchanges I refer readers to her exposition of their hopeless situation in London in 1788 and her shrewd proposal for extricating themselves (*English Experiment* 190–91).

Wise and subtle, Johnson recognized that Boswell's dependence on him drove a wedge into the harmony of minds and goals that even this troubled marriage could achieve. He tried to assure Margaret of *her* preeminence. I quote again, but exact and in full, his letter to her of 22 July 1777 acknowledging her gift of marmalade:

> Madam,
>
> Though I am well enough pleased with the taste of sweetmeats, very little of the pleasure which I received at the arrival of your jar of marmalade arose from eating it.[11] I received it as a token of friendship, as a proof of reconciliation, things much sweeter than sweetmeats, and upon this consideration I return you, dear Madam, my sincerest thanks. By having your kindness I think I have a double security for the continuance of Mr. Boswell's, which it is not to be expected that any man can long keep, when the influence of a lady so highly and so justly valued operates against him. Mr. Boswell will tell you that I was always faithful to your interest, and always endeavored to exalt you in his estimation. You must now do the same for me. We must all help one another, and you must now consider me, as, dear Madam,
>
> Your most obliged,
> And most humble servant,
> SAM. JOHNSON (*Life* 3: 129)

Six weeks later Johnson reinforced the message of this letter. He proposed to Boswell on 1 September 1777 that they contrive another "little adventure" like the tour of the Hebrides, but specified that Mrs. Boswell must have some part in the consultation as to what it should be (3: 131). Verbal assurance, though it contributed to the relaxation of Mrs. Boswell's attitude, could not alone persuade her of Johnson's sincerity. When words coalesced with cumulative action, when they induced Boswell to accept Lord Auchinleck's entail, restrained him from deserting her in the midst of her illness in 1782, and insisted on practical measures to guard her health, she responded to Johnson's friendship generously.

Boswell and Johnson were likely to have discussed Margaret Boswell's intransigence privately, in London; they may even have concerted, in part, the epistolary strategy by which Johnson tried to relax it. But because of the spontaneity, the wit, and the warmth of those letters addressed to a double audience I believe that the initiative and the strategy were Johnson's.

Boswell printed their correspondence chiefly to demonstrate from primary materials the range of Johnson's mind and to counteract his reputation for unkindness. The extraordinary solicitude which he summoned for Boswell is overmastered sometimes—and understandably—by harshness. But within the letters to Boswell—his own material at hand—lay unalloyed evidence, through another person, of Johnson's generous heart. His patient and tender efforts to prove himself a friend to Margaret Boswell recurring through a long stretch of the *Life* underscore an essential theme and counterbalance Johnson's less attractive traits.

Like many other letters in the *Life*, Boswell's correspondence with Johnson is abridged, and properly so. To have printed it entire would have introduced many irrelevancies and lengthened a work which troubled Boswell by its size. He was not obliged, moreover, to be witness against himself. Still, in proving Johnson's capacity for friendship Boswell did not always conquer his ego. He obviously exults over the declarations he earns or extracts. His discretion in the *Life of Johnson* as medium between the two persons most important to him is therefore the more remarkable. It suggests that Boswell knew himself to be at the center of the struggle.

Notes

1. The perverse pleasure of being a Jew and eating pork came later, 10 June 1784 (*Life* 4: 292).

2. In Boswell's journal Johnson says that he would "totter" about Boswell's place, a verb defined in Johnson's *Dictionary* as "to shake so as to threaten a fall." In the *Oxford English Dictionary* "toddle" is applied to an invalid or aged person as well as to a child and this very quotation from the *Life of Johnson* is cited as an example. To "toddle" as to "stroll" is illustrated from Ramsay's *Tea-Times Miscellanies*, 1733. Since the verbs appear to have been used interchangeably at the least, too much cannot be made of Boswell's emendation. Still, the connotations are suggestive, from a frail, toothless old age in the journal ("live mostly on milk") to childish dependency in the biography.

3. From a copy in the collections of the Yale Boswell Editions of Jasper John Boswell's papers at the Fondazione Sella, San Gerolamo, Biella, Italy. The excerpts are quoted by the generous permission of the Fondazione, Mr. Lodovico Sella, president. Johnson did not attend the wedding ceremony, but he signed Margaret and James's marriage contract, in London, as a witness (see *Boswell in Search of a Wife* 348, and illustration following).

4. "Your love of publication is offensive and disgusting, and will end, if it be not reformed, in a general distrust among all your friends" (11 February 1775). Boswell later published the verses in *Journal of a Tour to the Hebrides*, under the date 17 October 1773 (*Ominous Years* 63 and n. 9, 64).

5. Like Johnson, he was not present but signed the marriage contract as a witness (*In Search of a Wife* 348 and illustration following).

6. In reminiscing thus with Boswell on 24 March 1772, Paoli also praised Mrs. Boswell as having "something of the Italian manner, a frankness, an attention, and a politeness" (*Defence* 59). The description is worth having: Paoli was a shrewd judge of character.

7. C444. Margaret Stuart, wife of Lt.-Col. James Stuart, second son of the 3d Earl of Bute, MP, and deputy ranger of Richmond Park, herself managed both family and Park because her husband was hunting, attending the House of Commons, or drunken and idle. She, too, "exiled" from Scotland, lamented the absence of a faithful woman friend (C2606 and 2619).

8. A more painful instance of her deference before her marriage appears in a letter of 10 August 1769: "You are very good to allow me to correspond with Mrs. S.[Stuart]. I shall never abuse the confidence you put in me. I shall think it my duty to give up any acquaintance that is disagreeable to you, but I would willingly do it by degrees" (C426).

9. I owe this reminder to Professor John B. Radner, George Mason University. Johnson's omission is perplexing but not, I think, entirely questionable. The book is a generalized narrative in which even Boswell,

his companion, is introduced and characterized in half the first long sentence. Still, Johnson did not even mention that he stayed with the Boswells in Edinburgh, though he names his other hosts and often acknowledges their hospitality (Lachlan Mackinnon of Coirechatachan, for example [*Journey* 53] and Lady Macleod at Dunvegan [68]). Johnson also reports that en route to Auchinleck he and Boswell stopped two days at Mr. Campbell's, "a gentleman married to Mr. Boswell's sister" (either a lapse of memory or, given Johnson's hand, a printer's error for *Mrs.* Boswell's sister [*Journey* 161 and n. 6]). Yet Johnson has nothing to say about Campbell's place or the visit. Was Johnson ungracious, no matter how he felt about Margaret Boswell's welcome, or inconsistent because he wrote hurriedly and made slips (Freudian or otherwise) for which he later rebuked himself?

10. As above, n. 7, C444.

11. Boswell informs the reader of one of the rare "inaccuracies" in which he had detected Johnson: he had not yet opened the jar of marmalade (*Life* 3: 129 n. 1).

Appendix: Boswell's Meetings with Johnson, A New Count

HITOSHI SUWABE

On how many days did Boswell see Johnson during a friendship sustained for twenty-two years? This is a question most readers of Boswell's *Life of Johnson* must have had in mind at least once. Johnson's statement, "Nobody can write the life of a man, but those who have eat and drunk and lived in social intercourse with him" (*Life* 2: 166) may not be applicable to all biographies, but the number of hours Johnson and Boswell spent in each other's company is not an element one can ignore in a biography that makes us feel that we are in the very presence of Samuel Johnson. In fact, there have been at least three Johnsonians or Boswellians who counted and made public the days that biographer and subject met.

The first was John Wilson Croker, who announced in the Preface to his edition of Boswell's *Life of Johnson* that the total was 180, or 276 including the days they were together on their Scottish tour in 1773.[1] Leslie Stephen adopted Croker's finding when he wrote the life of Boswell for the *Dictionary of National Biography*.

The second to make a count was Philip A.W. Collins, who argued in *Notes and Queries* that Johnson and Boswell met on about 425 days.[2] His count seems trustworthy because it was based on the *Private Papers of James Boswell from Malahide Castle in the Collection of Lt.-Col. Ralph Heyward Isham*,[3] but, as Collins himself admitted, he got the number "by an extremely rough form of extrapolation" (164).

The third, and apparently decisive, count was made by Donald Greene, who meticulously illustrated their meetings by 327 black circles in all the calendered days from 1763 to 1784.[4] His calculation was based, however, only on Boswell's *Life of Johnson* and *Journal of a Tour to the Hebrides.*

It is well known that much of the *Life* was taken directly from Boswell's journal and revised; now that all the appropriate journals are available to us (actually, since 1981) in the trade edition of the Yale Editions of the Private Papers of James Boswell, it is time to re-count more strictly the days that Johnson and Boswell actually met. As Greene himself has said, "Ever since the earlier forms of Boswell's reports began to be available with the printing of the Malahide papers in the 1920s, careful

Johnson scholars have invariably turned to them, rather than to the *Life*, as the most authentic evidence available" (*New Questions, New Answers*, 127). This essay is an attempt to put his words into practice while reviewing Collins's too generous calculation.

The following list shows in consecutive numbers all the days that Boswell reports having seen Johnson, citing the volumes and the pages of the published journals in the Yale Editions of the Private Papers of James Boswell (the first page only when their meeting goes through several pages). The trade edition generally prints only fully written journal, however. On fifteen occasions that it fails and the editors have not reported Johnson-Boswell meetings in a summary of the missing period, I have been able to establish meetings from Boswell's rough notes printed in Isham's *Malahide* Papers (cited as MP). The passages corresponding to the journal in Boswell's *Life of Johnson* are specified by volume and page in the standard text edited by G.B. Hill and revised by L.F. Powell (Oxford: Clarendon Press, 1934–1964, reprinted 1971). Occasionally the *Life of Johnson* is not reported because Boswell has failed to date it precisely.

I have also cited meetings from reliable sources such as published letters. The consecutive numbers are interrupted in four points by question marks. They signify meetings reported in the *Life of Johnson* but not in the *Malahide* papers or in correspondence. The total number of days privately recorded is just 400. For readers who trust the circumstantial accuracy of the *Life*, the total is 404.

The volumes of journal in the Yale Editions of the Private Papers of James Boswell, and their abbreviations, to 1784, the year of the death of Johnson:

Boswell's London Journal 1762–1763: LJ
Boswell in Holland 1763–1764: BH
Boswell on the Grand Tour: Italy, Corsica, and France 1765–1766: GT2
Boswell in Search of a Wife 1766–1769: SW
Boswell for the Defence 1769–1774: BD
Boswell's Journal of a Tour to the Hebrides with Samuel Johnson, LL. D., 1773: TH
Boswell: The Ominous Years 1774–1776: OY
Boswell in Extremes 1776–1778: BE
Boswell Laird of Auchinleck 1778–1782: BLA
Boswell: The Applause of the Jury 1782–1785: BAJ

Serial Number of Days	Date		Yale Boswell Editions		*Life of Johnson*
	1763				
1	May	16	LJ	260	1: 392
2		24		267	396
3	June	13		278	399
?		15			399
4		25		282	401
5	July	1		286	417
6		5		289	421
7		6		291	422
8		9		298	426
9		14		300	426
10		19		310	434
11		20		312	437
12		22		317	443
13		26		322	452
14		28		325	452
15		30		328	457
16		31		331	463
17	Aug.	2		332	463
18		3		333	464
19		5	BH	2	464
20		6		2	471
	1766				
21	Feb.	12	GT2	296	2: 4
22		15		300	11
23		22		312	14
	1768				
24	Mar.	26	SW	146	47
25		27		152	52
26		28		153	54
27	May	2		165	59
28	June	7		175	63
29		8		177	66

Serial Number of Days	Date	Yale Boswell Editions	*Life of Johnson*
	1769		
30	Sep. 30	SW 311	2: 73
31	Oct. 2	310	
32	6	313	77
33	10	314	80
34	16	317	82
35	17	321	
36	19	322	91
37	20	325	96
38	26	325	98
39	27	333	107
40	31	348	
41	Nov. 10	343	110
	1772		
42	Mar. 21	BD 39	146
43	23	55	155
44	28	68	157
45	31	82	165
46	Apr. 5	93	171
47	6	96	173
48	9	102	178
49	10	104	179
50	11	109	183
51	15	121	186
52	17	126	189
53	18	127	189
54	19	128	190
55	22	MP 9: 256	
56	24	257	
57	27	259	
58	28	260	
59	29	260	
60	May 2	261	
61	4	262	

Serial Number of Days	Date	Yale Boswell Editions	*Life of Johnson*
62	May 8	BD 133	
63	9	*[5]	2: 195
64	11	BD 134	
	1773		
65	Apr. 3	159	209
66	7	168	211
67	8	171	213
68	9	171	214
69	11	173	215
70	13	180	217
71	15	182	220
72	19	183	226
73	21	183	227
74	27	183	229
75	29	183	232
76	30	184	235
77	May 1	184	242
78	7	185	246
79	9	MP 6: 140	259
80	10	BD 187	260
81–181	Aug. 14–Nov. 22	TH 11–393	6: 21–404
	1775		
182	Mar. 21	OY 87	2: 311
183	24	94	318
184	27	98	321
185	28	104	327
186	31	111	330
187	Apr. 1	112	330
188	2	115	334
189	5	123	338
190	6	125	340
191	7	131	345
192	8	135	349
193	10	137	350

Serial Number of Days	Date	Yale Boswell Editions	Life of Johnson
194	Apr. 14	142	352
195	16	OY 147	2: 360
196	18	149	361
197	May 6	*6	372
?	8		374
198	12	157	376
199	13	157	376
200	16	158	378
201	17	158	378
202	21	158	377
	1776		
203	Mar. 16	256	427
204	18	271	438
205	19	275	438
206	20	277	440
207	21	283	451
208	22	286	456
209	23	290	462
210	24	293	466
211	25	295	468
212	26	298	473
213	27	300	475
214	28	301	3: 2
215	29	302	4
216	31	306	7
217	Apr. 3	310	7
218	4	315	17
219	5	316	17
220	7	321	24
221	10	323	27
222	11	328	34
223	13	333	38
224	26	344	45
225	27	344	45
226	28	344	45
227	29	344	50

Serial Number of Days	Date	Yale Boswell Editions	Life of Johnson
228	Apr. 30	MP 11: 268	
229	May 5	MP 11: 270	3: 52
230	6	270	
231	7	271	52
232	8	272	52
233	9	OY 344	52
234	10	344	55
235	12	MP 11: 279	55
236	13	280	57
237	15	OY 345	66
238	16	352	80
	1777		
239	Sept. 14	BE 149	135
240	15	150	137
241	16	153	150
242	17	156	154
243	18	158	157
244	19	160	160
245	20	168	175
246	21	173	180
247	22	176	185
248	23	182	196
249	24	184	207
	1778		
250	Mar. 18	221	222
251	20	224	222
252	30	230	226
253	31	231	228
254	Apr. 3	234	230
255	4	240	238
256	5	243	
257	7	244	241
258	8	251	249
259	9	252	250

Serial Number of Days	Date	Yale Boswell Editions	*Life of Johnson*
260	Apr. 10	261	260
261	12	BE 271	3: 270
262	13	276	279
263	14	278	282
264	15	282	284
265	17	291	300
266	18	299	314
267	19	301	316
268	20	302	317
269	25	312	317
270	27	317	
271	28	318	324
272	29	322	331
273	30	327	336
274	May 2	328	337
275	8	328	338
276	9	331	341
277	10	332	342
278	12	338	344
279	13	342	351
280	16	344	354
281	17	345	356
282	18	349	
283	19	350	357
	1779		
284	Mar. 16	BLA 56	373
285	19	58	
286	23	58	
287	25	58	
288	26	58	375
289	27	59	
290	28	60	
291	29	60	377
292	31	61	377
293	Apr. 1	64	378
294	2	64	379

Serial Number of Days	Date	Yale Boswell Editions	*Life of Johnson*
295	Apr. 3	BLA 65	3: 380
296	4	65	380
297	6	69	
298	7	69	381
299	8	70	382
300	9	71	
301	10	72	
302	11	75	
303	12	76	
304	16	85	383
305	17	91	
306	18	92	
307	24	98	386
308	26	101	391
309	May 1	102	392
310	3	103	392
311	Oct. 4	139	400
312	6	*[7]	
313	10	140	400
314	12	143	407
315	14	*[8]	
	1781		
316	Mar. 20	292	4: 71
317	21	293	72
318	22	294	
319	26	295	
320	28	296	75
321	30	299	78
322	31	302	
323	Apr. 1	304	80
?	2		84
324	5	308	
325	6	308	87
326	7	309	88
327	10	316	

Serial Number of Days	Date	Yale Boswell Editions	*Life of Johnson*
328	Apr. 12	BLA 316	4: 88
329	13	321	90
330	15	323	91
331	20	327	96
332	22	329	
333	28	334	
334	30	337	
335	May 2	338	
336	7	347	
337	8	347	101
338	9	351	
339	17	359	
340	21	361	
341	25	362	
342	26	362	
343	29	364	
344	June 2	369	118
345	3	373	122
346	4	376	127
347	5	377	131
	1783		
348	Mar. 21	BAJ 73	164
349	22	77	169
350	23	79	171
351	25	85	
352	26	86	
353	28	87	
354	30	89	176
355	31	91	
356	Apr. 1	91	
357	2	93	
358	3	96	
359	10	98	198
360	12	99	200
361	18	100	203

Serial Number of Days	Date		Yale Boswell Editions		*Life of Johnson*	
362	Apr.	20	BAJ	109	4:	209
?		24				211
363		28		117		211
364		30		122		215
365	May	1		127		217
366		9		134		220
367		15		141		220
368		17		142		222
369		19		146		
370		21		146		
371		26		149		223
372		29		151		225
	1784					
373	May	6		210		271
374		9		210		272
375		10		210		272
376		13		211		272
377		15		211		273
378		16		213		277
379		17		214		278
380		18		214		279
381		19		215		279
382		20		217		
383		25		217		
384		30		220		281
385	June	3		225		283
386		9		231		286
387		10		231		288
388		11		234		293
389		12		236		298
390		13		239		305
391		14		241		307
392		15		241		308
393		16		246		311
394		22		248		326

Serial Number of Days	Date	Yale Boswell Editions	*Life of Johnson*
395	June 23	BAJ 249	328
396	24	249	330
397	25	250	330
398	27	250	332
399	29	253	336
400	30	254	4: 337

Notes

This article is a revision and a translation from the Japanese, by the author, of an account published in the *Journal of the Institute of Cultural Science,* Chuo University, Tokyo, August 1990.

1. *Life of Johnson,* ed. J.W. Croker (London: John Murray, 1831), 1: xii n.

2. "Boswell's Contact with Johnson," *Notes and Queries* (April 1956), 163–66. David L. Passler adopted Collins's calculation in Appendix Two of *Time, Form, and Style in Boswell's Life of Johnson* (New Haven and London: Yale University Press, 1971).

3. Hereafter referred to as *Malahide* papers. Professor Pottle and his assistants have provided a very useful key to the meetings and conversations between Johnson and Boswell recorded in this edition at the end of the volume of *Index* (London and New York: Oxford University Press, 1937), 19: 357–59.

4. "'Tis a Pretty Book, Mr. Boswell, But—," in *New Questions, New Answers,* 135–39.

5. *The Correspondence of James Boswell and John Johnston of Grange,* 281.

6. *The Letters of Samuel Johnson,* ed. R.W. Chapman, 3 vols. (Oxford: Clarendon Press, 1952), 2: 26.

7. Ibid. 306.

8. *Letters of James Boswell,* 2: 291.

Index

This is primarily an index of proper names, but a conscious effort has been made in headings ("rhetoric"), subheadings, and analyses to serve scholars of the various disciplines which the essays address. Writings and published works are indexed under the names of the authors, Boswell's relationships under the names of the persons concerned. Abbreviations are as follows:

(JB) James Boswell; (MMB) Margaret Montgomerie Boswell; (SJ) Samuel Johnson; (WJT) William Johnson Temple.

The index was compiled and edited by Irma S. Lustig, with the assistance of Constance Billé and Ben Cohen.

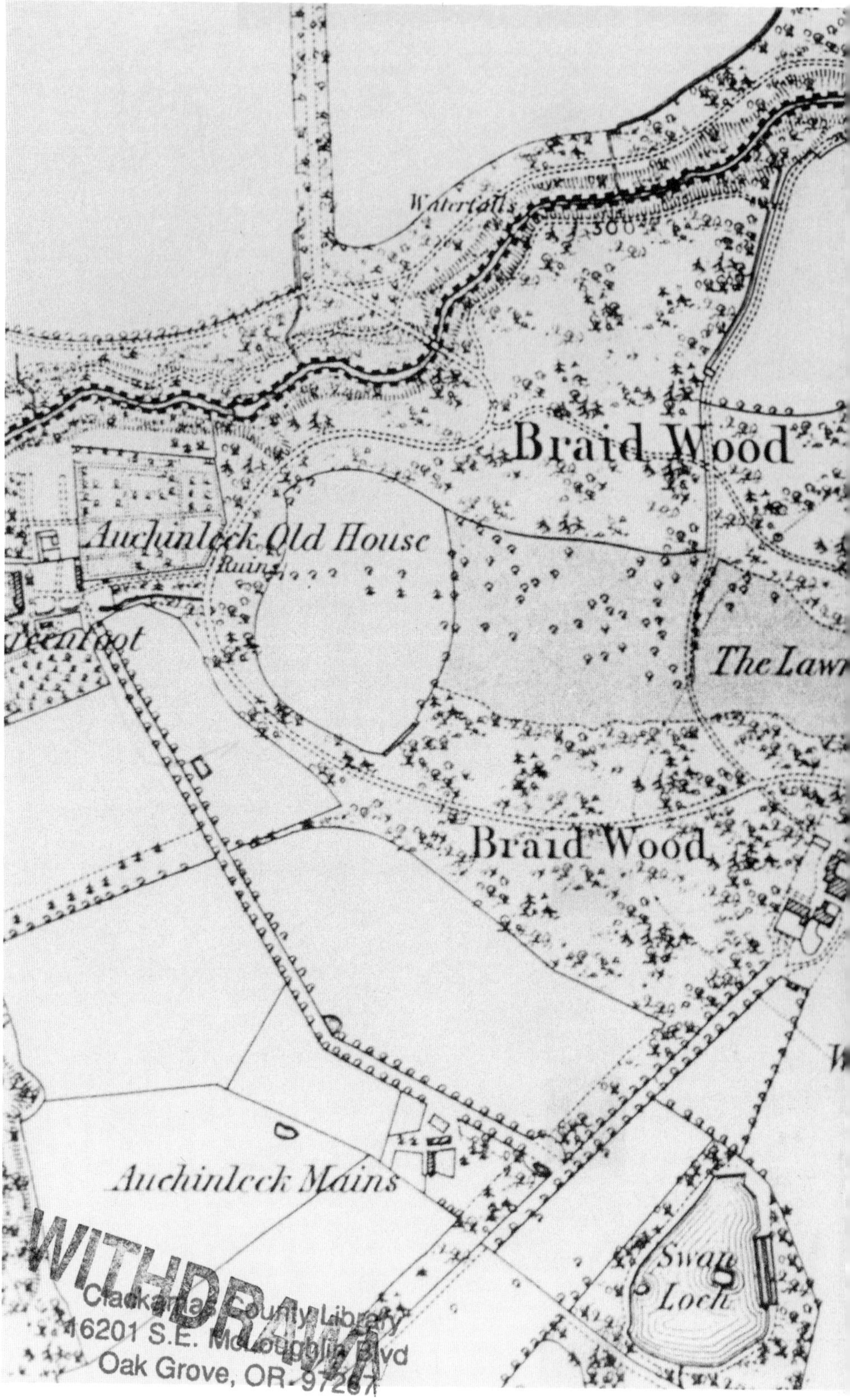

Waterfalls

300

Braid Wood

Auchinleck Old House

Ruins

Braid Wood

Auchinleck Mains

Swan Loch